SO-EES-463

Shakespeare's
Romance of the Word

Shakespeare's Romance of the Word

Maurice Hunt

Lewisburg
Bucknell University Press
London and Toronto: Associated University Presses

Associated University Presses
440 Forsgate Drive
Cranbury, NJ 08512

Associated University Presses
25 Sicilian Avenue
London WC1A 2QH, England

Associated University Presses
P.O. Box 488, Port Credit
Mississauga, Ontario
Canada L5G 4M2

The paper used in this publication meets the requirements
of the American National Standard for Permanence of Paper
for Printed Library Materials Z39.48-1984.

Library of Congress Cataloging-in-Publication Data

Hunt, Maurice, 1942–
    Shakespeare's romance of the word / Maurice Hunt.
        p.   cm.
    Includes bibliographical references.
    ISBN 0-8387-5188-1 (alk. paper)
    1. Shakespeare, William, 1564–1616—Tragicomedies. 2. Romances, English—History and criticism. 3. Tragicomedy. I. Title.
PR2981.5.H8   1990
822.3′3—dc20   89-46251
                                                                              CIP

To Pamela

Lux tua vita mihi

(Pericles, 2.2.21)

Contents

Acknowledgments

This book would not have been possible without the support of the Baylor University Research Committee, which generously provided several summer sabbaticals for its completion. I am indebted to Professors Robert Collmer and Darden Powers, Dean and Associate Dean respectively of Graduate Studies and Research. I would also like to thank Dr. James Barcus, Chairman of the English Department, and Dr. William Cooper, Dean of the College of Arts and Sciences, for their unfailing endorsement of my work.

Parts of *Shakespeare's Romance of the Word* originally appeared in essays published in *Essays in Literature, Texas Studies in Literature and Language, Studies in the Humanities, Bucknell Review, University of Mississippi Studies in English, Rocky Mountain Review of Language and Literature, Modern Language Studies, Journal of the Rocky Mountain Medieval and Renaissance Association,* and *Ball State University Forum.* I am grateful to the editors of these journals for permission to reprint material in either original or revised forms.

Professor Herbert Barrows of the University of Michigan first inspired my study of English literature; Professor Stephen Orgel of Stanford University became my role model for scrupulous scholarship. Neither of these individuals should be held accountable for any defects in this book. I am grateful to my copy editor, Janet Burton, and to my research assistants, Rick Diamond, Ann F. Oliver, and Kyle Keefer for their dedicated and painstaking labors; they have done more than any writer could ask of them. Finally, I want to express publicly my gratitude to the person to whom this book is dedicated, my wife—without whom this project would never have seen the light of day. The imagery of the Latin motto from *Pericles* forming my dedication of the book to her truly is apt (as only she knows).

Shakespeare's
Romance of the Word

1

Introduction

Simply put, my argument concerns Shakespeare's exploration of the word, first in its destructive dimensions and then in its redemptive workings, to illuminate a hitherto undescribed approach to his four last romances. In fact, Shakespeare's linguistic explorations in *Pericles, Cymbeline, The Winter's Tale,* and *The Tempest* make up a consistent dramatic design representing an alternative way of thinking about these plays as a group. Still, I wish to avoid overstating my claim. Offered at this late date in Shakespeare studies, my argument appears risky, to say the least; dramatic interpretation, flourishing in the watershed of Wittgensteinian linguistics and the New Criticism, has defined a Shakespeare self-reflexively brooding upon the nature of words themselves in their inherent limitations and potentialities. Recent studies of Shakespeare risk turning the dramatist into a linguistic philosopher (or a philosophical linguist) who used the vehicle of drama and the London stage to realize his contemplations about one of the chief mediums of his art. It remains doubtful that any playwright, let alone the multifaceted Shakespeare, primarily would write plays designed to please and instruct large crowds of mingled society for such a reason. Consequently, in my discussions of kinds of speech in *Pericles, Cymbeline, The Winter's Tale,* and *The Tempest,* I have tried to remember that words (and musings about words) play only one part in the total effect of a scene, act, or play.

Admittedly, individual essays of considerable merit exist that interpret various aspects of speech in the last plays. As the reader might guess, they mainly concern *The Winter's Tale* and *The Tempest.*[1] No one has yet pursued Shakespeare's linguistic dramaturgy from the riddle scene of *Pericles* to Prospero's epilogic prayer in *The Tempest.* In *Pericles, Cymbeline, The Winter's Tale,* and *The Tempest,* we find, in the broadest sense, the playwright representing different failures in speakers' communication or in words themselves complemented by new, extraordinary modes of expression. To a large extent, my work can be regarded as the obverse of Lawrence Danson's analysis of the language of Shakespearean tragedy.[2] Exploring the epistemological and linguistic universe of the tragedies, Danson has shown that solutions to vexed problems of knowing and expression remain unavailable to certain tragic protagonists. In the last romances, however, rare acts of expression and ways of knowing, often occurring in (and indeed made possible by) the reformative medium of pastoral, supersede and on occasion rectify earlier, flawed acts of understanding and speech. With the possible exception of *Pericles*, Shakespeare dramatizes the linguistic sequence outlined above in anything but a neat, compartmentalized manner. In fact, problematic language may erupt during a romance's latter acts, threatening to nullify both the positive effects of singular, mid-play modes of expression and the joyous ending prescribed by this dramatic genre. Nevertheless, near the end of each romance, potent words—sometimes mortal, sometimes divine—explicitly make possible characters' secular salvation.

My claim to a relatively original reading of the last romances rests upon the general statements made in the preceding paragraph. Like any interpreter of Shakespeare's plays, I hope that now and then I offer the reader a fresh way of thinking about a particular character, scene, or dramatic speech. Since the time of E. M. W. Tillyard's argument that the ethos of the last romances grows out of quasi-supernatural moments in the tragedies such as Cordelia's angelic effect upon awakened Lear, critics have customarily thought of the last romances as incorporating the experience of the tragedies in order to transcend it. By inviting comparison with Danson's approach, this book offers another way of thinking about the last plays in relation to the great tragedies, a way that associates the two groups of plays on the basis of Shakespeare's persistent interest in the complex dimensions of the word.

Ways of knowing and acts of speech cannot be neatly segregated in any analysis of either topic in Shakespearean drama. Speech reflects the color of ideas or habits of thought informing it, and vice versa. The Renaissance grasped this fact just as clearly as the twentieth century has, especially regarding speech's ability to restrict or enlarge the mind. As Keir Elam has recently shown, the opinion that a person's speech mirrors the quality and capacity of the speaker's mind surfaces frequently in the sixteenth and seventeenth centuries. Speech is "the image of Man *(mentis character),"* Thomas Puttenham wrote in 1589, "for man is but his minde, and as his minde is tempered and qualified, so are his speeches and language at large, and his manner of utterance the very warpe and woofe of his conceits." Concerning speech, Ben Jonson believed that "it springs out of the most retired and inmost parts of us, and is the image of the present of it, the mind."[3] Jonson's judgment on speech, delivered to Drummond of Hawthornedon and recorded in *Timber, or Discoveries* (1640–41), captures a pervasive Renaissance attitude— "Language most shewes a man; speake that I may see thee."[4] Less obvious perhaps is the converse opinion during the Renaissance—that the prior act of speech shapes the mind, that the mind in its nature ultimately resembles the quality of the articulating word. Concerning her original attempt to educate Caliban, Miranda says,

> . . . . When thou didst not, savage,
> Know thine own meaning, but wouldst gabble like
> A thing most brutish, I endowed thy purposes
> With words that made them known.[5]

$$(1.2.355\text{–}58)$$

Through Miranda, Shakespeare implies that our awareness of our ideas comes retrospectively from illuminating speech. The view of the interaction between speech and mind expressed in *The Tempest* represents a variation of the widespread Renaissance notion of Adamic speech. Focusing upon Genesis 2:19–20, wherein God parades the animals by Adam to see what he would name them, Renaissance commentators such as Mulcaster (1582) and Sylvester (1592) extrapolated the idea that Adam's naming the creatures instantaneously conferred knowledge of their essences.[6] By simply saying "tiger," Adam intuited the essence of tigerness. Such a judgment often made up the optimistic view of the word's ability to describe truth and confer knowledge in the Renaissance debate on the epistemological status of language.

One strain of modern linguistics lends support to the Elizabethan idea that speech furnishes and shapes the mind. According to Benjamin Whorf, "the study of language . . . shows that the forms of a person's thoughts are controlled by inexorable laws or patterns of which he is unconscious. . . . These patterns are the unperceived intricate systematizations of his own language. . . . Every language is a vast pattern-system, different from others, in which are culturally ordained the forms and categories by which the personality not only communicates, but also analyzes nature, notices or neglects types of relationship and phenomena, channels his reasoning, and builds the house of his consciousness."[7] Instead of saying, "Speak, that I might see thee," a supporter of the Sapir-Whorf hypothesis might say, "Think, that I might judge thy speech."[8] Despite criticisms, the Sapir-Whorf hypothesis has stimulated psycholinguists to describe the ways in which speech creates mind.[9] In the field of Shakespeare studies, Marion Trousdale's argument that verbal models determine ways of perceiving and interpreting not only literary texts but reality as well unintentionally validates the Sapir-Whorf hypothesis.[10] "In such a view of language," Trousdale remarks, "aspects of Othello's character," for example, "originate not in Othello but in the language codes used to describe him."[11] Asserting that Rudolph Agricola's *De Inventione Dialectica Libri Tres* (1515) involves "an exploration of the ultimate foundations of discourse," she concludes, "if what we know, we know only by means of common words, then it is in the structures of discourse that the sources of such knowledge must lie."[12]

In summary, the reciprocal interaction of speech and mind necessarily entails describing ways of knowing as well as acts of speaking during my treatment of the word. Word and mind form an organic whole violated by the assumption that a study of what Shakespeare's characters say can be conducted independent of how their thinking develops in the course of a play. Nonetheless, it will be important to distinguish between ways of thinking and linguistic acts at certain points in the following analysis.

The reader may be disappointed in not finding a first chapter sketching Renaissance theories of speech, its nature, and its function in various social and existential contexts. In the words of James L. Calderwood, such a comprehensive linguistic survey "would go a long way toward making a man look sad."[13] I have resisted the impulse to provide such a chapter for two reasons. First, excellent accounts of Renaissance and Classical attitudes toward speech exist elsewhere in Shakespeare studies.[14] Such accounts confirm that, within Shakespeare's lifetime, opinions about the word's ability to reflect truth and communicate ideas range from, on the one hand, optimistic Christian and Neo-Platonic/Hermetic doctrines of the salvatory Word and the divine rightness of names for things to, on the other, Baconian skepticism about language's inherent usefulness for intellectual analysis and scientific inquiry. Between these extremes, Elizabethans and Jacobeans rendered virtually every shade of possible opinion in the linguistic spectrum, and they did so in anything but an orderly fashion.[15] Second, application of relevant Renaissance theories of speech at appropriate moments in my argument seems more useful than does a survey of attitudes before a reader can understand what bearing any (or all) of them might have for the last romances. Shakespeare studies have benefited from twentieth-century linguistic events like the Sapir-Whorf hypothesis and Austin's and Searle's speech-act theory; insights derived from these modern linguistic approaches can supplement Renaissance doctrines of speech to illuminate Shakespeare's verbal concerns in the last romances. My methodology, then, is eclectic, incorporating what seems useful to clarify Shakespeare's various dramatizations of speech (and occasionally silence) in his last romances. Without more ado, let us turn to what Ben Jonson labeled Shakespeare's "mouldy tale"—*Pericles, Prince of Tyre.*

2

Pericles, Prince of Tyre

I shall approach my thesis about the importance of the word in *Pericles* by way of the play's most farcical dialogue. In *Shakespeare and the Confines of Art*, Philip Edwards remarks that "the uncouth fishermen who succour the shipwrecked Pericles are in the play only to show the warmth of kindness as a contrast to the previous coldness of both humanity and the elements."[1] While the low characters undoubtedly produce this dramatic impression, they play a more complex role in the play's design than the part suggested by Edwards. It has been widely noted that Shakespeare often comically distorts serious dramatic themes or values in order to call attention to them.[2] For example, after hearing the Porter at the gate, who can be unaware of Macbeth's tendency to equivocate damnably? The dramatist—Shakespeare presumably—employs this familiar technique early in *Pericles*.[3] One of the most amusing scenes of the play, the Prince's encounter with three rustic fishermen, burlesques and hence accentuates a motif central to several episodes and speeches that critics, for the most part, have ignored. In fact, Pericles' notorious passivity cannot be truly understood without reference to the motif, which concerns a bold verbal protest against evil.[4] The first tempest that Pericles endures washes him ashore in Simonides' Greece, where he overhears Pilch, Patch-breech, and their master describing the evils of their world.

> 3. *Fish.* Faith, master, I am thinking of the pour men that were cast away before us even now.
> 1. *Fish.* Alas, poor souls, it griev'd my heart to hear what pitiful cries they made to us to help them, when, well-a-day, we could scarce help ourselves.
> 3. *Fish.* Nay, master, said not I as much when I saw the porpoise, how he bounc'd and tumbled? they say they're half fish, half flesh; a plague on them, they ne'er come but I look to be wash'd! Master, I marvel how the fishes live in the sea.

18

1. *Fish.* Why, as men do a-land: the great ones eat up the little ones.
   I can compare our rich misers to nothing so fitly as to a whale:
   a' plays and tumbles, driving the poor fry before him, and at last
   devours them all at a mouthful. Such whales have I heard on
   a'th' land, who never leave gaping till they swallow'd the whole
   parish, church, steeple, bells, and all.

                                                    (2.1.18–34)

Such homespun philosophizing possesses a certain appeal.
The fishermen's fanciful speeches attract the audience that has
just heard Pericles' unspectacular poetry and the mainly limpid
expression of act 1.[5] Pericles might realize that the fisherman's
little allegory could apply to his own affairs. He has experienced
great Antiochus's treachery and the feelings of helplessness attending it. Like great fish, tyrannical men ruled by appetite can
and do eat up less powerful mortals, even when the latter are
princes. That fact, after all, moved Pericles, once he was safe in
Tyre, to tell Helicanus about Antiochus's vice and the sinful
king's possible attack upon their city. Nonetheless, Patch-breech,
not Pericles, completes the allegory and draws a moral:

3. *Fish.* But, master, if I had been the sexton, I would have been that
   day in the belfry.
2. *Fish.* Why, man?
3. *Fish.* Because he should have swallow'd me too; and when I had
   been in his belly, I would have kept such a jangling of the bells,
   that he should never have left till he cast bell, steeple, church,
   and parish up again.

                                                    (2.1.36–43)

The fishermen's talk of whales, sin, and the swallowing and
disgorging of a man, interwoven with mention of religious restoration, echoes the biblical story of Jonah. For Jacobeans, Jonah
was the most memorable figure swallowed by a whale. According to Norman Nathan, features of the Jonah story apparently impressed Shakespeare during the writing of *Pericles*.[6] Since the
moral of the story illuminates the play, a brief summary will be
helpful. Jonah found himself in the whale's belly because terrified sailors threw him overboard in order to appease divine
wrath, which had taken the form of a tempest battering their
ship.[7] Jonah freely became the sacrificial victim when he confessed that he was attempting to flee God's presence. His guilty
flight derived from his refusal to obey God's commandment that
he publicly proclaim ("cry against") the evil of Nineveh's citi-

zens. Jonah's error involved his failure to believe in Providence; he lacked faith that God would somehow use a public protest, which from a mortal viewpoint appeared dangerous, to bring forth good not only for the sinners but for the proclaimer himself. Resurrected from the beast, Jonah bravely enters the wicked city and, in an act of personal salvation, cries, "Yet forty days, and Nineveh shall be overthrown!" (Jonah 3:1–10). Immediately the Ninevites reform, proclaiming a fast, donning sack-cloth and averting ruin. Jonah's words, faithfully uttered, possess redemptive power.

In *Pericles*, Patch-breech's method for obtaining salvation whimsically recalls the moral of the Jonah story. By jangling the church bells, Patch-breech, if swallowed by leviathan, would work a personal and social resurrection. Despite the comic warping, the thematic connotations of his remark are clear. A vigorous jangling of church bells, a spiritual stirring, defeats a great villain and the evil associated with him. The nonverbal nature of the fisherman's protest does not detract from its verbal implications. Like Jonah, Patch-breech gains his salvation from the symbolic whale, from hellmouth, because he makes a bold spiritual protest against evil.[8] Within the generally serious context of romance, Shakespeare's viewer momentarily enjoys a comic rendering of a familiar truth.[9]

What importance can this truth have for Pericles? Hamlet before the Gravedigger demonstrates that Shakespeare on occasion conveys significant truths to the audience through homely speech to which a somewhat patronizing protagonist is ironically deaf.[10] Taken by the fishermen's colorful method, Pericles simply exclaims:

> How from the finny subject of the sea
> These fishers tell the infirmities of men;
> And from their wat'ry empire recollect
> All that may men approve or men detect!—
>
> (2.1.48–51)

At this dramatic moment, Pericles plays the role of the submissive hero.[11] Studied pathos informs his self-portrayal. In his own words, he is

> A man whom both the waters and the wind,
> In that vast tennis-court, hath made the ball

For them to play upon, entreats you pity him;
He asks of you, that never us'd to beg.

(2.1.59–62)

It is not surprising that Pericles, given his view of himself as acted upon rather than acting, overlooks Patch-breech's message about the redemptive effect of personal stirring. Stirring is generally preferable to passivity, and the Prince at this instant represents the less attractive quality. Regarding an energetic assertion of self, the fishermen have a comic advantage over Pericles in this scene. Instead of being foils who heighten the Prince's nobility, they are mainly spokesmen for pragmatic viewpoints that the hero cannot fully appreciate (2.1.63–65, 85–88). In its various forms, stir is an important value in *Pericles*.[12] By making Pericles passive, and by making him the butt of the fishermen's jokes, Shakespeare causes the viewer to value the energetic rustics' insights.[13] Pericles in Antiochus's court argued at length against the efficacy of a verbal protest against evil. In rejecting the linguistic form of virtuous stirring, he denies the value of the motif recommended by one of the play's major comic scenes.

Pericles' negative argument in Antioch results from the failure of certain extraordinary words to warn him of a lethal threat. At the play's outset, the Prince perceives the face of Antiochus's daughter as "the book of praises,"

where is read
Nothing but curious pleasures, as from thence
Sorrow were ever raz'd, and testy wrath
Could never be her mild companion.

(1.1.16–19)

In a Renaissance conceit described as conventional by Ernst Curtius, Pericles reads words in the text of his beloved's face.[14] Such words however are false; the beautiful, apparently innocent Daughter has been committing incest with her father for some time. Antiochus tries to drive Pericles away by pointing out the skulls of unsuccessful suitors and invoking another kind of visible language:

Yon sometimes famous princes, like thyself,
Drawn by report, advent'rous by desire,
Tell thee, with speechless tongues and semblance pale,

> That without covering save yon field of stars,
> Here they stand martyrs slain in Cupid's wars;
> And with dead cheeks advise thee to desist
> For going on death's net, whom none resist.
>
> (1.1.35–41)

While the treacherous words of a facial book entice Pericles, the significantly speechless language of Antiochus's macabre text fails to inform him of the danger in which he stands. Thus the Prince recklessly offers to read the riddle whose solution confers the Daughter as a bride upon the solver. From the riddle, Pericles learns that the Daughter whom he has been courting feeds incestuously upon her father's flesh. In the words of Northrop Frye, "if Pericles fails to solve the riddle, he must die; if he succeeds in solving it, he must die. The logic is that of the Arabian Nights."[15] The first consequence constitutes the gruesome penalty for failing to interpret Antiochus's enigma; the second reflects Antiochus's vicious resolve to keep his discovered vice secret. In either case, the word in the form of a riddle proves savagely destructive. Aware of the riddle's message, Pericles struggles to avoid both consequences. When pressed by suspicious Antiochus to expound the conundrum, the Prince, despite his horror, answers politicly:

> Great king,
> Few love to hear the sins they love to act;
> 'Twould braid yourself too near for me to tell it.
> Who has a book of all that monarchs do,
> He's more secure to keep it shut than shown;
> For vice repeated is like the wand'ring wind,
> Blows dust in others' eyes, to spread itself;
> And yet the end of all is bought thus dear,
> The breath is gone, and the sore eyes see clear
> To stop the air would hurt them. The blind mole casts
> Copp'd hills towards heaven, to tell the earth is throng'd
> By man's oppression; and the poor worm doth die for't.
> Kings are earth's gods; in vice their law's their will;
> And if Jove stray, who dares say Jove doth ill?
> It is enough you know; and it is fit,
> What being more known grows worse, to smother it.
> All love the womb that their first being bred,
> Then give my tongue like leave to love my head.
>
> (1.1.92–109)

Pericles risks death either by misinterpreting the riddle or by directly telling the King that he knows of the incest. This entrapping dilemma causes him to answer in obscure words. "To spread itself" (be widely broadcast), "vice repeated," in Pericles' opinion, must be like a "wand'ring wind" that blows dust in sinners' eyes. For his story's success and his own safety, the teller of a vicious tale must blind powerful sinners, his subjects, to the true application and meaning of his narrative.[16] But the sinners' delusion, their blinding, is only momentary. Pericles believes that the "breath" will be "gone": the special narration will eventually fail. The Prince implies that were he to broadcast Antiochus's incest, the tyrant's "sore" eyes would "see through" his veiled story, discovering a way to silence permanently the narrator. Thus Pericles vows that he will not be like the blind (unperceptive) mole whose protests against evil—its "Copp'd hills"—identify it and bring about its untimely death. He believes that evil "grows worse" when made more known; when sin is declared, not only the teller but innocent people associated with him are also sometimes vengefully struck down. Difficult poetry does not conceal Pericles' assurance that he will remain silent concerning incest. In terms of Pericles' complex metaphor, the vicious word blinds the faculty of sight; in due time, however, the pained eyes see their way to extinguish the word. Evil, whose knowledge is gained through the riddle, sets speaking, seeing, and hearing at odds with one another and restricts the faculties. Such a war among the faculties occurred when sin at the Fall originally impaired the act of knowing.[17] Shakespeare projects the Prince's present desire to be mute and deaf into the last act. Sitting in darkness, refusing to speak, and not crediting what he hears, the protagonist aboard his ship presents a powerful image of despair, acting out his earlier antiverbal attitude in a painful way that he could never have imagined.

Pericles remains true to the logic of his tortuous reply; he conceals Antiochus's incest once he has fled to Tyre. Melancholy, however, results from his harboring of the secret. Evil known but closely kept can fester, incapacitating the knower as much as evil contemplated does. In the negative silence wrought by Antiochus's riddle, Shakespeare builds into the design of *Pericles* a linguistic obstacle to the word's triumph. Elizabethans lacked a conceptual basis for the destructive verbal complement of the creative Johannine and Augustinian Word. The nearest they came were characterizations of the Devil as the grand equivocator, the father of lies, and of mankind's language as the confused product of Babel. Yet neither of these ideas amounts to the anticreative word, the terrible obverse of both John's Word (John 1:1–4) from which the world was made and Augustine's notion of human speech, fully expressive of thought because based on the analogy of the Word (Christ) that delivers God without diminishment.[18] For illustrations of the linguistic obverse, we must turn to Renaissance literature. Lear's "Never, never, never, never, never," undoubtedly the most nihilistic verse of trochaic poetry in world literature, approximates this prototypic anticreative (or decreative) word for which the Elizabethans had no metaphysical explanation.

The decreative force of Antiochus's riddle is clarified by speech-act theory developed during the past few decades.[19] J. L. Austin defines speech acts as either explicit or implicit illocutions of varying perlocutionary force. According to this linguistic philosopher, an illocution is "the performance of an act *in* saying something."[20] Thus when a minister declares, "I baptize this child in the name of . . . ," the utterance is properly an act done in speech (that of baptizing). According to speech act theorists, "the speaking of language is not merely the conveying of some conceptual content . . . but is primarily a mode of doing in its own right, namely the performing of acts 'such as making statements, giving commands, asking questions, making promises, and so on.'"[21] Austin characterizes the perlocutionary force of an utterance as "what we bring about or achieve *by* saying something, such as convincing, persuading, deterring, and even, say, surprising or misleading."[22] Unlike the categories of traditional grammar, Austin's concepts help us understand more clearly that Antiochus's riddle represents the antithesis of the creative word.

Classified grammatically, the riddle makes up a declarative statement metaphorically communicating not only Antiochus and the Daughter's incest but the unnatural intensity of their familial intimacy as well:

> I am no viper, yet I feed
> On mother's flesh which did me breed.
> I sought a husband, in which labour
> I found that kindness in a father.
> He's father, son, and husband mild;
> I mother, wife, and yet his child:
> How they may be, and yet in two,
> As you will live, resolve it you.

$$(1.1.65–72)$$

Regarded as a declarative statement ending in a command, the riddle is the Daughter's utterance—the "I's" of the enigma all refer to her. And yet Pericles reads rather than hears the riddle, an act reminding the informed auditor that the riddle is in fact Antiochus's. Regarded as Antiochus's speech act, the riddle constitutes neither a declarative statement nor a command. Considered as the performance of an act in speech (an illocution), it commits Antiochus to killing listening venturers (since solving the riddle will result in death as surely as misinterpreting it will). As a decreative word, the riddle undoes life as effectively as the Christian Word infuses it. Its perlocutionary force (what it brings about or achieves) devitalizes Pericles, muting him, forcing him to deny the moral promptings of his conscience, eventually draining the life from his cheeks and very being as melancholic stupor predominates. Vestiges of the belief that the royal word could create reality *ex nihilo* still surfaced during Jacobean times; as God's deputy, the ruler participated in the Johannine creativity of the divine word. In Antiochus's riddle and its destructive effect upon the Prince of Tyre, Shakespeare at the beginning of *Pericles* dramatizes a horrific parody of the nurturing word, a parody that initiates a tyrannical silence and broken life for Pericles. What creative word, we wonder, can match this decreative riddle, rectifying the chaos brought into being by it?

Still, it would be a mistake to imply that Pericles becomes victimized by decreative words. He *chooses* to pledge silence. By his commitment to silence, he virtuously desires to protect his subjects from Antiochus's retaliation. Pericles stated that "Kings are earth's gods; in vice their law's their will; / And if Jove stray, who dares say Jove doth ill?" As a rule, this saying might indict the speaker of a certain lack of courage, of a moral weakness blamable, for example, in the wavering Cleon who accedes to Dionyza's depraved plot against Marina. Applied to Pericles' predicament in Antioch, it can be appreciated, however, as ethical flattery by which a good ruler protects his people and himself from death. Regarded from one viewpoint, Pericles' attempt to convince Antiochus that he will not publish the crime deserves credit. Moreover, only a fool would berate a tyrant in his own court. In act 1, Pericles' situation contrasts with that of Jonah in one important respect: a deity does not order Shakespeare's character to "cry against" vice. Nevertheless, Shakespeare does evoke the tale of Jonah in the subsequent fisherman episode and does suggest that a declaration can defeat evil and restore good. While Antiochus has forced Pericles to deny this truth, Shakespeare thrusts it upon the viewer in scene after scene of the play. The theater audience thus wonders when Pericles can embrace and act out a truth whose worth, by act 5, has been repeatedly staged. Will Pericles be able to speak stirring words that characterize him as a redemptive hero instead of a helpless victim of the gods?[23]

In the play's early scenes, Shakespeare recasts his primary sources, focusing upon the good resulting from a verbal declaration of a special kind—that involving fault or evil. Ironically Pericles had to use words to tell Antiochus that he would not verbalize the tyrant's secret. Despite their oblique, clouded nature, these words betray Pericles by convincing Antiochus that the Prince is aware of his sin. Resolved to exterminate Pericles even in his own country, Antiochus conscripts an assassin, Thaliard. Thaliard at first unconsciously echoes the Prince's belief that the relating of a monarch's faults can only be harmful. Antiochus's confiding in a servant has created a reluctant henchman. Thaliard judges that

> he was a wise fellow and had good discretion that, being bid to ask what he would of the king, desir'd he might know none of his secrets: now do I see he had some reason for't, for if a king bid a man be a villain, he's bound by the indenture of his oath to be one.
>
> (1.3.3–8)

The remainder of this short scene reveals, however, the benefits of proclaiming a monarch's misdeeds. The "seal'd commission" (1.3.13), which Helicanus has slyly devised, does not "speak sufficiently" to the anxious citizens concerning Pericles' vanishing. They do not believe that their ruler is absent traveling. Consequently, Helicanus creates another white lie while Thaliard, undetected, eavesdrops. Helicanus declares that, because Antiochus was angry with Pericles for an unknown reason, the Prince penitently is toiling as a common sailor. In terms of the central passage in scene 1, the white lie represents a dramatic virtue. As *Hamlet* reveals, the divulging of a monarch's fault—the breaking of a seal on a commission—can be providential. Swayed by Helicanus's declaration, Thaliard decides that he will leave Pericles to the sea's anger and give up his murderous pursuit.[24] The playwright's poetry and prose may be flat; nevertheless, the scene helps shape a redemptive design.

The next scene of the play also refutes Pericles' ideas about the relationship between speech and evil. Suffering from severe hunger, Cleon, King of Tharsus, asks his queen, Dionyza,

> . . . shall we rest us here,
> And by relating tales of others' griefs,
> See if 'twill teach us to forget our own?
>
> (1.4.1–3)

Sad narratives, however, are counterproductive in Dionyza's opinion:

> That were to blow at fire in hope to quench it;
> For who digs hills because they do aspire
> Throws down one mountain to cast up a higher.
> O my distressed lord, even such our griefs are;
> Here they are but felt, and seen with mischief's eyes,
> But like to groves, being topp'd, they higher rise.
>
> (1.4.4–9)

Cleon, at any rate, decides to tell the story of Tharsus's "superfluous riots" in order to awaken divine comforters. By introducing his tale with the words, "This Tharsus, o'er which I have the government" (1.4.21), Cleon makes his story of his city's decline a mirror for magistrates in which the body politic's misrule of itself is reflected in the distraught King. The pathetic conclusion of his tale forms a moral for mankind:

> O, let those cities that of plenty's cup
> And her prosperities so largely taste,
> With their superfluous riots, hear these tears!
> The misery of Tharsus may be theirs.
>
> (1.4.52–55)

Cleon implies that the ruin of his city partly results from a monarch's fault—his own. His final plea coincides with the arrival of Pericles' fleet of ships. Cleon believes that a savage nation, aware of the vulnerability of Tharsus, expects an easy conquest of starving men. Pericles, admitting that "we have heard your miseries as far as Tyre" (1.4.88), informs him, however, that the ships bring the means for life. Cleon's onstage story resembles a tale reflecting a king's failure, one that appears to produce a comforter—a prince with a saving gift of grain. The dramatic sequence thus quickly refutes Dionyza's belief about the futility of telling certain stories. Uttered words prove providential. Furthermore, Pericles would never have set sail for any shore if he had followed his advice to Antiochus. Faced with Helicanus's criticism for hiding the root of his sadness, Pericles stated, "[H]eaven forbid / That kings should let their ears hear their faults hid!" (1.2.61–62). In keeping with this sentiment, the Prince then told Helicanus about the evil threatening them. This admission prompted the advice that Pericles travel for a while, words that prove fruitful for Cleon and his hungry subjects as well as for Pericles. In this instance, the Prince's unexpected admission is private. Only near the end of the play does Pericles experience the good resulting from a public declaration of royal evil.

In the second act, Shakespeare continues to focus upon the efficacy of protest—in this case a stirring verbal protest. Even though Pericles, his armor recovered, wins the offstage tourney and thus Thaisa's hand in marriage, as a "mean" knight he must demonstrate his worth to Simonides. Unfortunately, Pericles' passivity reaches new extremes in Simonides' hall of state. The Prince claims that his victory comes more by fortune than by merit (2.3.12); he avoids the seat of honor, stating that a lesser place is far more fit for him (2.3.23); he laments time's tyranny and his forlorn life (2.3.37–47); and he denies any skill in dancing (2.3.104). Later, he rejects Simonides' praise of his musical abilities, claiming that he is "the worst of all her scholars" (2.5.29–31). Moreover, when Simonides proposes that the stranger become Thaisa's tutor, Pericles declines: "I am unworthy for her schoolmaster" (2.5.40). Finally, when the King shows him Thaisa's love letter, Pericles fearfully exclaims,

> 'Tis the king's subtlety to have my life.—
> (Kneels.) O, seek not to entrap me, gracious lord,
> A stranger and distressed gentleman,
> That never aim'd so high to love your daughter,
> But bent all offices to honour her.
>
> (2.5.44–48)

Such pithless sentiments convince neither the audience nor Simonides that Pericles deserves Thaisa. The hero balks at assuming any role requiring mastery, whether it be one of lover, schoolmaster, or son-in-law to a king. Clearly, Pericles' experience of venturing for Antiochus's daughter, which he finds reflected in a seemingly similar contest for the beautiful Thaisa, has intellectually crippled him. Brooding upon Antiochus's manners, Pericles concluded:

> How courtesy would seem to cover sin,
> When what is done is like an hypocrite,
> The which is good in nothing but in sight!
>
> (1.1.122–24)

The more courteous that Simonides appears, the more Pericles imagines that he is as inwardly devilish as the earlier fair-speaking giver of a lovely daughter through a trial. For the marriage to occur, Simonides must jar Pericles from his dogmatic opinion about appearance and reality. Critics have often noted that Simonides succeeds by playing the role of the heavy father in the manner that Prospero later does vis-à-vis Ferdinand. While his worthiness must also be proved, Ferdinand, unlike Pericles, does not need to be freed from an imprisoning idea. Nevertheless, Pericles, like Ferdinand, strongly reacts to the apparently hostile father's claims that the young man represents a traitor. In both plays, the reaction is a stirring protest:

> *Sim.* Traitor, thou liest.
> *Per.*   Traitor?
> *Sim.*   Ay, traitor.
> *Per.* Even in his throat—unless it be the king—
>   That calls me traitor, I return the lie.
> *Sim.* (*Aside.*) Now, by the gods, I do applaud his courage.
> *Per.* My actions are as noble as my thoughts,
>   That never relish'd of a base descent,
>   I came unto your court for honour's cause,
>   And not to be a rebel to her state;
>   And he that otherwise accounts of me,
>   This sword shall prove he's honour's enemy.
>
> (2.5.54–63)

By this vigorous verbal protest, Pericles redeems himself not only in Simonides' eyes but in those of the theater audience also. Dramatically, this speech—not the tourney—wins Thaisa. No longer passive, Pericles learns that Simonides' role was assumed and that one assumption will not cover superficially similar cases.[25] The swiftness of the change in Pericles' stated regard for Thaisa amounts to regrettable drama. Promising, in only one line of blank verse, to love Thaisa as much as life does the blood fostering it, Pericles does not permit much character analysis. In light of Shakespeare's linguistic thesis, however, his bold telling a king of his error amounts to a special triumph.

Despite this personal victory, Pericles, in the middle scenes of the play, reveals a mistaken idea of the word's power, mainly because he confuses the proper responses to metaphysical and moral evil. In Shakespeare's last plays, what appears to be metaphysical evil usually deserves silence. Because he lacks the knowledge of Diana's providence, Pericles bewails every woe. Having lost the material evidence of his heritage in the first tempest endured, the Prince laments,

> Yet cease your ire, you angry stars of heaven!
> Wind, rain, and thunder, remember, earthly man
> Is but a substance that must yield to you;
> And I, as fits my nature, do obey you.
> Alas, the seas hath cast me on the rocks,
> Wash'd me from shore to shore, and left me breath
> Nothing to think on but ensuing death.
> Let it suffice the greatness of your powers
> To have bereft a prince of all his fortunes;
> And having thrown him from your wat'ry grave,
> Here to have death in peace is all he'll crave.
>
> (2.1.1–11)

What begins as an angry command quickly becomes a somewhat spiritless complaint. According to John F. Danby, we hear in this speech "the cliché of resignation instead of the vast moment of spiritual forces that turns on 'patience.'"[26] Appearing at the beginning of the fisherman episode, Pericles' complaint contrasts with the rustics' comparatively stirring speech and with their lesson concerning the value of stir.

In his study of *Pericles*, Danby distinguishes between Stoic patience, which he equates with apathy, and active Christian patience *(patiens)*, which he describes as a "release of charity."[27] While Pericles is often charitable, Danby judges that, in complaints like the speech quoted above, the protagonist expresses an imperfect attitude. In the play's most famous passage (3.1.56–64), Pericles imagines Thaisa's body, "scarcely coffin'd," plummeting through the sea to the ooze, where "the belching whale" and "humming water" overwhelm her corpse, "lying with simple shells." Expressed in remarkable poetry, these images cannot obscure Pericles' mistaken belief that the gods are indifferent to human value. In Danby's analysis of the arresting speech, Pericles "fully realizes death's final 'apathie'—away from the storm, on the sea's floor, 'lying with simple shells': an apathy which is the opposite of patience as death is the opposite of life."[28] In the Prince's vision, the whale's belching suggests a bestial indifference to human redemption; the image evokes Jonah's experience only to deny its truth. Pericles' poetry finally becomes stirred, imaginatively original; yet its faithless content paradoxically concerns stasis—the gradual ceasing of all movement and loss of human value.

Like Posthumus and Leontes, Pericles does not understand that the gods inflict suffering upon elected men and women in order to refine their souls and develop spiritual states of mind. The hero of late Shakespearean romance learns that metaphysical evil is not evil after all. Rather, it consists of "crosses" that a ruling god or goddess lays upon him in order to make his final joys more delightful for having been delayed. Pericles complains pointlessly to Neptune and Aeolus, for example, measuring the gods by mortal wishes:

> The god of this great vast, rebuke these surges,
> Which wash both heaven and hell; and thou that hast
> Upon the winds command, bind them in brass,
> Having call'd them from the deep! O, still
> The deaf'ning, dreadful thunders; gently quench
> Thy nimble sulphurous flashes!
>
> (3.1.1–6)

Regarded in light of the play's verbal dramaturgy, the word "rebuke" deserves special consideration in this passage. Pericles urges Neptune to speak against the unruly waves. But like Jupiter in *Cymbeline* and Apollo in *The Winter's Tale*, Diana does not make Pericles capable of receiving spiritual truths by "gently quenching" rough forces of suffering, the necessary schoolmasters of the soul. By stilling the raging sounds of the sea, wind, and atmosphere, Neptune and Aeolus, in Pericles' conception, would work the stasis that the Prince usually desires but from which he does not develop character. Finally, when Thaisa appears to die during childbirth, Pericles indicts all the Olympian deities:

> O you gods!
> Why do you make us love your goodly gifts,
> And snatch them straight away? We here below

> Recall not what we give, and therein may
> Use honour with you.
>
> (3.1.22–26)

Lychorida's reaction to these words—"Patience, good sir" (3.1.26)—unequivocally indicates that Shakespeare, at least, did not intend them to reflect a refined virtue. Even though Pericles' imaginatively existential vision of the gods' indifference to human worth proves mistaken in the complete context of *Pericles*, his immediate reaction to his philosophical discovery helps preserve comatose, apparently dead Thaisa. Her physical salvation hinges upon the salvatory word. Immediately after his vision of Thaisa's sinking body, Pericles exclaims,

> O Lychorida,
> Bid Nestor bring me spices, ink and paper,
> My casket and my jewels; and bid Nicander
> Bring me the satin coffer.
>
> (3.1.64–67)

If Pericles believes that neither Nature nor the gods will save Thaisa, then he has reason to impress a human signature upon his wife's loss. The word written by pen and ink—not the reward of jewels—works Thaisa's preservation. Cerimon labors to revive Thaisa mainly because Pericles' words inform him that she is a queen. She thus survives because the King affectionately includes her "passport" with her senseless body.

After Thaisa's sea "burial," Pericles' complaints cease; apparently he grasps the futility of addressing the gods about metaphysical evils. When Dionyza later hypocritically laments Thaisa's loss, Pericles admits that

> We cannot but obey
> The powers above us. Could I rage and roar
> As doth the sea she lies in, yet the end
> Must be as 'tis.
>
> (3.3.9–12)

With these words Pericles expresses the proper attitude toward metaphysical evil in the world of the last romances—faithful silence.[29] Yet as happens so often in the play, his triumph is short-lived; Marina's "death" shatters Pericles' spirit and he sinks into the absolute apathy of despair.

Moral evil, on the other hand, warrants verbal rebuke, a point left to Marina to demonstrate during her trials in the Mytilene brothel. Like Pericles in Antiochus's court, Marina would hear no evil. For example, she stops her ears when the Bawd tells her that she shall "taste gentlemen of all fashions . . . " and "have the difference of all complexions" (4.2.74–76). Marina also resembles her father in petitioning the gods to end her suffering:

> For me,
> That am a maid, though most ungentle fortune
> Have plac'd me in this sty, where, since I came,
> Diseases have been sold dearer than physic—
> That the gods
> Would set me free from this unhallow'd place,
> Though they did change me to the meanest bird
> That flies i'th' purer air!
>
> (4.4.94–101)

Like Pericles, Marina does not realize that her painful bondage to the fallen world amounts to a phase in a divine plan. Both Marina and Pericles lack Thaisa's ability to endure adversity patiently by trusting the gods, especially Diana, to bring events to their own divine end. Nonetheless, an important difference between the characters emerges. Marina complains to the gods; however she never makes Pericles' mistake of blindly indicting them. More important, Marina knows that moral evil deserves vigorous chastisement. No one, Pericles stated, dares to tell an earthly Jove that he acts wrongly. Marina, on the contrary, courageously risks telling the erring Governor of Mytilene that he dishonors himself by visiting the stews. While critics have often compared Marina's youthful innocence to that of Miranda, Marina's name does not signify a passive character, as the Latin gerund does in the case of Prospero's daughter. At first Lysimachus thinks that Marina's whorish dwelling place "proclaims" her to be "a creature of sale" (4.6.76–77). But her brave declaration that a virtuous man would never enter a sty gives Lysimachus a good opinion of her:

Mar. Do you know this house to be a place of such resort, and will come into't? I hear say you're of honourable parts and are the governor of this place.
. . . .
If you were born to honour, show it now;
If put upon you, make the judgement good
That thought you worthy of it.

Lys. How's this? how's this? Some more; be sage.

(4.6.78–80, 91–94)

Marina's biting, fearless criticism of a ruler's faults prompts (not retards) good understanding:

Lys.   I did not think
    Thou couldst have spoke so well; ne'er dreamt thou couldst.
    Had I brought hither a corrupted mind,
    Thy speech had alter'd it.

(4.6.101–4)

Despite his disclaimer, Lysimachus has brought a degraded mind to the brothel and Marina's sharp words have altered it. After hearing her, he guiltily denies his lust:

            For me, be you thoughten
        That I came with no ill intent; for to me
        The very doors and windows savour vilely.

(4.6.108–10)

Marina's stirring verbal protest proves redemptive for Lysimachus and those patrons subjected to it.[30] Her role provides a corrective commentary upon Pericles' idea about the futility of speaking out against evil. Shakespeare earlier hinted at the transformational power of Marina's speech. It has often been noted that Marina incarnates the moment of her birth at sea through a symbolic voice capturing the storm and its sounds. She verbally recreates for Leonine Pericles' and the sailors' brave industry during the tempest accompanying her birth, even assuming the voices of different men amid the imagined roar (4.1.49-64). By recreating an originally terrifying moment through charmingly innocent speech, Marina stylistically suggests that the unhappy events of that moment are finally innocent—as they in fact are within the scheme of Diana's providence. Equally important, she reveals her special gift for verbally metamorphosing disaster into something less threatening. Lysimachus's comic turnaround in his imaginative valuing of the doors and windows of the brothel stresses how thoroughly her fearless speech revolutionizes sight into a moral faculty.[31] In act 5, however, the change occurs in the opposite fashion. There, Pericles' visions of Marina as Justice and Patience cause him to revalue her speech.

At the beginning of the last act, melancholy Pericles remains concealed behind a curtain on board his ship, withdrawn from the gods who seemingly reclaim their gifts just as mysteriously as they give them. Helicanus then presents him as a dismal spectacle that stresses the vanity of speech and sight. "May we not see him?" Lysimachus asks. Helicanus replies:

>   You may;
>   But bootless is your sight; he will not speak
>   To any.
> Lys.   Yet let me obtain my wish.
> Hel. Behold him. *(Pericles discovered.)*
>   This was a goodly person,
>   Till the disaster that, one mortal night,
>   Drove him to this.
> Lys. Sir king, all hail! the gods preserve you!
>   Hail, royal sir!
> Hel. It is in vain; he will not speak to you.
>
>   (5.1.32–40)

In this episode, Pericles profoundly dramatizes his original reaction to sin; seeing and hearing no evil was his professed wish after learning of vice. His isolation ironically reflects this desire, not mankind's solitude in a cruel world. A challenger of her father's dramatic spectacle, Marina confronts it, finally shattering it and introducing her father to the restorative virtues of a story retold.

At first, Lysimachus believes that Marina's "sweet harmony" and "other chosen attractions" will "allure, / And make a batt'ry" through Pericles' "deafen'd ports" (5.1.44–46). Marina's song, however, makes no impact by itself; her physic will be her woeful story:

>   . . . she speaks,
>   My lord, that, may be, hath endur'd a grief
>   Might equal yours, if both were justly weigh'd.
>   Though wayward fortune did malign my state,
>   My derivation was from ancestors
>   Who stood equivalent with mighty kings. . . .
>
>   (5.1.86–91)

Hearing these words, Pericles sees the unknown maiden in a new light:

>   . . . my queen's square brows;
>   Her stature to an inch; as wand-like straight;

> As silver-voic'd; her eyes as jewel-like
> And cas'd as richly; in pace another Juno;
> Who starves the ears she feeds, and makes them hungry
> The more she gives them speech.
>
> (5.1.108–13)

A beautiful sufferer, Marina forces Pericles to revise his conviction that grief should look grievous. Transcendental imagination occurs when terrible suffering abates somewhat; Pericles, by a psychological reflex, adopts a view as brilliant as his painful vision was dark. After his great denial of speech, the word rings with a silver tone in his ears, and he fully enjoys its simple reality. Marina fears that her story of suffering will "seem / Like lies, disdain'd in the reporting" (5.1.118–19). Pericles, however, insists that his supreme vision will guarantee the truth of any words she speaks:

> Prithee, speak;
> Falseness cannot come from thee, for thou look'st
> Modest as Justice, and thou seem'st a palace
> For the crown'd Truth to dwell in. I will believe thee,
> And make my senses credit thy relation
> To points that seem impossible . . .
>
> (5.1.119–24)

In Pericles' eyes, Marina's heavenly beauty makes her speech resound truthfully in his ears, and her musical words intensify his rare view. Word and vision wonderfully complement each other, making possible a familiar Platonic coincidence.[32]

> Tell thy story;
> If thine consider'd prove the thousandth part
> Of my endurance, thou art a man, and I
> Have suffer'd like a girl; yet thou dost look
> Like Patience gazing on kings' graves, and smiling
> Extremity out of act. What were thy friends?
> How lost thou them? Thy name, my most kind virgin?
> Recount, I do beseech you. Come, sit by me.
>
> (5.1.134–41)

Trusted "by the syllable" (5.1.167), Marina's narration of Cleon's and Dionyza's treachery, bloodthirsty Leonine's attack, and the pirates' mercenary rescue positively identifies Pericles' lost daughter. Marina opens the book of monarchs' faults. Her words of evils suffered have a homeopathic effect when one grief drives out another and Pericles is fully revived.[33] Cerimon's recovery of Thaisa depended upon "still and woeful music" (3.2.90) whereby one bitterness expelled another. Marina invites her listeners to remember her trials and imagine her martyr-like faith, comparing these images with personal woes whenever the latter seem extreme. Pericles does say that if Marina's story proves the thousandth part of his misfortunes, he has not suffered manfully.

Marina's invitation extends to the theater audience as well as to Pericles. Pericles' advice that every book of monarchs' acts be kept closed contrasts with Shakespeare's decision to open Gower's and Twine's volumes and stage (publicly proclaim) the chief deeds of Pericles' life. According to Gower, lords and ladies have read the saga of Pericles "for restoratives" (Chorus 1.7–8). Shakespeare's sorrowful play can revitalize its viewer by presenting images of griefs greater than any suffered or imagined possible. Marina's brief tale is such an image. It is the composite—in fact, the miniature—of the play in its cathartic working. Just as her tale of suffering displaces Pericles' grief, promoting his recovery and making possible the formal ending of romance, so the larger tale of Pericles works upon the viewer's woes, placing them in perspective. The word proves to be restorative metadramatically as well as dramatically. A tale involving a monarch's faults can redeem not only a king but a society as well.[34]

Gower's periodic dumb shows and his commentaries upon them have predisposed the viewer of *Pericles* to believe by act 5 that the spoken word and vision acquire a special virtue when they interact for complete understanding. In the Chorus to act 2, for example, Gower first tells the viewer that Pericles is safe and honored in Tharsus; then he announces, "tidings to the contrary / Are brought your eyes; what need speak I?" (Chorus 2.15–16). Onstage this pantomime occurs:

> *Enter, at one door,* Pericles *talking with* Cleon; *all the train with them. Enter, at another door, a* Gentleman, *with a letter to* Pericles; Pericles *shows the letter to* Cleon; Pericles *gives the* Messenger *a reward, and knights him. Exit* Pericles *at one door, and* Cleon *at another.*

If performed spiritedly, the spectacle exemplifies the epistemology originally formulated in *The Rape of Lucrece*:

To see sad sights moves more than hear them told,
For then the eye interprets to the ear
The heavy motion that it doth behold,
When every part a part of woe doth bear.

                                    (1324–27)

While the dumb show under consideration possesses this affective merit, the theater audience remains perplexed about the
meaning of the distressing emotions portrayed. The viewer requires Gower's resumed speech to know that the letter in the
dumb show comes from Helicanus, the faithful counselor gov-
erning Tyre, who notifies Pericles that the assassin Thaliard has
stopped there in his pursuit of him. When Gower explains that
Helicanus advises further flight, the viewer grasps the meaning
of the rushed exits at the dumb show's close. Eye and ear thus
explicitly complement each other for knowledge; directly speaking of a monarch's faults has clarified understanding. Gower
prefaces the initially ambiguous dumb show of act 3, complete
with another messenger, a new letter, and the same quick de-
partures of Pericles and Thaisa—exits that are in this case
joyous—with the assurance "What's dumb in show I'll plain
with speech" (Chorus 3.14). Rather than acquiring negative connotations, Gower's "plain" signifies "explains"—a welcomed activity. Thus the viewer hears that Helicanus has told Pericles that
Antiochus and the Daughter are dead and that Tyre's lords will
deprive the Prince of rule unless he returns immediately. By act
4, Shakespeare's instruction for harmonizing the eye and ear has
become emphatic. Regarding the actors in the dumb show of Marina's tomb, Gower requests that the viewer "like motes and
shadows see them move awhile." Then he promises, "Your ears
unto your eyes I'll reconcile" (4.4.22).[35] The more enigmatic the
dumb show's spectacle, the more the viewer appreciates the enlightenment given by the spoken word; the more plain the poetic
word as choral narrative, the more he or she values the power
of the vision. In summary, through the choral technique of *Pericles*, Shakespeare highlights the interaction of faculties crucial
to the protagonist's final recovery, pointedly underscoring the
word's clarifying power.[36]

Pericles' dream-vision of Diana is part of the linguistic design
under discussion. The deity who visited the seventeenth-century stage often bodied forth a Neo-Platonic virtue proper to itself.[37] Were their rare pageant not dissolved, Ceres and Juno, for
example, would have chastely taught Ferdinand and Miranda

the Idea of Married Fertility by joining them in symbolic dance with April's nymphs and August's reapers.[38] Given the dramatic context and Diana's symbolic meaning, Shakespeare's informed playgoer awaits Pericles' sudden knowledge of Chastity.[39] However, instead of the intuition of Chastity, Pericles receives from Diana the command to travel to Ephesus, offer sacrifice upon her altar there, and give both his and Marina's trials "repetition to the life" before the assembled worshippers. In this instance, giving a tale repetition to the life does not entail describing events exactly as they happened; rather, the goddess directs Pericles to narrate a story of suffering in such stirring words that it lives in listeners' minds. His fulfillment of Diana's bidding is letter-perfect:

> Hail, Dian! to perform thy just command,
> I here confess myself the king of Tyre;
> Who, frighted from my country, did wed
> At Pentapolis the fair Thaisa.
> At sea in childbed died she, but brought forth
> A maid-child call'd Marina; who, O goddess,
> Wears yet thy silver livery. She at Tharsus
> Was nurs'd with Cleon, who at fourteen years
> He sought to murder; but her better stars
> Brought her to Mytilene; 'gainst whose shore
> Riding, her fortunes brought the maid aboard us,
> Where, by her own most clear remembrance, she
> Made known herself my daughter.
>
> (5.3.1–13)

Pericles obeys a deity's command to tell a story involving evil (the evil of a king) even as his counterpart Jonah finally divulged the wickedness of Nineveh in an act pleasing to God and assuring salvation. Pericles' faithfully told story is restorative; his public narration makes his identity known to the nun Thaisa, who faints upon hearing this revelation. Revived a second time by Cerimon, she threatens to recreate the play's original conflict:

> O, let me look!
> If he be none of mine, my sanctity
> Will to my sense bend no licentious ear,
> But curb it, spite of seeing.
>
> (5.3.28–31)

Now, however, no radical conflict in knowing presents itself. The viewer realizes that the problem has been resolved; all the faculties cooperate in revealing husband and wife to each other. Thaisa's eyes and ears record the truth; Pericles is a "Great sir" (5.3.26). Gower predicted that Pericles would prove awful both in deed and word. Antiochus's greatness was merely totalitarian force; the King of Tyre, on the other hand, inspires awe because he humbly submits to divine edict. Great in this sense, he practices an active faith far different from his passive obedience to what he supposed was the gods' will. Thaisa's vision of her husband opens her ears to his bizarre yet true narrative of the family's preservation. The efficacious working of words has re-created the sanctity of the family as only the theater audience can fully appreciate.

After the royal family's reunion, Gower speaks the Epilogue. He explains that Fame conveyed Cleon and Dionyza's plot against Marina to the ears of Tharsus's citizens. Outraged, they burned the rulers in their palace: "The gods for murder seemed so content / To punish; although not done, but meant" (Epilogue. 15–16). After supposedly murdering Marina, Dionyza taunted her conscience-stricken husband:

> Be one of those that thinks
> The petty wrens of Tharsus will fly hence,
> And open this to Pericles.

(4.3.21–23)

While birds do not miraculously "open" the fault to Pericles' ears, an earthly power—fame—inevitably does disclose the crime to Cleon and Dionyza's subjects. Instead of a god's lightning bolt, the common telling of a story of monarchs' faults brings about the tyrants' ruin. That dramatic point, however, is hardly necessary for the viewer aware of a verbal truth in Pericles.[40]

3

Cymbeline

By making redemptive speech depend upon the relative strength of characters' inner faith, Shakespeare in *Pericles* conforms to Margreta De Grazia's description of an Elizabethan rather than Jacobean attitude toward the speaker/speech relationship. In an important essay, this critic has argued that Elizabethan writers generally depicted prideful speakers (rather than flaws within language) as bearing the responsibility for perverting potentially divine speech.[1] She remarks that "for Augustine, as well as for sixteenth-century Scriptural exegetes and commentators, the Word of 'charity' incarnated in Christ and instilled in the disciples at Pentecost was the antidote to Babel."[2] In other words, speakers were praiseworthy or blamable to the degree that love infused their words. In *Pericles*, a certain faith in either the efficacy of the word or the goodness of the gods (and on occasion in both) takes the place of love as the ethical touchstone for speech. Admittedly, De Grazia almost certainly oversimplifies her argument by claiming that "in the sixteenth century, it was assumed that defects in men brought about confused speech; in the seventeenth, it became widely held that confused speech brings on many of the defects in man."[3] In fact, strains of nominalism appear in the sixteenth century, while optimistic views about the ability of words to convey truth surface late in the period of Baconian skepticism.[4] Still, regarded in light of her many illustrations, De Grazia's analysis of a dominant Elizabethan attitude toward language illuminates *Pericles*. If characters do not boldly or faithfully speak at key moments, they risk becoming the cause of their own ruin. Their salvation lies, in Christian fashion, in the word, providentially rewarded when uttered by the Prince of Tyre, Cleon, and Marina.

After the profound linguistic skepticism of the great tragedies, Shakespeare's depiction in *Pericles* of speakers working their own redemption or damnation through words is particularly Elizabethan in its optimism concerning one's linguistic control

41

of one's destiny. In *The Garden of Eloquence* (1577), Henry Peacham argued that "to the end that this sovereign rule of reason, might spread abroad her bewtifull branches, and that wisdome might bring forth most plentifully her sweete and pleasant fruites, for the common use and utility of mankind, the lord God hath joyned to the mind of man speech, which he hath made the instrument of our understanding, and key of conceptions . . . and here is it that we do so far passe and excell all other creatures, and not they, in that we have the gifte of speech and reason, and not they."[5] In this respect, the play is distinctly pre-Baconian in its linguistic cosmos. Still, in using the Jonah story to exemplify miraculous speech, Shakespeare in *Pericles* demonstrates a positive linguistic belief persisting at least as late as 1622. During his sermon preached on Easter Monday of that year, John Donne alludes to the tale of Jonah to define the creative word of God: "In the act of Creation, the Will of God, was the Word of God; his Will that it should be, was his saying, Let it be. Of which it is a convenient example which is in the Prophet *Jonah, the Lord spoke unto the Fish, and it vomited Jonah upon the dry Land;* that is, God would have the Fish to do it, and it did it."[6] While Shakespeare does not dramatize this aspect of the Jonah story in *Pericles*, Donne's comment suggests that the playwright may have been drawing upon a homiletic motif when he highlights the redemptive verbal dimension of a well-known biblical episode.

If *Pericles* represents essentially sanguine assumptions about language, *Cymbeline* constitutes a confirming gloss on Bacon's dark ruminations on words in *The Advancement of Learning* (1605) and *The Novum Organum* (1620). Borrowing Polonius's stage distinctions, we may agree that, in *Cymbeline*, Shakespeare presents a compendium of "tragedy, comedy, history, pastoral, pastoral-comical, historical-pastoral, tragical-historical, tragical-comical-historical-pastoral, scene individable, [and] poem unlimited" (*Ham.* 2.2.396–400). These kinds of drama are subordinated to two major types in *Cymbeline*, one of which Polonius does not mention: romantic and historical.[7] The historical matter—Cymbeline's refusal of the tribute due Augustus, the consequent Roman invasion of Britain, and the fierce battle that the Welsh exiles help the British King to win—surfaces as a primary subject in act 3. Cymbeline's breaking of political faith with Rome thus gives dramatic place to Posthumus's breaking of the faith appropriate to married love—the subject of the first two acts. Posthumus's breaking of his married faith proceeds from both certain defects within speech itself and misguided scientific inquiry. In fact, in keeping with the assumption of organic interaction between mind and speech, the linguistic defects and the method of intellectual inquiry are related in *Cymbeline*. By the end of act 2, the relationship has destroyed Posthumus's most cherished idea, that of Imogen's beautiful goodness, and reduced his language to ugly invective against women. Later, however, a humble empirical way of thinking, once registered in speech, confers architectonic self-knowledge upon the play's protagonist.

The problematical interaction of thought and speech typical of *Cymbeline* is most immediately noticeable in the play's often-remarked, troublesome style. The corrugated style of *Cymbeline* has often appeared to interpreters much as the speechless Pisanio, burdened by Posthumus's command that he murder his mistress, does to Imogen:

> One but painted thus
> Would be interpreted a thing perplex'd
> Beyond self-explication.
>
> (3.4.6–8)

"In narration," Samuel Johnson memorably pronounced in his Preface (1765), Shakespeare often "affects a disproportionate pomp of diction and a wearisome train of circumlocution, and tells the incident imperfectly in many words, which might have been more plainly delivered in few. . . . Not that always where the language is intricate the thought is subtle, or the image always great where the line is bulky; the equality of words to things is very often neglected, and trivial sentiments and vulgar ideas disappoint the attention, to which they are recommended by sonorous epithets and swelling figures."[8] Dr. Johnson's famous indictment includes a certain obtuseness of expression on Shakespeare's part as well as the implied violation of neoclassical principles of decorum: "It is incident to him to be now and then entangled with an unwieldy sentiment, which he cannot well express, and will not reject; he struggles with it a while, and if it continues stubborn, comprises it in words such as occur, and leaves it to be disentangled and evolved by those who have more leisure to bestow upon it."[9] Rather than amounting to a defect within an undisciplined artist, Shakespeare's perplexed style may represent a bold, conscious stroke on his part. Critics are only beginning to investigate the possibility that Shakespeare's crabbed, convoluted, and tumid verse, whether in *Cymbeline* or elsewhere, at times artistically reflects a similarly embroiled state of mind within characters.[10]

The two gentlemen of Cymbeline's court who begin the dramatic action do not merely neglect the equality of words to things; Shakespeare flagrantly controverts the dictum in their speech. First Gentleman's remark forms perhaps the most cryptic opening speech in Shakespearean drama:

> You do not meet a man but frowns: our bloods
> No more obey the heavens than our courtiers
> Still seem as does the king.[11]
>
> (1.1.1–3)

Frank Kermode judges that "*Cymbeline* is the only play in the canon which has characters given to such tensely obscure ways of expressing themselves that not only the audience but the other characters find it hard to make out what they mean."[12] Evidently, Cymbeline's courtiers appear differently than does Cymbeline himself. A peculiar disobedience involving "blood" pervades the court, but its cause and nature remain obscure to the audience. Since the courtiers wear frowns, the viewer is tempted to believe at this early moment that the King acts otherwise than troubled. Nothing in the gentleman's next speech violates this possible expectation:

> His daughter, and the heir of's kingdom (whom
> He purpos'd to his wife's sole son—a widow
> That late he married) hath referr'd herself
> Unto a poor but worthy gentleman. She's wedded,
> Her husband banish'd; she imprison'd, all
> Is outward sorrow, though I think the king
> Be touch'd at very heart.
>
> (1.1.4–10)

The viewer now comprehends the several reasons for the pervasive unhappiness at court, but he or she still does not definitely know how the inwardly vexed Cymbeline "seems." Consequently the spectator remains without a key for unlocking the thought of the ambiguous opening statement. Only upon a restatement does First Gentleman's primary meaning become apparent:

But not a courtier,
Although they wear their faces to the bent
Of the king's looks, hath a heart that is not
Glad at the thing they scowl at.

(1.1.12–15)

First Gentleman thus simply means that the courtiers are grieved outwardly, as Cymbeline is; unlike him, however, they are inwardly joyous over Imogen's and Posthumus's wedding.

Some viewers of this play might argue that contrivance in the courtiers' speech is unremarkable; often initial dialogue between minor Shakespearean characters rapidly introduces several major dramatic issues, usually in a compressed moment that encourages verbal ellipses. The courtier's turgid language, requiring fifteen lines of verse to clarify a rather uninvolved truth about appearances and emotional realities, could represent, nevertheless, the kind of writing that Dr. Johnson regretted.[13] Regarded retrospectively, the gentlemen's dialogue signals Shakespeare's special concern in *Cymbeline* with a speaker's struggle to fashion meaning through statement and restatement. First Gentleman alters his original remark until words more accurately convey his thought. This habit of mind can be called empirical in the broadest sense. Instead of being deduced from an unambiguous utterance, meaning is gradually induced from a primary, ambiguous saying through repeated linguistic "trials."[14] Certainly this stylistic trait of Shakespeare's appears elsewhere in his work; it in fact uniformly characterizes his dramaturgy as much as it marks everyday conversation between people. No sooner, for example, does First Gentleman begin portraying Posthumus's marriage than he must clarify a possibly uncomplimentary ambiguity in his speech:

and he that hath her
(I mean, that married her, alack good man,
And therefore banish'd) . . .

(1.1.17–19)

In this context, the phrase "hath her" could mean "sexually possessed her"; the gentleman, startled by his unruly words, must graciously modify his imprecise speech.[15] What distinguishes *Cymbeline* is the notable degree of complexity accompanying the process of statement and restatement, a degree calling attention to the properties of language itself.

In this ambitious late romance, a failing within speech itself (rather than the speaker) often accounts for the tortuous efforts of speakers to clarify an original ambiguous statement. During their discussion of Imogen's and Posthumus's exceptional natures, the two courtiers suggest that a rarity cannot be voiced in words without inadvertent linguistic slander. Although he cannot boast of material riches, Posthumus, according to First Gentleman,

> is a creature such
> As, to seek through the regions of the earth
> For one his like; there would be something failing
> In him that should compare. I do not think
> So fair an outward, and such stuff within
> Endows a man, but he.
>
> (1.1.19–24)

Impressed, Second Gentleman observes, "You speak him far" (1.1.24). First Gentleman in turn disagrees, but instead of coining more spectacular terms, as the viewer might expect, he rather obscurely says,

> I do extend him, sir, within himself,
> Crush him together, rather than unfold
> His measure duly.
>
> (1.1.25–27)

The gentleman's intentions, not his admittedly colorless words, must constitute Posthumus's eulogy. He implies that words and syntax cannot wield matter more magnificent than themselves; the most well-meaning praise of Posthumus's virtue appears inadequate when spoken. The dramatic problem is neither that hyperbole fails ridiculously, as it did in *Troilus and Cressida*, nor that the hero lacks excellence—nor even that his worth is artificially divided into outer and inner qualities. The difficulty lies in the fact that his virtue, as the courtiers imagine it, remains so unparalleled that restatements cannot authentically represent it.

To emphasize a verbal insufficiency, Shakespeare makes the idiom in which First Gentleman casts his belief that he cannot describe Posthumus's virtue labored and somewhat disparaging to the hero. Posthumus's excellence becomes lost in the perplexing accordion-like effect of the lines quoted above. When the viewer hears them spoken quickly in the theater, Posthumus's value suddenly expands with the word "extends," just as rapidly contracts in the phrase "crush him together," and abruptly increases again in the word "unfold" and the remainder of the passage. The speech anticipates Polixenes' labored attempt in *The Winter's Tale* to forge normal words, by themselves insufficient to convey his gratitude to Leontes, into an original image of thanks, Metaphysical in its arithmetic ingenuity (*WT.* 1.2.1–10). Specific lines later in *Cymbeline* neatly describe the viewer's feeling that a vast difference exists between Posthumus's virtue and First Gentleman's lame representation of it. Iachimo tells the company in Rome that Imogen's marriage to Posthumus "words him (I doubt not) a great deal from the matter" (1.5.16–17).[16]

The unintentional slander that results from imperfect ways of speaking and knowing creates the opportunity for the more conventional type of slander that pervades *Cymbeline*. A radical problem in speaking that gives Iachimo the means to realize his jealous plot makes possible the Italian's poisoning of Posthumus's faith. To be sure, tensions exist in Imogen's and Posthumus's married love which make us uncomfortable. Their speaking of their affection in terms of buying and selling gives limiting connotations of commercial price to a quality that they claim is infinite. Regarded from the perspective of pure faith, Posthumus's introduction of an alternative to Imogen's truth becomes unnecessary. In his opinion, she is

> therewithal the best, or let her beauty
> Look through a casement to allure false hearts,
> And be false with them.
>
> (2.4.33–35)

An absolutely faithful lover would not admit this doubt, which puts Posthumus in a mood to accept more readily the notion that his wife might be an adulteress.[17] Iachimo, however, does not use such a questionable doubt as a chink in Posthumus's faith that can be widened.

Iachimo capitalizes instead upon the disparities between Posthumus's incomparable idea of Imogen and the alien words and jewel by which the protagonist struggles to make it understandable not only to others but to himself as well. A Frenchman in Philario's house begins the chain of events that leads to the wager when he recalls that Posthumus once praised Imogen in language as grand as the terms that the members of the present gathering have used to extol their mistresses. Then Posthumus believed that his beloved was

more fair, virtuous, wise, chaste, constant, qualified and less attempt-
able than any the rarest of our ladies in France.

(1.5.61–63)

Upon Iachimo's ridicule of such hyperbole, Posthumus maintains that her virtue and his opinion have not altered with time.
Attentive to the form of the Briton's praise, Iachimo calls attention to the making of verbal comparisons, which becomes a
source of trouble in the present dispute:

As fair, and as good—a kind of hand-in-hand comparison—had been
something too fair, and too good for any lady in Britany.

(1.5.72–74)

The insult is double. In Iachimo's mind, Posthumus has "out-
spoken"—overshot—Imogen's value, even though the Briton's
comparisons for Imogen make up a common epithet. Iachimo's
sarcastic phrase, "a kind of hand-in-hand comparison," suggests
that "as fair, and as good" amounts to a predictable linguistic
formula—one cliché draws forth the other.
    Pressing Posthumus to believe that he can easily lose every-
thing related to his love, Iachimo says,

Your ring may be stolen too: your brace of unprizable estimations,
the one is but frail and the other casual; a cunning thief, or a (that
way) accomplished courtier, would hazard the winning both of first
and last.

(1.5.92–97)

While the word "unprizable" chiefly means "inestimable" in the
passage, it also has overtones of "worthless." When "a (that
way) accomplished courtier" can with carnal purposes use Posthumus's well-meant words in his courtship of any woman, they,
by implication, cannot be unique ways of expressing Imogen's
rarity—or the rarity of any woman, for that matter. Such words
are public property available to any base fellow; voicings of them
infrequently reveal individual speakers' good and evil motives.[18]
Thus they remain imprecise symbols. The dramatic problem becomes essentially that which Bacon describes in The Novum Organum:

There are also Idols formed by the intercourse and association of
men with each other, which I call Idols of the Market-Place, on ac-

count of the commerce and consort of men there. For it is by discourse that men associate; and words are imposed according to the
apprehension of the vulgar. And therefore the ill and unfit choice of
words wonderfully obstructs the understanding. . . . For men believe
that their reason governs words; but it is also true that words react
on the understanding; and this it is that has rendered philosophy and
the sciences sophistical and inactive. Now words, being commonly
framed and applied according to the capacity of the vulgar, follow
those lines of division which are most obvious to the vulgar understanding. And whenever an understanding of greater acuteness or a
more diligent observation would alter those lines to suit the true divisions of nature, words stand in the way and resist the change.[19]

While Bacon's interest lies in asserting that precise philosophic
and scientific inquiry can never be reliably conducted through
common language, his generalizations about the leveling effects
of speech apply to *Cymbeline*.[20] Words in this play are generally
formed in such popular senses and define things by such broad
lines that they, even in restatements, cannot convey singular
truths.[21] Rare values, whether held as an idea or condensed in
art, remain essentially untranslatable into speech.

Many of the memorable details of the second wager scene
drive home this point. The rich tapestry woven with the story
of Cleopatra's meeting on the Cydnus with Mark Antony, a
chimney-piece of chaste Diana bathing, the roof worked with
golden cherubs, and the andirons wrought into two winking Cu
pids are artifacts in Imogen's bedchamber so marvelous that
Iachimo claims he has never seen figures "so likely to report
themselves" (2.4.83). So lifelike is this compelling art that only
motion and breath are lacking. The tapestry and andirons unfortunately have latent erotic values that intensify the notion of
promiscuous passion that Iachimo is attempting to implant in
Posthumus's mind.[22] For Jacobeans, Cleopatra on occasion dou-
bled for *Venus Cupiditas*. It was the cupidinous Venus who often
surrounded herself with golden cherubs and winking Cupids.[23]
By minutely describing these objects, Iachimo hopes to convince
Posthumus that he has spent the night with Imogen, gazing upon
these beauties amid his sport:

> Sir, my circumstances,
> Being so near the truth, as I will make them,
> Must first induce you to believe. . . .
>
> (2.4.61–63)

But Iachimo's account of the fine features of these art objects does not constitute proof of his wife's adultery in Posthumus's opinion. Iachimo might have heard a vivid narration of them in either Britain or Rome and not been struck by a first-hand viewing. Referring to the chimney-piece of Diana, Posthumus says,

> This is a thing
> Which you might from relation likewise reap,
> Being, as it is, much spoke of.
>
> (2.4.85–87)

Once a speaker verbally counterfeits the art objects, they forfeit their veridical power. This judgment applies not only to the slanderous use to which Iachimo would put them but also to their communicative value in general. Transferred to words, their meanings lack unique imaginative appeal. For example, the tapestry's residual moral about erotic love is apparently caught by Iachimo's remark that "Cydnus swell'd above the banks, or for / The press of boats, or pride" (2.4.71–72).[24] Nevertheless the art objects lose their inspirational force when Iachimo's narration rather flatly conveys their meanings. An inferior medium of expression in effect approximates their specialness without communicating the imaginative conviction that only they themselves directly do.

The report of the beautiful art in Imogen's bedchamber thus reiterates more narrowly the basic problem of knowing that is set more broadly in the wager scenes. Unique values are lost when they are expressed through a lessening verbal medium. Imogen can be known truly in terms of Imogen; she is her own precious self-referent. She exists, after all, on a plane of value different from that of the diamond ring and bracelet to which Posthumus and Iachimo reduce her during their wrangling. Even the precious objects that the lovers substitute for inadequate words fail them. In fact, appropriated by enemies, such communicative substitutes can be used to invert the special message intended by their original status as love-gifts. At the beginning of the debate, Iachimo seizes upon Posthumus's diamond ring as a vehicle for his belief that Imogen does not equal the perfect woman:

If she went before others I have seen, as that diamond of yours out-lustres many I have beheld, I could not believe she excelled many:

but I have not seen the most precious diamond that is, nor you the
lady.

(1.5.74–79)

Iachimo argues that the limited sample from which Posthumus
draws his conclusion invalidates his claim concerning Imogen's
rarity. Posthumus simply has not compared Imogen to a large
number of women; a poor empiricist at the play's beginning, he
has tested his claim in too few situations for it to merit the status
of a universal truth.

By dwelling upon the ring, Iachimo encourages Posthumus to
equate Imogen's worth with an inappropriate object, just as Iago
does when he insinuates that Desdemona's handkerchief could
be symbolic of her honor. At this point Iachimo does not succeed
in getting Posthumus to identify Imogen with the diamond:

Post. I prais'd her as I rated her: so do I my stone.
Iach. What do you esteem it at?
Post. More than the world enjoys.
Iach. Either your unparagon'd mistress is dead, or she's outprized
  by a trifle.
Post. You are mistaken: the one may be sold or given, or if there were
  wealth enough for the purchase, or merit for the gift. The other
  is not a thing for sale, and only the gift of the gods.

(1.5.80–88)

After Iachimo has returned from Britain with his evidence, Posthumus unfortunately uses the diamond ring as a metaphor for
Imogen's honor. He thus makes the association that Iachimo contrived in the first wager scene. Concerning Iachimo's success,
Posthumus asks, "Sparkles this stone as it was wont, or is't not
/ Too dull for your good wearing?" (2.4.40–41). In his mind, Imogen's chastity now gives luster and hence worth to the ring.
Rather than properly being on another level of value, her chastity
has become synonymous with the diamond which, in the absence of adequate words, expresses it. Now Iachimo surprisingly
insists that Imogen and the ring cannot be equated: "if I have lost
it, / I should have lost the worth of it in gold" (2.4.41–42).
Upon her discovery that her bracelet is missing, Imogen said, "I
hope it be not gone to tell my lord / That I kiss aught but he"
(2.3.148–49). Once a material object expresses values, those values are subsequently known chiefly in terms of the object. Be-

cause Imogen's chastity has come to be esteemed as a material article (a ring), another material object (a bracelet which Iachimo produces) appropriately proclaims her reputed adultery. Just as nurture cannot supply the words, nature cannot provide the metaphorical objects for expressing without slander Posthumus's ideas of Imogen and married chastity. These ideas can be grasped only in their uncommunicable singularity, in what makes them unlike anything else in creation.

Posthumus's intellectual error thus consists of his exposing his rare idea of Imogen to the world of words and comparable objects, which inevitably debase it. Speaking in iron conceptions tarnishes Posthumus's golden intuition. Like Cordelia, who found no words fit for her devotion, he should have loved and courageously remained silent before Iachimo's taunts. Words, however, of course cannot by themselves mislead a completely well-intentioned speaker. Nevertheless, when words fail a speaker or compromise his or her ideas, they necessarily impact the mind's search for truth or confirmation. Failed words testify to the organic interaction of speech and mind, simply because thought takes a different, often disastrous course once it can no longer rely on words to give preconceptions adequate form. This phenomenon helps to explain Posthumus's other epistemological error—his abuse of scientific inquiry. Posthumus apparently considers himself driven to test Imogen's integrity physically once words fail to shape and preserve his idea of her rarity. Abandoning descriptive words as a measuring device altogether, he joins with Iachimo in a perilous assaying of her worth. Posthumus's and Iachimo's testing of Imogen's married chastity seems—in the detached manner by which they finally agree upon it—to resemble a scientific experiment designed to estimate the degree of an object's preciousness. But such testing of mortals to discover their spiritual mettle in *Cymbeline* remains the god Jupiter's privilege. By proudly conducting a cruel experiment, Posthumus and Iachimo associate themselves with a debased "scientist," the Queen. No longer content with making perfumes, distilling, and preserving—arts learned from the good doctor Cornelius—the Queen seeks poisonous compounds, which bring on death slowly. She intends to give these deadly drugs to Imogen, so that her son Cloten can ascend easily to Cymbeline's throne. Thus she must deceive Cornelius concerning her motive for desiring poisons. His reaction to the reason she fabricates forms an ironic commentary upon the moral destruction that Posthumus's and Iachimo's illegitimate testing of Imogen brings upon the testers themselves. "Having thus far proceeded," the Queen asks,

> is't not meet
> That I did amplify my judgment in
> Other conclusions? I will try the forces
> Of these thy compounds on such creatures as
> We count not worth the hanging (but none human)
> To try the vigour of them, and apply
> Allayments to their act, and by them gather
> Their several virtues, and effects.
>
> (1.6.15–23)

The referents of the pronouns in the last three verses of this speech appear ambiguous. By gesturing first to the box of drugs that she holds, the Queen specifies the vigor of the compounds, which she would try by paralyzing an onstage cat and dog (toward which the actress might point). By means of the animals, she believes that she can gather the several virtues and effects of the drugs. Cornelius immediately identifies the evil of such a seemingly disinterested empiricism:

> Your highness
> Shall from this practice but make hard your heart:
> Besides, the seeing these effects will be
> Both noisome and infectious.
>
> (1.4.23–26)

The Queen's heart, however, has already been hardened. The doctor's judgment describes the callousness that Posthumus develops from his mistaken testing of Imogen for her several qualities. Posthumus's savage diatribe against women testifies to the infected knowledge resulting from his ill-advised experiment. By giving the Queen harmless drugs rather than lethal compounds (and so stupefying but preserving Imogen), Cornelius resembles Jupiter, who troubles elected mortals in order to refine their souls and lead them to greater happiness. Consistent with the god's benign aim, the Queen's and Posthumus's punishments for their sacrilegious acts are different. Unregenerate, the Queen dies raving; contrite, Posthumus suffers terribly but grows to be a husband worthy of Imogen.

Posthumus finally knows Imogen in the last stage of his wager by one of the most common recognition devices of romance: a mole significantly shaped like a star—a pentangle. The hero does

not credit a traditional figure of divinity because he no longer
desires to believe that his wife is the gods' creation.[25] Posthumus's infected will reveals itself after his erected wit cannot
sustain its heavenly idea. His intellectual fall is complete. Enraged, he declares,

> Let there be no honour
> Where there is beauty: truth, where semblance: love,
> Where there's another man. The vows of women
> Of no more bondage be to where they are made
> Than they are to their virtues, which is nothing.
>
> (2.4.108–12)

Posthumus in this passage unknowingly sets an important condition for later scenes of the play. "Fair and good" verbal comparisons have not been able to indicate how Imogen's inner truth and
outward beauty constitute an integral whole. The unique binding
of her virtues into a transcendent whole occurs in Wales during
Arviragus's elegy. In the Welsh mountains, Shakespeare depicts
a natural language that does not slander a remarkable idea in its
expression.

Enduring adversity, Imogen, disguised as Fidele, takes the benign but life-suspending drugs that Cornelius substituted for the
Queen's poison and so appears dead to her brothers and Belarius. In his elegy for her, Arviragus depicts her beauty by means
of a Renaissance pastoral convention:

> With fairest flowers
> Whilst summer lasts, and I live here, Fidele,
> I'll sweeten thy sad grave: thou shalt not lack
> The flower that's like thy face, pale primrose, nor
> The azur'd harebell, like thy veins: no, nor
> The leaf of eglantine, whom not to slander,
> Out-sweet'ned not thy breath: the ruddock would
> With charitable bill (O bill, sore shaming
> Those rich-left heirs, that let their fathers lie
> Without a monument!) bring thee all this;
> Yea, and furr'd moss besides. When flowers are none,
> To winter-ground thy corse—
>
> (4.2.218–29)

Writers of pastoral romance often expressed the heroine's physical beauty by means of flowers. For example, Clitophon, in *The
Loves of Clitophon and Leucippe* by Achilles Tatius, asserts:

But still *Leucippes* countenance seemed to me stil to surpasse the glittering shewe of the Peacocks traine, for her bewtie might contend very well with the flowers of the Gardaine: the forme of the Daffadill did shine in her forhead, the colour of the Rose did glister in her cheekes, the brightnesse of the Violet did appeare in her eyes, her haire did imitate the curling of the Vine, and such was the admirable bewtie of her face.[26]

Natural flowers unequivocally express Arviragus's idea of Imogen's beauty; the primrose communicates the loveliness of her face, the harebell that of her veins, and the eglantine leaf that of her breath. In Arviragus's estimation, the eglantine is not slandered; her breath's sweetness is no more nor no less than the leaf's. Arviragus's flower-statement observes, in Bacon's words, "the true divisions of nature" more accurately than conventional speech does. Competition between words and intuitions does not materialize in the elegy; elevated thought smoothly becomes elevated artistic speech without slander. Nor do things and words (res et verba) perpetuate their long-standing communicative intransigence in Wales; a flower not only prompts but also conveys Arviragus's eloquence. Marion Trousdale has argued that "the single most important belief about the nature of language in the sixteenth century" concerned "the disjunction between words and things."[27] According to Trousdale, "things were thought to be in many different senses and could be described in a variety of ways. Such disjunction meant that language use was by definition a conscious endeavor and that there was always a recognized gap between the thought or the res and the words on the page."[28] This inevitable gap also exists between res as objects and the words used to portray them. Arviragus bridges this gap when he uses a res (a unique flower) as a nonverbal vehicle to convey the idea of Imogen's beauty (res in another sense). When one kind of res originally expresses another res, the linguistic compromise of meaning never occurs.

Barren winter, however, mars Arviragus's elegaic art. Transient summer blossoms and the speaker's impermanent residence make the flowers' testimonial power ultimately relative. Nevertheless, late in the play Imogen suggests that the pastoral realm fosters true speech. Discovering Arviragus's and Guiderius's identity, she declares,

> O, never say hereafter
> But I am truest speaker. You call'd me brother,

When I was but your sister: I you brothers,
When ye were so indeed.

(5.5.376–79)

Even Belarius's words on occasion possess a physically compelling power in Wales. "When on my three-foot stool I sit, and tell / The warlike feats I have done," the old man confides, Guiderius's

>   spirits fly out
> Into my story: say "Thus mine enemy fell,
> And thus I set my foot on's neck," even then
> The princely blood flows in his cheek, he sweats,
> Strains his young nerves, and puts himself in posture
> That acts my words. The younger brother, Cadwal,
> Once Arviragus, in as like a figure
> Strikes life into my speech, and shows much more
> His own conceiving.

(3.3.89–98)

Rarely has the uttered word exerted such a plastic effect. By means of this immediate, near-perfect mimesis, the uttered word almost seems to assume the corporeal shape of its meaning. Word and thing become a single expressive whole, immune from the intervening forces that compromise the uttered word's message.

In light of the problems with language in the play's wager scenes, Arviragus's dramatization of "truest speaker" in his elegy gains a special relevance.[29] Still, language does not easily attain ideal power in Wales. Boldly, Shakespeare incorporates several different failures of speech within the pastoral experience linguistically regenerative for Imogen. Understanding the deficiencies of Welsh language intensifies our appreciation of the word's eventual triumph in Imogen's pastoral role playing.

Throughout *Cymbeline*, Shakespeare suggests that the reliability of speech remains intimately connected with visual and auditory perspectives. Perspectives, whether in art or in life, exist only because intrusive space distorts visual and auditory messages, creating the illusion that represented objects or sounds at a distance are in fact small or indistinct. Imogen expects to derive the following benefits from residing in Rome near Posthumus—the drastic reduction of space and thus the virtual elimination of falsifying perspectives. Pisanio implies that such benefits justify Imogen's long and dangerous journey over the sea to (from an English viewpoint) the sink of corruption. According to the good servant, although Posthumus's "actions [in Rome] were not visible, yet / Report should render him hourly" to Imogen's ear "as truly as he moves" (3.4.150–52). Roman report should be more truthful than British report, simply because the distorting perspectives of time and space in which words move have been virtually abolished. It would obviously be better still if Posthumus's actions were visible to Imogen's eye, a situation that would eliminate the possibility that slanderous accidents might change lovers' vows.

Shakespeare explicitly links false words and falsifying perspectives in one of Imogen's early Welsh speeches. Fallible eyes create deceiving perspectives in the Welsh mountains, causing misunderstanding and introducing error and suffering into Imogen's life. She misses the way to Milford Haven (and presumably to Posthumus) because the road, when viewed from a mountain top, seemed much closer than it proved in truth. Imogen laments that

> Milford,
> When from the mountain-top Pisanio show'd thee,
> Thou was within a ken.
>
> (3.6.4–6)

Thus the natural slander attending a visual way of knowing reinforces, even compounds verbal slander—the lying of two beggars who mislead Imogen (3.6.8–14)—even as both types worked together to undermine Posthumus during the wager scenes. During act 1, the relationship between slanderous visual perspectives and language is the other way around. Shakespeare verbally portrays Posthumus's exile from Britain within a receding visual perspective so that the audience keenly feels the inadequacy of sensory knowledge. In regard to Posthumus, Pisanio tells Imogen that

> for so long
> As he could make me with this eye, or ear,
> Distinguish him from others, he did keep
> The deck, with glove, or hat, or handkerchief,
> Still waving, as the fits and stirs of's mind
> Could best express how slow his soul sail'd on,
> How swift his ship.
>
> (1.4.8–14)

Distance and the failing senses translate Posthumus's passion-ate gestures into proverbial (and hence conventional-sounding) speech. Posthumus's waving gloves, hat, and handkerchief con-vert to a maxim about slow souls and swift ships. Deficient vi-sual and auditory perspectives directly contribute to relatively unoriginal speech, which necessarily cannot be unique because it must substitute for unknown (or poorly known) perceptions.

The epistemological and expressive deficiencies related to sensory perspectives reappear during Belarius's unorthodox to-pographical instruction of the young Princes. Belarius mistakenly believes that visual perspectives add meaning to his narratives and sayings. For example, he commands Arviragus and Guider-ius to scale a nearby mountain in order to understand existen-tially the saying "place sets off":

> Now for our mountain sport, up to yond hill!
> Your legs are young: I'll tread these flats. Consider,
> When you above perceive me like a crow,
> That it is place which lessens and sets off,
> And you may then revolve what tales I have told you
> Of courts, of princes; of the tricks in war.
> This service is not service, so being done,
> But being so allow'd. To apprehend thus,
> Draws us a profit from all things we see.
>
> (3.3.10–18)

The somewhat pedantic Belarius whimsically would utilize a lit-eral perspective to teach his young charges about an imaginary one, which offers a lesson about the relativity of social class, court favors, and service. Furthermore, Belarius believes that his previously told stories of "courts, of princes; of the tricks in war" would gain significance for Arviragus and Guiderius from the visually understood proverb about place setting off value. In this respect, a way of seeing and the word would reinforce each other to provoke a sudden insight within Belarius's pupils. But the Princes complain that such unusual learning has little meaning for them; they lack the alternate courtly experience that would allow them to appreciate Belarius's axioms:

> Gui. Out of your proof you speak: we poor unfledg'd,
>   Have never wing'd from view o' th' nest; nor know not
>   What air's from home. Haply this life is best
>   (If quiet life be best) sweeter to you
>   That have a sharper known, well corresponding

With your stiff age; but unto us it is
A cell of ignorance, travelling a-bed,
A prison, or a debtor that not dares
To stride a limit.

                                                    (3.3.27–35)

In other words, Arviragus and Guiderius lack the experiential dimension by which they might judge the relative worth of an idea or saying presented in their primary field of life. Their Welsh existence is flat—without depth; they cannot grasp the value of their savage pursuits, to say nothing of the incomprehensible abstractions that Belarius evokes from an alien, enticing world. As Guiderius states, the secluded life against which the young men chafe has become sweet to Belarius because he has known a sharper existence in court.[30]

Not only do the Princes grumble about their impoverished existence; they also imply that their savage manner of life limits their speech. At one point, Arviragus, replying to Belarius's praise of the secluded life, makes an assumption about the origin of speech:

                                    What should we speak of
                    When we are old as you? When we shall hear
                    The rain and wind beat dark December? How
                    In this our pinching cave shall we discourse
                    The freezing hours away?

                                                    (3.3.35–39)

Arviragus assumes that speech is the product of experience. The deeper assumption is that the word, in its richness or originality, reflects the quality of experience out of which it arises. "We have seen nothing," Arviragus states:

                    We are beastly: subtle as the fox for prey,
                    Like warlike as the wolf for what we eat:
                    Our valour is to chase what flies. . . .

                                                    (3.3.39–42)

Hunting beasts, feeding upon them, the Princes possess the animal vigor and ferocious valor conferred by an uncultivated life. Their language mirrors this life; it is not shaped by sophisticated rhythms or refined forms as the language of the court characters often is. That is not to say that courtiers' speech represents an ideal; it, conversely, could profit from an infusion of the natural vigor often heard in Arviragus's and Guiderius's talk. Ideally, the richest speech would be that of a character equally instructed by Nature and Art. Granted these distinctions, the young Princes would benefit from a refining social influence upon their language.

In retrospect, we judge that the eloquence of Arviragus's flower elegy and the great dirge constitute exceptions to the rule of the Princes' speech. What, then, accounts for their moving poetic speech on those occasions? The answer lies in the continuation of the episode under discussion. Belarius's response to Arviragus's candid self-portrait—"How you speak!"—suggests more than a rebuke for ingratitude; the phrase reveals Belarius's perhaps unintentional, ironic agreement with Arviragus's assumptions about the inspiration for speech. The exclamation "How you speak" conveys Belarius's distress that the young men's relatively unadorned speech reflects their limited understandings. Belarius tells the Princes that they would not speak as they do if they felt the "city's usuries . . . knowingly" (3.3.45–46). Through his remark, he inadvertently touches upon a source of imaginative speech, whether spoken in the court or country—experiential passion. Arviragus and Guiderius feel death "knowingly" when their beloved Fidele appears to die. The haunting words of Arviragus's elegy and of the rare dirge, "Fear no more the heat o' th' sun," move auditors because they are inspired by profound feelings of love and grief; the occasion of Fidele's "death" for a moment makes possible especially poetic expression. Generally, however, the Princes' idiom remains naive, reflecting their uncomplicated minds, even as Imogen's speech is usually "tuneful" and that of the psychopath Cloten arrhythmic.[31]

While Arviragus and Guiderius long for the city, court-bred Imogen expands her understanding through her harsh pastoral trials. For the play's heroine, alternate experience does not invest sayings with extra meaning so much as it teaches truths contrary to courtly report. Her very first words in Wales signify that she has already learned a truth unknown to a princess:

> I see a man's life is a tedious one,
> I have tir'd myself: and for two nights together
> Have made the ground my bed.
>
> (3.6.1–3)

Imogen learns that mountaineers can be "kind creatures":

> Gods, what lies I have heard!
> Our courtiers say all's savage but at court;
> Experience, O, thou disprov'st report!
> Th' emperious seas breed monsters; for the dish
> Poor tributary rivers as sweet fish. . . .

(4.2.32–36)

Here experience corrects verbal report, so much so that previous words are now regarded as lies. Primarily, however, Imogen's experience in Wales inculcates married fidelity to the degree that eventually the details of her life charge the word faithfulness (her name Fidele) with absolute, cleansed meaning. How that occurs requires extended analysis. Learning that her husband has accused her, Imogen too easily believes that an Italian whore has betrayed him (3.4.49–50). Once in Wales, she continues to doubt Posthumus's faith. She pardons the two beggars who give her false directions to Milford Haven by claiming that, while poor people may be driven by need, Posthumus's great lies of love have no imaginable cause (3.6.9–15). And she would change her sex to be the rustics' companion since she thinks that her husband has selfishly broken his vow (3.7.59–61). Faithful Pisanio, however, is not so credulous. Shakespeare introduces Pisanio into Cymbeline partly as a measure of loyalty revealing that the main characters' faith lacks requisite strength. The good servant correctly suspects that

>   it cannot be
> But that my master is abus'd: some villain,
> Ay, and singular in his art, hath done you both
> This cursed injury.

(3.4.120–23)

Imogen on the contrary believes that "some Roman courtezan" has, and Pisanio must repeat, "No, on my life" (3.4.124). By comparison, her view is not so complimentary to her husband.

This last point, however, must not be overstated. Imogen's love for Posthumus, which she never fully loses, proves basically resilient; unlike his corresponding opinion, her belief that "men's vows are women's traitors" (3.4.54) is fleeting. In the words of Robert G. Hunter, Posthumus "cannot succeed in destroying the love that is felt for him. Imogen's love, like God's for man, remains constant and is available to her erring husband when, penitent, he once more desires it."[32] This judgment is basically correct, except for the suggestion of divine constancy—a nineteenth-century critical legacy. While Imogen's affection constitutes the most remarkable example of love in the play, she does not exemplify flawless humanity, as the Victorians imagined.[33] Deeply angered by her husband's betrayal, Imogen rearranges the past in a typically human fashion so that it reflects her revised ideas of her own worth and Posthumus's meanness:

> And thou, Posthumus, thou that didst set up
> My disobedience 'gainst the king my father,
> And make me put into contempt the suits
> Of princely fellows, shalt hereafter find
> It is no act of common passage, but
> A strain of rareness: And I grieve myself
> To think, when thou shalt be disedg'd by her
> That now thou tirest on, how thy memory
> Will then be pang'd by me.
>
> (3.4.88–96)

Imogen may grieve for Posthumus's future remorse; yet her stronger desire is for his severe punishment. Her healthy self-esteem causes her to imagine herself the rare wife who, rejected for a lesser woman, inflicts the punishment of regret. Imogen's and Posthumus's marriage appears to have been a mutual decision; by claiming that Posthumus caused her to spurn other (more worthy) suitors and to rebel against her father Cymbeline, Imogen shifts the blame. To distort the past so that it reveals one's own importance is not really a blamable failing. Nevertheless, in Imogen, such a tendency, coupled with her assumption of Posthumus's lustful pleasures, indicates that her unusual love could undergo further refining.

When Imogen adopts the alias "Fidele" as part of her masculine disguise, she suggests that her experience in Wales involves her faith. In fact, she has chosen a word for her name that she will recharge with the meaning that presumably attended its original coinage. Walter R. Davis has explained how a character in a Renaissance prose romance like Henry Robart's *The Historie of Pheander The Mayden Knight* (c. 1595) or Richard Johnson's *Tom a Lincolne* (1607) occasionally adopts a persona along with a disguise, gradually learning a related Platonic Idea or an ideal, such as chivalry, by enacting it and so making it part of his or her inmost being.[34] This romance motif offers the only precedent for Shakespeare's complex use of disguise and role-playing as the major agents for expanding Imogen's knowledge of herself and her marriage to Posthumus. After Guiderius proves himself the best woodsman during the deer hunt, he becomes the lord of a feast at which Arviragus and Belarius play the roles of cook and servant respectively. Imogen acts the part of their housewife, dutifully cutting their root diet into letters for an alphabet soup (4.2.45–51). By means of her quaint experience, Shakespeare keeps his focus upon the word—the letter in this case. Imogen's culinary/educational activity not only suggests the nonprimitive nurture she would extend to her verbally starved brothers but also constitutes the faithful service by which she will fulfill a word—Fidele. Appropriately, the means of this linguistic fulfillment involves faithful linguistic service—her creation of the alphabet soup. By her original housewifery, Imogen reaffirms her wifely faith, which has been thrown into question. That the reaffirmation of Imogen's faith in Wales refers to her marriage is suggested by Guiderius's allusion to Juno. Struck by the fanciful nature of Fidele's culinary art, he exclaims:

> But his neat cookery! he cut our roots in characters,
> And sauced our broths, as Juno had been sick,
> And he her dieter.
>
> (4.2.49–51)

The seventeenth-century Juno was primarily regarded as the goddess of marriage, as her role in Prospero's masque reveals. Guiderius's remark applies not so much to the local incident but, metaphorically, to Imogen's pastoral service as a whole. Through her faithful Welsh service, Imogen, in his opinion, cures the goddess of marriage—that is, she makes healthy a languishing marriage (her own).

Imogen thus does not reaffirm her faith by any miraculous means. Suffering Posthumus's imagined death teaches her how much she loves him. When she thinks that Cloten's bloody trunk is her husband's, Jupiter is not perversely demonstrating that love lies at the mercy of ocular knowledge. Imogen learns that her husband's supposed infidelity is a minor evil compared with his ultimate loss. She thus experiences the play's educative dynamic; a greater grief displaces an extreme sorrow.[35] Through her drawn-out suffering of adversity, Imogen understands that her most intense joy involves Posthumus's well-being. Consequently she is prepared for her reunion with him. Thus, when the Roman

Lucius demands that she identify the headless body upon which she lies stretched, Imogen speaks of her husband in the noblest terms:

> Richard du Champ: *(Aside)* if I do lie, and do
> No harm by it, though the gods hear, I hope
> They'll pardon it.
>
> (4.2.377–79)

Giving her husband a knight's name, Imogen in a verbal phrase confers upon him the honor that his deeds in battle will show that he deserves. In the sense that her dignified name for Posthumus reflects her reconstituted love for him, Imogen's words do not make up a spoken lie. Lucius suggests that such devotion amounts to an extreme example of faith. Learning her assumed name, Fidele, he pronounces, "Thou dost approve thyself the very same: / Thy name well fits thy faith; thy faith thy name" (4.2.380–81). In other words, in Wales Imogen's persona gradually becomes part of her, so much so that her assumed name is the major instance in the play of a word that absolutely expresses an idea.[36]

Imogen's experimental role in Wales revitalizes other corroded words in addition to the term faithfulness. When Lucius, condemned to death after his capture, magnanimously pleads for the life of his "boy" Fidele, he does so by praising those qualities of Imogen that have been on trial, thus indicating that their strength is no longer in question. "Never master had / A page so kind," he insists,

> so duteous, diligent,
> So tender over his occasions, true,
> So feat, so nurse-like. . . .
>
> (5.5.85–88)

With reference to Imogen's remarkable service, certain terms such as "duteous," "diligent," and "tender" lose their social encrustations and regain an evocative clarity of meaning, Shakespeare's interest in linguistic cleansing resembling a Baconian preoccupation.

Not only does it cleanse words and augment knowledge; the experience of suffering in *Cymbeline* also corrects the conventional-sounding ideas that characters repeatedly voice throughout the play. We learned during Arviragus's elegy that suffering could impact speech, rendering it relatively original and imaginative. In passage after passage, the characters of this late romance interpret dramatic events by means of verbal *sententiae*. As Pisanio, for example, watches Imogen react to the letter directing him to murder her, he construes her grief in terms of a Renaissance commonplace of slander:

> What shall I need to draw my sword? the paper
> Hath cut her throat already. No, 'tis slander,
> Whose edge is sharper than the sword, whose tongue
> Outvenoms all the worms of Nile, whose breath
> Rides on the posting winds, and doth belie
> All corners of the world. Kings, queens, and states,
> Maids, matrons, nay, the secrets of the grave
> This viperous slander enters.
>
> (3.4.32–39)

A character in *Cymbeline* often begins with one interpretation of an event, catches himself when he realizes that the interpretation does not precisely fit the dramatic situation, and qualifies his first idea with additional ones. So Pisanio, in the speech above, first believes that Posthumus's vengeful letter has undone Imogen, disagrees with himself in the second verse of the passage, and then portrays the slander that has struck her, quarreling with himself for greater clarity in the penultimate line.[37] While this process (described earlier as made up of linguistic "trials") appears to be one of increasing specificity, on occasion the effect is the opposite; the qualifying ideas lead the speaker away from a complex dramatic situation into conventional expression where distinctions are blurred. Sententious sayings often become corrupting verbal frames of reference that prevent the incidents of this play from being understood purely in their own terms. In this case, the criterion for slander is exacting to an Olympian degree. *Only* a bird in hand is, strictly speaking, worth two in the bush. Any experience in which one actually holds something that can potentially be possessed in abundance naturally is bound to have dimensions that the saying about birds and bushes cannot encompass. Thus, any saying has only one context for the most precise understanding—the original one that bred it, of which it in turn gives the clearest interpretation. Any other application suffers from the distortions of metaphor. When Cornelius reports the Queen's death, Cymbeline finds some consolation in the sayings, perhaps proverbial, that bad news best becomes a physician and that, while medicine can lengthen life, death will seize the doctor too (5.5.27–30). Such common sayings work against the King's eventual understanding of the courage that the physician showed when he removed the deathly drugs from the chest that the Queen gave Pisanio. Similarly, Belarius curtails inquiry into Imogen's "death" by apostrophizing melancholy (4.2.203–9); Cymbeline into the Queen's evil by moralizing woman (5.5.47–48); Lucius into Imogen's failure to plead for his life by stereotyping the falsity of boys and girls (5.5.106–7), and so on.

Verbal commonplaces in *Cymbeline* repeatedly warp the meaning of a quality, an event, a character's words—a subject that superficially resembles the commonplace's meaning but in fact proves dissimilar. Imogen focuses upon this warping during her speech concerning Posthumus's imagined disloyalty. To her credit, Imogen does not stress Posthumus's lack of worth, or even the universal frailty of the opposite sex—the theme of his corresponding diatribe (2.5). Instead, she worries that, because of Posthumus's betrayal of her trust, women will distrust the good seeming of honest men. Like false Aeneas and weeping Sinon, Posthumus will become a precedent causing the words of true lovers, who are like him in everything but his deceit, to be misinterpreted and so condemned:

> All good seeming,
> By thy revolt, O husband, shall be thought
> Put on for villainy; not born where't grows,
> But worn a bait for ladies . . . .
> True honest men, being heard like false Aeneas,
> Were in his time thought false: And Sinon's weeping
> Did scandal many a holy tear, took pity
> From most true wretchedness: so thou, Posthumus,
> Wilt lay the leaven on all proper men;
> Goodly and gallant shall be false and perjur'd
> From thy great fail. . . .
>
> (3.4.54–64)

In other words, Posthumus will become a familiar archetype, slanderously stereotyping the good speech of someone like him but crucially different in moral nature. "The subtlety of nature is greater many times over than the subtlety of the senses and understanding," Bacon noted, "so that all those specious meditations, speculations, and glosses in which men indulge are quite from the purpose."[38]

When he reacts to Jupiter's epiphany, Posthumus initially illustrates the adverse relationship between speech and knowledge discussed above. Having suffered intensely and experienced remorse for his plan to murder Imogen, Posthumus attempts penance by recklessly fighting with Cymbeline's forces and thus sacrificing his life on Imogen's behalf. A distressed victor, he then dresses as a Roman in order to be executed as a prisoner of war. When he awakens in prison, Posthumus does not realize that his strange dream of the prior night possesses redemptive potential, for he first construes his vision in terms of an idea that sounds like a courtly saying. Dejected, he says that

> Poor wretches, that depend
> On greatness' favour, dream as I have done,
> Wake, and find nothing.
>
> (5.4.127–29)

Such a verbalization amounts to an interpretative framework that threatens to keep Posthumus from giving any importance to his dream-vision. But he chides himself before a commonplace obscures the extraordinary content of his dream:

> But, alas, I swerve:
> Many dream not to find, neither deserve,
> And yet are steep'd in favours; so am I,
> That have this golden chance, and know not why.
>
> (5.4.129 32)

Convinced that he does not deserve "this golden chance," Posthumus gratefully values the vision of his recreated family given by the dream.

Posthumus's remorse for his rash command for Imogen's death has helped forge a new humility, which entails a greater degree of self-knowledge. Immediately before his dream-vision, he petitioned the gods:

> For Imogen's dear life take mine, and though
> 'Tis not so dear, yet 'tis a life; you coin'd it:
> 'Tween man and man they weigh not every stamp;
> Though light, take pieces for the figure's sake:
> You rather, mine being yours: and so, great powers,
> If you will take this audit, take his life,
> And cancel these cold bonds.[39]
>
> (5.4.22–28)

Once asleep, Posthumus in his mind's eye sees Jupiter, Sicilius, his mother, and the young Leonati, his brothers, but he does not hear their words. In this respect, he differs from Pericles, who both sees Diana and hears her silver command that he recount his miseries at Ephesus. Were Posthumus to have heard Jupiter's verbal assurance that he would eventually be "lord of lady Imogen" and "happier much by his affliction made," he would know why he has been "steep'd in favours." Unlike Pericles (and the theater audience), he cannot benefit from the directly heard divine word. Instead, in a greater test of his faith, he must trust the riddling words of a book, a tablet left behind by the mute (to his ears) figures of the dream-vision:

> A book? O rare one,
> Be not, as is our fangled world, a garment
> Nobler than that it covers. Let thy effects
> So follow, to be most unlike our courtiers,
> As good as promise.
>
> (5.4.133–37)

Genuine modesty and penitence offer a better context for appreciating the dream-vision and tablet than a court saying does. Concerning the enigmatic oracle, Posthumus announces,

> Be what it is,
> The action of my life is like it, which
> I'll keep, if but for sympathy.
>
> (5.5.149–51)

Deepening his self-knowledge in the process, the hero understands one of the play's most crucial events by means of his own special punishment for proudly testing his wife. In the manner of a well-intentioned empiricist, he lucidly interprets experience in terms of the unique context out of which it emerges, thus avoiding the distorting medium of preconceived sayings (see note 14). Posthumus thus retains the divine word inscribed in the arcane tablet about a lion's whelp embraced by tender air that will be the sole proof that Jupiter has assisted the characters from despair to happiness. Only the most tenuous idea of correspondence, of "sympathy," between a singular, enigmatic life and an obscure riddle prevents Posthumus from throwing away the tablet. For his romantic salvation, Posthumus must possess an absolute faith in the truth of the divine word, purposely twisted into a riddle to test that faith. While intelligible, mortal sayings in *Cymbeline* have usually corrupted to some degree the events or ideas that they would convey. Unintelligible as a riddle, the divine word paradoxically fits the strange shape of providential experience, interpreting it for those who have enlightened ears to hear and hearts to know.

Unlike Antiochus's riddle, Jupiter's does not permit easy interpretation. The enlightenment of its hearers' ears comes slowly, in fact only after they have seen its terms acted out. For that acting to trigger interpretation, the words of characters' narratives preparing the riddle's interpretation must conform to prior experience as neatly as the linguistic medium allows. The several discoveries and stories of the last scene of *Cymbeline* reveal their experience to the characters basically in terms of those experiences themselves. Shakespeare presents the totality of experience in the play through successive narrations without the alien sayings that, as frames of reference, might misrepresent events and warp their true meanings. In detail and vigor, words approximate experience as well as narrative permits. By means of Iachimo's protracted story of intrigue (5.5.153–208), Shakespeare rather elvishly makes this point. The dramatist desires to lay words to the very curve of experience; Iachimo's eccentric words, imaginative ellipses, and digressive detail so catch and repeat the form of his complex betrayal that they draw the spellbound Posthumus out of his part as a Roman soldier into a compulsive reenactment of his sin when the story reaches that stage. In his true identity, he rehearses his former hatred for his wife by unknowingly striking Imogen when she would quiet his guilty ravings. In other words, a lively narrative so purely recreates an experience that the hero is catapulted into the spirit of the latter. Nonetheless, experience can rarely be understood in its own terms, for the simple reason that the tautology precludes an interpretive perspective upon events—the somewhat removed vantage point necessary for judgment and the assigning of values. Traditionally, art has provided this perspective upon experience. Iachimo's episodic narrative, however, in one respect works against art's interpretive function. While one standard for art involves its mimicry of life, Shakespeare implies in this episode that, when the principle is rigorously observed, art in effect duplicates experience, losing the special powers of enlightenment that come from the aesthetic distancing and reorganization of life.[40]

For the world of *Cymbeline*, Jupiter's artistic riddle supplies

the liberating perspective upon experience. Without the transla-
tive perspective that Jupiter's word provides, narratives of the
characters' actions in Cymbeline, no matter how vital or truthful,
would as a whole stand bare, made up of wonderful accidents
that might have no greater significance. Shakespeare in Cymbeline especially focuses upon the human yearning for the imposed design that makes episodic experience meaningful. Upon
learning of the Queen's evil plot against him, Cymbeline protests
that

> Mine eyes
> Were not in fault, for she was beautiful:
> Mine ears that heard her flattery, nor my heart
> That thought her like her seeming. It had been vicious
> To have mistrusted her. . . .

(5.5.62–66)

According to a Christian view, people do not viciously mistrust
the report of the eyes and ears because they know that any evil
carried unintentionally by them is somehow part of a benign
scheme. And if the senses report apparent evil, the report is
given the most charitable interpretation because they know that
such an act forwards Providence. In all other surviving versions
of the wager story, the villain persuades an old woman to conceal him in a chest in the heroine's bedchamber.[41] Imogen, without question, accepts Iachimo and his chest into her safekeeping
after he has debased Posthumus and her marriage and acted
churlishly toward her. By the dramatic adaptation, Shakespeare
emphasizes Imogen's martyr-like trust that her eyes and ears tell
her of no real evil.[42] The deeds that her charity prompts in this
case become necessary links in the chain of painful events that
creates her permanent happiness. She, however, has no intuition
of her destiny when she openly receives Iachimo.

Thus, Imogen and Cymbeline deserve credit when they give
sensory knowledge the most charitable construction, for when
they do, they have no reason to believe that normal charity fulfills a celestial plan. So that they do not have to remain creatures
of blind faith, the specific knowledge of Jupiter's providence is
redemptive for the characters of Cymbeline. They deduce the existence of Jupiter's design retrospectively, from his revealed
oracular word and their experiences.[43] Understanding divine
providence by means of natural events and earthly experiences
reveals a seventeenth-century shift in interest from heavenly to

terrestrial affairs. According to Wilbur Sanders, "the implication seems to be that these matters can be legitimately discussed on the naturalistic plane."[44] Writing in *The History of the World* (1614), Sir Walter Raleigh observes that

> The example of God's universall Providence is seene in his creature. The Father provideth for his children: beasts and birds and all livings for their young ones. If Providence be found in second Fathers, much more in the first and Universall: and if there be a naturall loving care in men, and beasts, much more in God, who hath formed this nature, and whose Divine love was the beginning, and is the bond of the Universall.[45]

Deducing the fact of providence from mundane experiences and the behavior of creatures becomes more certain when the divine word, even when expressed in riddles, provides the key for interpreting earthly happenings.

The oracular word becomes comprehensible when its terms are experienced in the last scene, acted out before the Roman Soothsayer, Philarmonus. Only then can the sage decree that the riddle is fulfilled: King Cymbeline is the lofty cedar whose lopped branches, grafted to him again, are his lost sons. "Leonatus" Posthumus is the lion's whelp, and

> The piece of tender air, thy virtuous daughter
> Which we call *mollis aer*; and *mollis aer*
> We term it *mulier*: which *mulier* I divine
> Is this most constant wife, who even now,
> Answering the letter of the oracle,
> Unknown to you, unsought, were clipp'd about
> With this most tender air.
>
> (5.5.447–53)

"It is not easy to conjecture why Shakespeare should have introduced this ludicrous scroll," Samuel Taylor Coleridge confessed, "which answers no one purpose, either propulsive, or explicatory, unless as a joke on etymology."[46] By demonstrating the interpretive power of the divine word, especially by contrast with the several failed or inadequate instances of mortal language in the play, Jupiter's scroll serves a primary dramatic purpose. Philarmonus can venture his etymology of "wife," one well-established in Shakespeare's day, because he has seen Imogen in the joyful act of embracing her husband.[47] Making the lovers' embrace the key to clarifying the divine word and finally apprehending a divine plan is appropriate, for their clasping proves that Jupiter's ethic of delaying joy to make it delightful has been successful. Posthumus and Imogen's love has at last answered the "letter" of Jupiter's providence. Conversely, their experience recharges words such as "wife" and "brave-born" ("Leo-natus") with a pristine quality of meaning, a quality resembling the purity inherent in the words' original creation. Their embrace amounts to a triumphant gesture of love that inspires Posthumus to say, "Hang there like fruit, my soul, / Till the tree die" (5.5.263–64). Tennyson considered these words to be "among the tenderest lines in Shakespeare."[48] That one of the simplest and most natural gestures of love should be the event by which the knotted strands of this tragicomedy's plot are unravelled is striking. The simpler and more gracious the actor and actress's embrace, the more deeply the beholder will reflect upon the mystery that Shakespeare has fashioned—the fact that love, essentially and unpremeditatedly offered, can make possible changes of heart, even historical revolution. Cymbeline's redefinition of his own and Britain's place in the world follows from the mood that the vision of intertwined Posthumus and Imogen creates within him and the other observers. One simple act of love leads indirectly to the archetypal one; Britain's peace with Rome makes possible the Pax Augustus, a necessary condition for the birth of Christ.[49]

Moreover, Posthumus's image for the embrace—that of fruit and tree—nicely conveys his charitable idea of the bond between man and wife, a bond so empathetic that Posthumus would change nature's pattern and make the nourished as important as the nourisher, the fruit as important as the tree. Posthumus fashions from the moment an original symbol by which he conceives of his love, uttering heart-felt poetic words expressive of his new knowledge of his unselfish role in marriage. As has happened previously, a well-told tale moves its auditors to act out its consequences. The acting in this case does not take the form of a verbal cliché, but originally grows out of experience to give birth to a rich metaphor. Posthumus's image suggests an inversion of the Christian symbol for the experience of sin, and therefore a prelapsarian purity for the lovers. Those who are jarred from construing life in terms of preconceived verbalizations and can patiently wait for each action to dictate its own context for understanding articulate their happiness when they learn that their experiences have assumed the form of an enabling figure of speech.

Still, Shakespeare will not let us leave the theater until he emphasizes that any human claim to professional authority in the verbal translation of divinity remains suspect. The right reading of Jupiter's other, equally ambiguous revelation—the Soothsayer's dream-vision—proves exceedingly difficult. In the vision, Philarmonus saw

> Jove's bird, the Roman eagle, wing'd
> From the spongy south to this part of the west,
> There vanish'd in the sunbeams. . . .
>
> (4.2.348–50)

The Soothsayer first thought that the vision predicts victory for the Roman host; by his western flight, Jupiter's bird is glorified. But after the British defeat the Roman legions and peace reigns, he decides that it foretells that imperial Caesar, the winged eagle, shall again unite with "radiant" Cymbeline in the west (5.5.468–77). An equivocal vision thus gains true meaning only when the Soothsayer can retrospectively see that experience fulfills it, however roughly, for some tension still exists in the interpretation.[50] Rome is absorbed within Britain ("vanish'd in the sunbeams") in the Soothsayer's definitive reading, while it is tiny Britain's immersion, signified by the paying of the tribute, within the Roman Empire that makes possible the Peace of Augustus. Divine ideas are never directly or easily divulged in this play but remain far removed mysteries confirming Shakespeare's conservative attitude toward the accessibility of celestial knowledge. In the working of Philarmonus's mind upon the hard facts of experience, we observe not only a final instance of an empirical method in *Cymbeline* but also the mystery of the divine word, resistant to every effort to force its predestined meaning.

4

The Winter's Tale

Rather than analyzing the language of *Cymbeline* from the Baconian (or empirical) viewpoint, one could study the play's speeches through the lens of contextualism. The term "contextualism" refers to what linguists such as Bronislaw Malinowski and J. R. Firth have described as an utterance's context of situation, "the whole cultural setting in which the speech act is located."[1] According to Firth, "the central concept of the whole of semantics considered in this way is the context of situation. In that context are the human participant or participants, what they say, and what is going on."[2] Obviously, situational contexts often help determine the value of words in speeches. Clearly, the male, nationalistic atmosphere of Philario's house colors the Frenchman's account of Imogen's virtues for the characters onstage; a competitive, "men's-club" context authorizes his adjectives, making them worthy of attack.[3] A contextual focus, nonetheless, does not illuminate the language of *Cymbeline* to the degree that the approach taken in the previous chapter does. Such is not the case with *The Winter's Tale*. In this later romance, Shakespeare continues to dramatize problems intrinsic to speech as a communicative medium. However, in *The Winter's Tale* the playwright accentuates the role of an utterance's context in corrupting or enhancing meaning. More precisely, he focuses upon the play between words and their contexts during the creation of meaning. This interaction undergoes a distinct shift in the course of the play. In Leontes' Sicilia, words by themselves appear either deficient for speakers' purposes or unreflective of reality. Thus they especially depend upon situational contexts for their value. Later, in Bohemia, Shakespeare reveals that words at moments can transform auditors' perspectives upon their world, eventually forging new, life-giving contexts making possible Leontes' and Hermione's reunion. The word, first lacking and misleading, thus finally becomes the means to grace in *The Winter's Tale*.[4]

Granted this shift of emphasis, Shakespeare makes linguistic deficiency the actual subject of the play's first episode. Having felt it, we can later appreciate the characters' need to find or construct the best context for a potentially inadequate utterance (rather than their desire to employ contextless words). In scene 1, Archidamus, a Bohemian lord, tries without much success to make known the munificence that Camillo will enjoy the following summer when he visits Polixenes' court. Compared to Leontes' remarkable hospitality, the Bohemians' entertainment, in Archidamus's verbalization, will in its failings make the hosts ashamed. Still, he insists:

> we will be justified in our loves: for indeed—
> Cam. Beseech you—
> Arch. Verily I speak it in the freedom of my knowledge: we cannot
>   with such magnificence—in so rare—I know not what to say—
>   We will give you sleepy drinks, that your senses (unintelligent
>   of our insufficience) may, though they cannot praise us, as little
>   accuse us.
>
> (1.1.8–16)

When he cannot find words as generous as his idea of munificence, Archidamus's courtesy becomes less than ideal. Unable to express clearly his intuition, he would drug the hearer's senses; Archidamus makes the mildest of threats when he speaks of stupefying Camillo. Such an unfortunate change of tone, while playful, occurs because language is unable to convey genuine gratitude. Archidamus "knows not what to say." In apology, he exclaims: "Believe me, I speak as my understanding instructs me, and as mine honesty puts it to utterance" (1.1.19–20). This apology indicates that the problem lies not so much within Archidamus as within the mode of speech; he is speaking with the best intentions in the relative freedom of his knowledge.[5] By swearing "verily" that speech fails him, Archidamus uses one of the most truthful expressive symbols; the writer of the Homily "Against Swearing and Perjury" notes: "Thus did our Saviour Christ swear divers times, saying, Verily, Verily."[6] Archidamus relies upon a catchword (a specially charged, contextless term) because language generally fails him. Shakespeare thus focuses not upon a fallen speaker but upon an unsatisfactory medium of communication. The question is precisely that raised by the opening dialogue of the gentlemen in Cymbeline. How can common speech convey singular ideas?

For *The Winter's Tale*, the answer to this question involves the complex nature of an utterance's setting.[7] Context initially becomes a dramatic subject in the play in Polixenes' speech of leavetaking from Sicilia. In a passage of haunting rhythms, Polixenes, speaking the first dramatic words heard in Leontes' court, strains mightily to thank the King for his hospitality:

> Nine changes of the watery star hath been
> The shepherd's note since we have left our throne
> Without a burden. Time as long again
> Would be fill'd up, my brother, with our thanks;
> And yet we should, for perpetuity,
> Go hence in debt: and therefore, like a cipher
> (Yet standing in rich place) I multiply
> With one "We thank you" many thousands moe
> That go before it.
>
> (1.2.1–9)

Polixenes labors in his speech because the usual expression of gratitude cannot ideally convey his profound affection. Heartless utterances of the phrase, after all, could sound to the ear exactly like Polixenes' genuine "thank you." In this respect, Polixenes' common "thank you" might be regarded as a "cipher"—a communicative zero—when compared to the unparalleled love to be expressed. It is only by a witticism, based upon arithmetic and Metaphysical in its intricacy, that Polixenes places his phrase of thanks in a context in which its minimal value is ingeniously increased. "Standing in rich place," one "thank you," like the zero in a large number, multiplies the worth of preceding phrases (digits) many times. The image of the cipher, moreover, can apply to Polixenes as well as to his phrase of thanks. In a Protestant view popular in Renaissance London, unaccommodated man was "nothing"—an equation memorably made in Shakespeare's plays.[8] Polixenes may be "nothing" because he is Adam's fallen heir; yet he is also a king. As King of Bohemia, Polixenes stands in one of the richest social places. Consequently, the words that he coins, like his currency, have utmost value even though they may be confused with counterfeits. Because he is a creative source, the king's expression of gratitude can legitimately multiply, unlike a lord's or commoner's. In other words, the social status of a speaker creates a context within which his words become either dross or gold.[9] Furthermore, Polixenes stands next to a queen, one who is visibly pregnant; thus the "rich place" to which he refers also has a literal meaning. Spoken near a fertile lady, his "thank you" multiplies.[10] This last reading is confirmed by a passage in *Henry VIII*. Regarding the ambitious Wolsey, Norfolk—in the Folio text—observes that

> O gives us note,
> The force of his owne merit makes his way
> A guift that heaven gives for him, which buyes
> A place next to the King.

Hilda Hulme, in her commentary on these lines, explains that, regarded from Norfolk's perspective, "Wolsey is nothing; he is 0, a cipher among numbers, to 'note' or fill a place, himself of no value. But . . . 'a Cypher (Yet standing in rich place)' can 'multiply' . . . and Wolsey stands in a 'place next to the King.'"[11]

In summary, the significance of Polixenes' striking speech depends upon several contexts—syntactical, social, physical. Taken as a whole, these elevating contexts form a single complex setting within which Polixenes for the moment succeeds.[12] In Polixenes' remarkable speech, Shakespeare defines a dramatic principle for his play. A special "standing" in an enhancing "place"—a crucial positioning within a valuable context—often enriches key ideas, characters, and especially words in *The Winter's Tale*. As Polixenes reveals, creative contexts can increase the value of common speech so that an utterance communicates an excellent sentiment or thought. His verbal success is fragile, however; it exists only so long as auditors agree that a larger social context invests the verbal accomplishment with worth.

Polixenes expresses his thanks, but Leontes persists in demanding that the Bohemian King remain in Sicilia. The tension building around Polixenes' leavetaking is temporarily relieved when Hermione persuades Leontes' friend to prolong his visit. The social context of Hermione's speech, rather than her words themselves, makes possible this resolution. The Queen apparently believes in an inviolable order of speech acts that gives statements their different worths. Pressed by Leontes to speak to Polixenes, Hermione states that she intended to remain silent until her husband drew oaths from his fellow King, for in her opinion an oath is an utterance more sincere than any saying:[13]

> To tell, he longs to see his son, were strong:
> But let him *say* so then, and let him go;

> But let him *swear* so, and he shall not stay,
> We'll thwack him hence with distaffs.[14]
>
> (1.2.34–37, italics mine)

Hermione playfully focuses upon Polixenes' oath—"I may not, verily"—in his response to her request that he remain in Leontes' court:

> Verily!
> You put me off with limber vows; but I,
> Though you would seek t'unsphere the stars with oaths,
> Should yet say "Sir, no going." Verily,
> You shall not go: a lady's Verily's
> As potent as a lord's. Will you go yet?
> Force me to keep you as a prisoner,
> Not like a guest: so you shall pay your fees
> When you depart, and save your thanks? How say you?
> My prisoner? or my guest? By your dread "Verily,"
> One of them you shall be.
>
> (1.2.46–56)

Even though Hermione jokingly calls Polixenes' vows weak ("limber"), in the Queen's terms he has made an absolute declaration.[15] He has *sworn* that *truly* he may not stay. In Searle's taxonomy of speech acts, Polixenes' utterance amounts to a double (doubly strengthened) representative. Yet the Queen insists that a lady's "truly" remains as potent as any gentleman's; in fact, the code of refined manners makes her word more powerful than a lord's. Polixenes appears aware of the linguistic and courteous contexts imposed by Hermione, for he gallantly yields to her argument:

> Your guest then, madam:
> To be your prisoner should import offending;
> Which is for me less easy to commit
> Than you to punish.
>
> (1.2.56–59)

Hermione and Polixenes have traded precious statements in a game of verbal fencing until the Queen deals the unreturnable blow.[16] Hermione's "verily" (equal linguistically to Polixenes') succeeds in this instance because of its special place in a shared context. Without enriching contexts, tacitly accepted by speaker and listener, the worths of pleas and self-defenses—all words, in fact—would fluctuate wildly, depending upon private appraisals which are now inflated, now debased.

Leontes appears ignorant of the creative linguistic contexts within which his wife and friend achieve harmony. Having felt Adam's curse, Leontes suffers from a tainted imagination:

> How blest am I
> In my just censure! in my true opinion!
> Alack, for lesser knowledge! how accurs'd
> In being so blest! There may be in the cup
> A spider steep'd, and one may drink, depart,
> And yet partake no venom (for his knowledge
> Is not infected); but if one present
> Th' abhorr'd ingredient to his eye, make known
> How he hath drunk, he cracks his gorge, his sides,
> With violent hefts. I have drunk, and seen the spider.
>
> (2.1.36–45)

Leontes' infected knowledge grows when the King interprets reality through warped linguistic contexts. Within his twisted frame of reference, Hermione and Polixenes are "paddling palms," "pinching fingers," "making practis'd smiles," and sighing "as 'twere / The mort o' the' deer." Repeatedly the corrupt context of Leontes' mad jealousy condenses the vile connotations of words. For example, he believes that Hermione and Polixenes deceitfully take advantage of the festivity attending the Bohemian monarch's visit:

> This entertainment
> May a free face put on, derive a liberty
> From heartiness, from bounty, fertile bosom,
> And well become the agent: 't may, I grant. . . .
>
> (1.2.111–14)

Leontes repeats his word "entertainment"—"O, that is entertainment / My bosom likes not, nor my brows" (1.2.118–19)—charging it, through a new context, with the uncomplimentary meaning of dalliance.

As the above example indicates, Leontes has a delicate ear for verbal shades of meaning. When Camillo at one point answers Leontes' question concerning the reason for Polixenes' change of plans with the reply "at the good queen's entreaty," the King makes a fine distinction:

> At the queen's be't; "good" should be pertinent,
> But so it is, it is not.
>
> (1.2.221–22)

By depriving the Queen of the epithet "good," Leontes appears to possess a sacrosanct notion of the value and aptness of words. His prior verbal tyranny, however, causes the playgoer instantly to reject this conclusion. Noticing Mamillius's smudged nose, Leontes tells the child that he must be "neat." By "neat," Leontes merely means "clean." But the King soon wrenches the word loose from its moorings in his statement, places it in his own illicit context for interpretation, and broods upon its bestial overtones:

> not neat, but cleanly, captain:
> And yet the steer, the heifer and the calf
> Are all call'd neat.
>
> (1.2.123–25)

Mamillius amounts to a "wanton calf" because Hermione, regarded from Leontes' viewpoint, acts lasciviously, even bestially. Leontes' depraved context for knowing reality has quickly precipitated the word's grossest meaning. Contexts are most flagrantly violated, however, when Leontes rips Camillo's well-meant words out of his servant's utterances, setting them in his own grid of mad meaning.

Leontes attempts to confirm his doubts by forcing Camillo into saying that he also witnessed Hermione's lustful courtship. Camillo's simple commentary upon the scene before him unfortunately sounds like agreement to Leontes' tainted ear. The King makes a leading remark about Polixenes' decision to lengthen his visit, and Camillo politely says: "You had much ado to make his anchor hold: / When you cast out, it still came home" (1.2.213–14). Forming his thought in an anchor image works against Camillo's aim of absolutely clear, uninvolved report, simply because metaphor by nature is highly connotative discourse. In Leontes' mind, the anchor image applies, if to anything, to Hermione's imagined "hold" upon Polixenes. Leontes breathlessly asks, "Didst note it?" Camillo, in turn, neutrally summarizes the facts: "He would not stay at your petitions; made / His business more material" (1.2.215–16). Camillo's words have an unfortunate breadth of meaning that allows them to make different sense within a false context. In Camillo's utterance—"He

... made / His business more material"—the word "business" denotes "private affairs." But within the context of Leontes' jealousy, the term refers to adultery; Polixenes' imagined adultery was more important (more "material") in detaining him than Leontes' pleas were. That Leontes understands Camillo's remark in such a perverse manner becomes evident from his excited response to it—"Didst perceive it?"

> [*Aside*] They're here with me already; whisp'ring, rounding
> "Sicilia is a so-forth"; 'tis far gone,
> When I shall gust it last.
>
> (1.2.216-19)

When Leontes states that intelligences inferior to Camillo's "perchance are to this business purblind" (1.2.227–28), the counselor suddenly realizes that the King is using the term "business" in an unknown sense: "Business, my lord? I think most understand / Bohemia stays here longer" (1.2.229–30). As the wager scenes of *Cymbeline* demonstrated, a common word can carry widely varying private meanings and yet create virtually identical auricular soundings (with which the word's meaning is identified). Language has come full circle; Camillo simply resorts to voicing the phrase— "stays longer"—with which Leontes began their dialogue (1.2.212). Leontes' "Ha?" (1.2.230) indicates that he pretends not to have heard Camillo clearly. But the latter, now on guard, only repeats the phrase "stays here longer" (1.2.230). When Camillo explains that Polixenes remains in Sicilia to satisfy Leontes' and Hermione's pleas, he effectively ends the game of meaning "what you will." Once he cannot find meanings in Camillo's words that feed his fantasy, Leontes angrily unveils it, causing the stunned Camillo to protest in a way that leads to his ominous dismissal.

The above episode illustrates Leontes' sustained linguistic totalitarianism. He continually refuses to acknowledge and share verbal contexts that could promote good understanding. Because speech is inherently ambiguous, the social context in which words are spoken and heard generally insures that a reasonable similarity exists between intended meaning and understood significance. In his spiritual isolation, Leontes believes that his autocratic words create their own private contexts for understanding, or that, in their "truth," they need no accompanying settings for interpretation. Leontes' words often exist as malign forces in the void created by his withdrawal from human community. He insists, for example, that Camillo can merely "say" and "justify" that Hermione is a "hobby-horse" and deserves a name "as rank as any flax-wench that puts to / Before her troth-plight" (1.2.277-78). In Leontes' opinion, an act of willful speech fixes character forever. Verbally transforming Hermione's character will forge a fact:

> Leon.   Say it be, 'tis true.
> Cam. No, no, my lord.
> Leon.   It is: you lie, you lie:
>   I say thou liest, Camillo, and I hate thee,
>   Pronounce thee a gross lout, a mindless slave,
>   Or else a hovering temporizer . . .
>
> (1.2.298–302)

In the above speech, Leontes recreates Camillo's character to suit his fancy simply by "pronouncing." It would be difficult to find a more vivid example of despotic speech in Shakespeare's nontragic drama. Only Lear, whose tyrannical word also exists in a great self-created vacuum, outdoes Leontes.

If the words by which he creates his evil "facts" are nothing, Leontes believes that

> . . . the world, and all that's in't, is nothing,
> The covering sky is nothing, Bohemia nothing,
> My wife is nothing, nor nothing have these nothings,
> If this be nothing.
>
> (1.2.293–96)

In *The Winter's Tale*, Shakespeare plays upon the Renaissance homographic identity between "world" and "word," suggesting that Leontes' illusory world is a travesty of the true creation that God made from nothing through the Word which existed in the beginning.[17] Essentially Leontes has confused the nature of God's creative Word with that of his own as God's deputy. For John, the Christian God created heaven and earth through his Word, which mysteriously caused a palpable reality to spring into being (John 1:1–4). "It will be recalled," David Patterson writes, "that in the Hebraic view everything comes into being by virtue of the word, or *davhar*, which is 'an aspect of the continuous divine creative force itself.'"[18] As a miracle, the Word's unaided creation of a world obviously lies outside any taxonomy of speech acts. If human declarations have any materially creative power, later, nonlinguistic deeds confer it. (Copying the name in a registry and painting it on the bow make the verbal christening of a ship a creative speech act.) This fact suggests that outside agencies play a key role in making speech creative. As regards the creativity of speech acts, Stanley Fish has remarked that "the only thing that performative or illocutionary acts produce is recognition on the part of a hearer that the procedures constitutive of a particular act have been invoked."[19] In short, Leontes can verbally create values only when auditors agree that the royal speaker, represented subject, and setting all have the qualities requisite for the creation of them. By withholding his assent, Camillo, like Paulina and other characters in the play, prevents Leontes' words from attaining the status of extraordinary speech acts.

In contrast to Leontes' abuse of speech and understanding, Polixenes' and Camillo's attention to (and respect for) the intended meanings of sayings (especially their nuances) abets Apollo's providence in *The Winter's Tale*. Camillo's remark that he dares not know why Leontes frowns upon Polixenes draws this reaction from the frightened King:

> How, dare not? do not? Do you know, and dare not?
> Be intelligent to me: 'tis thereabouts:
> For, to yourself, what you do know, you must,
> And cannot say you dare not.
>
> (1.2.377–80)

Once again the abstraction of knowledge from an ambiguous statement becomes Shakespeare's dramatic focus. On this occasion, however, the speakers have a mutual understanding of the denotations of their words and, most important, a respect for the precise shadings of their speech. In the process of correcting Camillo's "dare" to "do," Polixenes discovers that the servant is fearful, perhaps of something within the glowering Leontes; Camillo, however, will not speak candidly until Polixenes has defined a gracious context within which his words will be understood. He is wiser after his run-in with Leontes. The gracious context materializes when Polixenes admits that Camillo, in contrast to Leontes' "lout" and "slave," is a "gentleman" who is "clerk-like experienc'd" (1.2.391–92) and begs him "by all the parts of man / Which honour does acknowledge" (ll. 400–401) to discover his grave secret. Once an honorable context again lends value to Camillo's speech, he quickly reveals Leontes' shocking plot, trusting that he will be believed:

> Sir, I will tell you;
> Since I am charg'd in honour, and by him
> That I think honourable.
>
> (1.2.406–8)

"Charg'd" in this context means "invested" as well as "com-
manded." Camillo's words about Leontes' strange hatred for Polixenes thus gain credence from the positive ambience in which
they are spoken.

Such an ambience is denied Hermione during her unjust trial.
Hermione speaks as "a fellow of the royal bed," "a great king's
daughter," and "the mother to a hopeful prince," who is rightly
indignant at having to defend herself before a gaping crowd. Her
effort to set her words within an ennobling context fails, however. Hermione, in Leontes' infected opinion, has forfeited the
priceless status conferred by wifehood, motherhood, and aristocratic birth. Wrathfully, the King strips his Queen of her social
identities, terming her simply a "thing" (2.1.82). The eloquent
words that she utters in her self-defense do not move him because, in his view, they issue from a physical cipher and so must
themselves be worthless. Hermione seems to recognize that no
wholesome context gives meaning to her plea:

> Since what I am to say, must be but that
> Which contradicts my accusation, and
> The testimony on my part, no other
> But what comes from myself, it shall scarce boot me
> To say "not guilty": mine integrity,
> Being counted falsehood, shall, as I express it,
> Be so receiv'd.
>
> (3.2.22–28)

Leontes believes that it is common knowledge that those who are
boldly vicious impudently deny their deeds; the stereotypic idea
of propriety dictates that conclusion. Hermione replies, "That's
true enough, / Though 'tis a saying, sir, not due to me." Leontes
asks, "You will not own it?" (3.2.57–59). As things apparently
with lives of their own, conventional-sounding sayings may be
recklessly tagged to a character whom they in truth do not describe. Their independence of their engendering contexts allows
appliers of them like Leontes not only to abuse their application
but also to controvert the original communicative purpose that

led to their coining. Moreover, Leontes' conventional idea of adulteresses slanders Hermione:

> As you were past all shame
> (Those of your fact are so) so past all truth,
> Which to deny, concerns more than avails. . . .
>
> (3.2.84–86)

Since adulteresses naturally deny their deeds, and since Hermione amounts to an adulteress in Leontes' imagination, he expects that she *should* deny, in the most heart-rending terms, the accusation made against her. Were she to admit her guilt, Leontes would be at a loss regarding her worth. The dramatic problem resembles that presented during the wager scene of *Cymbeline:* common statements pervert the truth when they are applied to rare characters whom they in fact do not portray.

Despite the linguistic problems described above, Hermione during her trial bravely speaks with measured dignity, trusting that "powers divine" will vindicate her. Her faith soon proves justified. Apollo swiftly shatters Leontes' false creation of words with the true, the divine word, the ultimately life-fulfilling oracle. Shakespeare takes dramatic pains to establish a divine context for a predictive statement that, by implication, achieves perfection. The authority of Apollo's words—that "Hermione is chaste; Polixenes blameless; Camillo a true subject; Leontes a jealous tyrant; his innocent babe truly begotten; and [that] the king shall live without an heir, if that which is lost be not found"—may be questioned when considered out of context. As read by the Officer to Leontes in Sicilia, they certainly appear unadorned and arbitrary. Apollo's words, however, originally issued from a "delicate" climate, "sweet" air, and "fertile" isle; the temple in which they were first heard surpasses "the common praise it bears." The "grave" priests' habits were "celestial" and their behavior was reverent, while the preceding sacrifice was "ceremonious, solemn and unearthly" (3.1.1–11). The enriching context that Cleomenes and Dion strive to recreate charges Apollo's words with value, mainly because the god's speech, as originally heard, was so genuinely authoritative that immediately it caused Leontes' officers to revalue the surroundings in which it was uttered. "The burst / And the ear-deaf'ning voice o' th' Oracle" so ravished Cleomenes' hearing that he, by his own admission, "was nothing" (3.1.8–11).

Removed from the circumstances of the oracle's utterance, Leontes rejects the almighty word when plainly read to him; immediately thereafter Mamillius dies, a fact that instantly dispels the King's delusion. While Leontes quickly, sanely begs Apollo's pardon for his sins, he still retains his profane belief that his contextless word creates reality:

> I'll reconcile me to Polixenes,
> New woo my queen, recall the good Camillo,
> Whom I proclaim a man of truth, of mercy. . . .
>
> (3.2.155–57)

Such proclamations are too easy, too unrelated to how truthful utterances are contextually forged and confirmed. Only Time, or Apollo, can prove Camillo's virtues—or those of Hermione and Polixenes for that matter. The declaration of a guilty moment does not make men and women truthful or merciful. Eventually the character who ignored and twisted contexts necessary for communion moves in a world seemingly without dimension—a blank landscape offering no comfort. In Paulina's unforgettable vision,

> A thousand knees
> Ten thousand years together, naked, fasting,
> Upon a barren mountain, and still winter
> In storm perpetual, could not move the gods
> To look that way thou wert.
>
> (3.2.210–14)

It is to Paulina's credit that she has strived mightily to prevent Leontes' self-destruction. Her efforts began in act 2. Initially she believes that Leontes may see Hermione's truth reflected in the Queen's daughter, the gracious infant Perdita. In her opinion, "the silence often of pure innocence / Persuades, when speaking fails" (2.2.41–42). Thus Paulina verbalizes the paradoxically silent eloquence of the infant daughter's face:

> Behold, my lords,
> Although the print be little, the whole matter
> And copy of the father: eye, nose, lip;
> The trick of's frown; his forehead; nay, the valley,
> The pretty dimples of his chin and cheek; his smiles;
> The very mould and frame of hand, nail, finger. . . .
>
> (2.3.97–102)

In other words, the babe Perdita's appearance may signify a certain wholesomeness better than any verbal translation of the quality could. Paulina merely lists Perdita's "speaking" traits; she does not attempt to verbally recreate their nonauricular message. When in doubt about signification, one might turn to the *res* itself as signifier rather than the *verba* representing it. A vision of the child, nonetheless, does not purify Leontes' thought; through his mind's ear he hears nothing. Semiotic signification fails. Paulina still appears "a gross hag" in Leontes' eyes, and Perdita remains Polixenes' "brat." Great creating nature cannot overcome Leontes' delusion through its singular, silent expression.

Consequently, Paulina resorts to her primary method of attacking Leontes' madness through bitter words. Paulina's hyperboles are merely examples of Leontes' "free speech" taken to a punitive extreme. In the middle scenes of the play, Shakespeare somewhat comically stages a measure-for-measure cure, inflicted by a boundless tongue upon a despotic speaker whose disrespect for the laws of language has been unlimited. Paulina's casting herself in the role of Leontes' reprover possesses a verbal dimension; she represents the play's most stinging "tongue":

> If I prove honey-mouth'd, let my tongue blister,
> And never to my red-look'd anger be
> The trumpet any more.
>
> (2.2.33–35)

Paulina will be Hermione's "advocate to th' loud'st" (2.2.39):

> I'll use that tongue I have: if wit flow from't
> As boldness from my bosom, let't not be doubted
> I shall do good.
>
> (2.2.52–54)

When she presents the babe Perdita to Leontes, she formulates the verbal principle that she practices:

> I
> Do come with words as medicinal as true,
> Honest, as either, to purge him of that humour
> That presses him from sleep.
>
> (2.3.36–39)

Paulina's notion is homeopathic; a volley of words helps expel a lunacy strengthened by an earlier spate. Camillo's honest speech was ridiculed when Leontes depicted him as cowardly, negligent, and foolish; Paulina, however, possesses the contrary qualities of audacity, courage, and wit. In this respect, Shakespeare has conceived Camillo and Paulina, characters who later marry, as antitheses, even though Camillo's portrait is undeserved. Superseding Camillo's polite disclaimers, Paulina's audacious words attempt to dispel Leontes' "humour" through their sheer force.

The comic justice of Paulina's method remains inescapable. Leontes in his rage would not allow Camillo's phrase "at the good queen's entreaty"; hypocritically, the King insisted that a word like "good" should always pertain to its subject. In the complementary episode, Paulina loudly reasserts the word's aptness for Hermione, tormenting Leontes by her insistence:

> Paul.   I say, I come
>   From your good queen.
> Leon.   Good queen!
> Paul. Good queen, my lord, qood queen: I say good queen,
>   And would by combat make her good, so were I
>   A man, the worst about you.
>
> (2.3.57–61)

Such a vociferous claim scarcely needs physical combat for proof. After this tirade, Leontes does not make willful distinctions again. Like "the burst / And the ear-deaf'ning voice" of Apollo's oracle, Paulina's tirade reduces its auditor to "nothing." The analogy reminds us that Paulina's stinging tongue constitutes the earthly vehicle of Apollo's providence.

Still, Paulina's homeopathic reproof at first fails to transform Leontes, mainly because he hears it within defensive, insulating contexts that allow him to dismiss it. By calling Paulina "dame Partlet" and "Lady Margery" and by claiming that she has "unroosted" Antigonus, Leontes stereotypes her as the henpecking wife whose reproof simply equals "noise" (2.3.39). Leontes believes that Paulina is merely "a callat / Of boundless tongue, who late hath beat her husband, / And now baits me!" (2.3.90–92). The King's unsuitable context for hearing Paulina's words thus causes her reproof to seem trivial and blameworthy at first. This context prevails until the report of Mamillius's death. The dramatic phenomenon of a worse grief driving out a

lesser misery, articulated by Edgar in *King Lear* and apparent in
Cymbeline, explains Leontes' sudden recovery of sanity. Apollo
practices spiritual homeopathy as Jupiter does, but his technique
is harsher, requiring literal sacrifice. Once the divine physician
has touched the King, Paulina's mortal version of the god's cure
becomes effective. Heard within the new context of Leontes'
humble, penitent mood, Paulina's rough words suddenly become wise sayings rather than shrewish complaints; the King accepts her caustic statements as well as her method of healing:

> Go on, go on:
> Thou canst not speak too much; I have deserv'd
> All tongues to talk their bitt'rest.
>
> (3.2.214–16)

> Thou didst speak but well
> When most the truth: which I receive much better
> Than to be pitied of thee.
>
> (3.2.232–34)

As these last words reveal, Paulina has undermined Leontes'
self-pity. Leontes' cold privation accords with a particular self-
denial necessary for contrition and salvation. In light of her
name, Paulina's harsh but purifying words evoke the image of
Pauline Christianity;[20] she is the blessed thorn in the King's
flesh.[21] The Pauline notion of mortification and renewal provides
a setting for Leontes' self-abasement and penance. Thus the
blank, emotionally wintry world in which Leontes wanders retains one important context that promises spiritual recovery.

In the summer-like Bohemian scenes of the play, Shakespeare
focuses upon extraordinary acts of expression; pastoral modes of
communication again offer alternatives to fallen courtly speech.
Since Time shapes events in *The Winter's Tale*, critics have likened the play's structure to that of the hourglass.[22] The great sea
storm, the loss of Antigonus, the finding of Perdita—these events
mark a narrow passage that opens upon the expansive pastoral scene. One of the most colorful in Shakespearean drama,
this scene (4.4) represents the obverse of the dark Sicilian episode. Dramatic ideas presented in Sicilia are repeated—formally
"mirrored"—in Bohemia, but usually with redemptive differences.[23] The differences generally are the result of the benign
rather than corrupting contexts in which major ideas reappear.
Because of these contexts, ideas and characters during the pas-

toral scene often stand in enriching places (to use a key metadramatic phrase of the play). A consideration of the most notorious speech in the play and its staging in Bohemia clarifies the role played by context in Shakespeare's redemptive "mirroring" technique.

First, let us consider the speech as a self-contained entity, divorced from its relevance for the play as a whole. This consideration becomes easier once an auditor realizes that Leontes' utterance in a situational sense echoes in a vacuum; as the work of a monarch whose psychosis divorces him from reality, the speech almost immediately (1.2.138) floats free from the situational context of its utterance. When a speaker despotically insists upon creating a private, unreal world through words, language itself aids in the task by allowing the crystallization of the meaning chosen in its pluralistic field of significance. This interplay between a fallen speaker and malleable language is nowhere more apparent in *The Winter's Tale* than in Leontes' apostrophe to Affection, which has been a crux for almost every editor of the play. "Come, sir page," Leontes commands Mamillius:

> Look on me with your welkin eye: sweet villain!
> Most dear'st, my collop! Can thy dam?—may't be?—
> Affection! thy intention stabs the centre:
> Thou dost make possible things not so held,
> Communicat'st with dreams;—How can this be?—
> With what's unreal thou coactive art,
> And fellow'st nothing: then 'tis very credent
> Thou may'st co-join with something; and thou dost,
> (And that beyond commission) and I find it,
> (And that to the infection of my brains
> And hard'ning of my brows).
>
> (1.2.136–46)

Charles Frey notes that Leontes "takes shape in our consciousness . . . from his full-scale attack upon 'affection' as leading to 'infection' of his brains . . . because it coacts with the unreal and is fellow to 'nothing.'"[24] Leontes' reflections seem to "prove"—at least in the King's mind—that Hermione is an adulteress; the dense speech appears to involve discovery, for the comment about hardening of the brows alludes to being cuckolded. But critical interpretation has often stopped at this point. The passage has been dismissed as amounting to no more than a madman's cryptic mutterings. For one group of critics, the speech's incomprehensibility constitutes a measure of Leontes' delusion.[25] Those commentators who have attempted to explain the speech have focused, for the most part, upon the obscure process of thought by which Leontes reaches his mistaken conclusion as well as upon the King's peculiar language.[26]

The difficulty of Leontes' speech partly derives from its unusual Latinate diction, which faintly resembles the characteristic style of *Troilus and Cressida* and other linguistically tangled plays of the middle period. Of the nine words of Latin origin in the passage, "many of them are what may be called low-frequency words in that Shakespeare used them very rarely (let us say, arbitrarily, five times or less), if at all, in the rest of his work. While 'affection,' 'possible,' 'commission,' and 'infection' appear innumerable times, 'intention' is found only once (and not in this sense), with 'communicat'st,' 'co-active,' and 'co-join' used for the only time. 'Co-active,' meaning 'acting in concert,' is the first recorded usage in this sense in English. 'Credent' is used in *Measure for Measure* and *Hamlet* but not, as here, meaning 'credible.' 'Co-join' is recorded only twice in the language."[27] Regarded in light of this abstract diction, the precise meanings of "affection" and "intention" provide the keys for unlocking the passage's significance. These ambiguous terms, however, seem to carry special—perhaps technical—meanings.[28] For instance, Hallett Smith, quoting Cooper's *Thesaurus Linguae Romanae et Britannicae* (1582 ed.), equates Leontes' affection with the Ciceronian notion of *affectio*—an abrupt mental seizure that, in Smith's reading, the King addresses in the passage.[29] But rather than a sudden perturbation of mind or body, animosity, or lust— all possible seventeenth-century glosses for the word—the play suggests that the word "affection" bears its common meaning of "liking" or "love."[30]

Leontes' speech does not record his violent seizure of jealousy; the seizure, strictly speaking, has already occurred. When Hermione gives her hand to Polixenes, Leontes cries, "Too hot, too hot!" His exclamation signals the appearance of his jealousy at least thirty lines prior to the notorious speech concerning affection.[31] Leontes appears preoccupied in his musings on affection with verifying an existing doubt. His doubts momentarily vanish, however, under the benign influence of Mamillius's "welkin eye," into which he gazes. The adjective "welkin" suggests "something providential and life-giving, and not merely 'clear and blue like the sky.'"[32] Mamillius's gracious eye is akin to

Apollo's, with which it is associated through the play's imagery of sight and blindness.[33] Under Mamillius's aspect, Leontes becomes convinced that the child is his son; in relief, he affectionately says, "sweet villain! / Most dear'st, my collop!" Unequivocal epithets for intense love express Leontes' faith. When the King's thoughts return to the question of Hermione's constancy ("Can thy dam!—may't be?"), the affection that he has been feeling for Mamillius enters into them, and he skeptically theorizes about love's nature. Leontes judges that love combines with dreams in lovers' minds and gives birth to fantasies—to nothing real. The wispy blending of affection and dream gives Leontes precedent for his belief that affection enters into something actual—his wife's and friend's supposed scheming:

> . . . then 'tis very credent
> Thou may'st co-join with something; and thou dost,
> (And that beyond commission). . . .

Leontes has created his own soul-shaking reality solely through words; he deduces a fact exclusively from an illusory linguistic fabrication. Leontes' speech represents a prime example of the linguistic hypothesis that what one says (or can say) equals what one knows.

Having considered how the linguistic dynamics (and deficiencies) of Leontes' critically infamous speech help create its meaning, the reader can better appreciate its importance for Shakespeare's contextual dramaturgy in this last romance. "Affection! thy intention stabs the centre," Leontes cries out. "Intention" was a technical term in Renaissance philosophy for the conceptions of the imagination. "The images or conceptions of phantasy, possessing a kind of preconceptual determination"—Paul Oskar Kristeller writes in his account of Neo-Platonic philosophy—"are called intentions, after the scholastic tradition. In forming these intentions the Soul shows its productive force; for it forms the images of the sense impressions 'through phantasy and preserves them in memory.'"[34] In this view, the word "intention" became a synonym for "image," the product of an active imagination.[35] Leontes' exclamation thus concerns love's fantastic image. In the speech, love's image, its intention, takes shape primarily as a dreaming lover's fantasy. By means of this image, Leontes believes that he "stabs the centre" (discovers the "truth" about Hermione). The King deduces evil from the reality of love's innocent image; if something romantically ideal and ephemeral exists, then something coarsely selfish and tangible must be an equal, perhaps greater possibility. Or so Leontes believes. Since lovers easily create ephemeral images in their minds, lustful scheming must be a certainty. Leontes completely perverts the positive relationship between love and knowledge. Instead of ennobling him in a traditional manner by their alternating influences, love—affection—in the speech verifies the most infected knowledge, and reason and imagination turn love into lust. At least they do so in Leontes' mind. Virtuous qualities, joining in promising ways, become pitch when the intellectual context of their articulation is degrading. However, the qualities, in the same combination, become redemptive in *The Winter's Tale* when their interpretative context is wholesome.

To those qualities like time and nature which critics have found repeated with a difference in Bohemia, imagination and love can be added. These qualities blend in a pastoral ecstasy of mind that replaces (and so redeems) Leontes' vile union of them in his speech on affection. This blending occurs only when a series of progressively rich contexts, earlier ones set concentrically within later, more inclusive ones, charge the dramatic atmosphere until a flashpoint is reached and intellectual ecstasy is experienced. Significantly, remarkable acts of expression accompany this ecstasy.

The first context emerges when Perdita, costumed as the Roman goddess of flowers, greets her guests at the sheep-shearing festival by giving them flowers or herbs symbolic of the ages of man.[36] Like Arviragus's flowers in *Cymbeline*, Perdita's flowers and herbs constitute a kind of natural expression superior to court speech. Polixenes and Camillo have disguised themselves in white beards in order to spy upon Florizel in an effort to discover the cause of the young man's periodic disappearances from court. Taken in by their disguise, Perdita thus initially gives them herbs symbolic of the December when the soul should prepare its spiritual accounts. Polixenes capitalizes upon her gift of rosemary and rue (signifying remembrance and penitence) to fix his false identity:

> Shepherdess—
> A fair one are you—well you fit our ages
> With flowers of winter. . . .
>
> (4.4.77–79)

Like Leontes, Polixenes is physically in the late-summer or early-

autumn of his life (both Kings are in their mid-forties).[37] Nonetheless, because Polixenes' destructive mood can be defined as
wintry,[38] his case illustrates the judgment that Perdita's flowers
"suit precisely the moral [inner] situations of the recipients."[39]
Since the flowers are singularly spotted and hued, they are
uniquely beautiful. They thus apparently can function as adequate expressive vehicles for Perdita's singular feelings of welcome. Unlike the stereotypic language available to Polixenes, or
to any courtier, they would not slander an uncommon thought
during its communication. Perdita's guests of middle age receive
flowers of midsummer—hot lavender, mints, savory, marjoram,
and marigolds—all of which are precisely symbolic of the viril-
ity of this time of life. By means of special utterances, in which
res literally take the place of verba, Perdita has the opportunity
to do what, according to Leontes, is rarely done in a lifetime—
speak to purpose (1.2.88–89).

Still, the effectiveness of Perdita's gracious "statements" derives mainly from the unrivaled setting in which they appear.
Her gesture of offering, caught in a moment of time, forms an extended tableau, which, in its totality, makes up the complete
statement of hospitality. The brilliantly robed Perdita, the flowers themselves, the bright day, the pastoral landscape—these elements compose the tableau's features. Because the superlative
combining of the tableau's elements will never precisely repeat
itself, the larger statement of hospitality must be prized because
it is fleeting. But for an instant everything that grows reflects perfection, and the goddess of flowers utters her essence in an image
of beauty and youth and grace. Standing in the rich place described, Perdita enhances her inherently wonderful expressions
of welcome.

Perdita's act of distributing flowers and herbs becomes the
standard for communication in the play—at least it holds that
status at the moment of its performance. Yet the nearness of the
act's perfection requires comment. Considered as a pastoral utterance, Perdita's flower-speech is explicitly natural and thus un-
spoiled; considered from a cultured Renaissance viewpoint, the
speech, however, remains categorically limited because unim-
proved by art. Because Perdita will not permit art to remedy nature, she cannot ideally welcome men of late summer and early
autumn. Her garden lacks the grafted hybrids (carnations and
streaked gilly-flowers) for complementing their times of life. In
her opinion, these hybrid growths are bastards, symbolic of autumn, the season mixed of summer and winter. While the rose-

mary and rue fit Polixenes' January mood, the grafted flowers would be apt for his physical age. While superlative, Perdita's welcome thus is not absolutely superlative. Moreover, she lacks the natural symbols for praising Florizel's springtime of life and chastely communicating her love for him. She yearns in September for the flowers of spring symbolic of both Florizel's and her own time of life.[40] Without the expressive "words" daffodils, violets, or primroses, Perdita feels compelled to convey her passion in the unsatisfactory terms of either rape or sterility. She laments the absence of the spring flowers that frightened Proserpina dropped when Pluto abducted her from Sicily to the Underworld. "Now, my fair'st friend," she tells Florizel,

> I would I had some flowers o'th' spring, that might
> Become your time of day; and yours, and yours,
>   [*To Mopsa and the other girls*]
> That wear upon your virgin branches yet
> Your maidenheads growing: O Proserpina,
> For the flowers now that, frighted, thou let'st fall
> From Dis's waggon! daffodils,
> That come before the swallow dares, and take
> The winds of March with beauty; violets, dim,
> But sweeter than the lids of Juno's eyes
> Or Cytherea's breath; pale primroses,
> That die unmarried, ere they can behold
> Bright Phoebus in his strength (a malady
> Most incident to maids); bold oxlips and
> The crown imperial; lilies of all kinds,
> The flower-de-luce being one. O, these I lack,
> To make you garlands of; and my sweet friend,
> To strew him o'er and o'er!

(4.4.112–29)

Florizel could understand Perdita's plight, typical of the springtime of life, in the flowers that she describes but which are unavailable to her. By their provocative beauty and poignant transience, they make up her indirect argument that Florizel should seize the day nobly in courtship and marriage; pale primroses do die unmarried—a malady most incident to maids like Perdita. Furthermore, the flowers would be excellent vehicles for chastely expressing her refined passion for her beloved. M. M. Mahood has remarked that "the great flower passage is full of what Herrick calls a 'cleanly wantonness': the violets are as sweet as the breath of Venus, the primroses lovesick, the oxlips

inviting, and the daffodils 'take' the air in a triple sense—
enchant, seize, and come out for exercise and pleasure."[41] Such
messages, however, can only come from the offered flowers
themselves; despite her exquisite poetry, Perdita's portrayal of
the effects of the flowers amounts to a translation—a reduction—
of the ideas that only the flowers themselves can convey. Florizel
could better know through the flowers themselves frank but honest desires and fears that, if boldly stated in direct speech, might
make Perdita appear a country wench, brazenly announcing
what she would physically give and take. As expressed, Perdita's
description of the effects of the flowers rings with innuendoes
reflecting seizure and rape. Clearly, a greater context for expression is needed in *The Winter's Tale*. That liberating context becomes Florizel's creation; yet Perdita resists it. To understand her
resistance, first consider her character in light of an aspect of nature in *The Winter's Tale* that has escaped critical commentary.

Critics have often noted that the younger generation of this
play, rendered innocent by idyllic Nature, atones for the sins of
its fathers through its love and faith in a brave new world.
G. Wilson Knight, for example, believes that nature exerts the
restorative power in the play; he finds his text in Paulina's opinion that "the law and process of great Nature" have freed the infant Perdita from the womb and certified that hereditary sin has
not touched her.[42] The reader ought to question the validity of
Paulina's belief, however. Adam's sinful legacy was a Renaissance commonplace to which Polixenes referred in act 1. Strong,
potentially corrupting spirits reared each king's weaker blood,
and presumably adult Florizel and Perdita have felt their force
to some degree. Obviously, the young lovers are not corrupt; virtue and reason have mastered unruly passions. At their young
ages and in their nobility, Florizel and especially Perdita maintain control of their sensual desires. In Knight's view Florizel
and particularly Perdita become Nature's agents for remedying
its own disorders. Perdita, however, does not acquire her symbolic status as easily as critics have interpreted allegorically her
role and the Bohemian scenes generally. As a natural restorative,
she, like Mamillius, made no effect upon Leontes; great Nature
by itself seemingly cannot minister to a mind diseased. It is
worth noting that divine intervention and artistically induced
penance work the spiritual cures of *The Winter's Tale*.

Paulina's account of Perdita's natural likeness to her father is
usually the point of departure for the critical argument for great
creating Nature. Yet critics rarely quote the text in full. If they

did, another equally important feature of Nature would become apparent. The well-known speech also includes the following lines:

> And thou, good goddess Nature, which hast made it
> So like to him that got it, if thou hast
> The ordering of the mind too, 'mongst all colours
> No yellow in't, lest she suspect, as he does,
> Her children not her husband's!
>
> (2.3.103–7)

Paulina speculates that Nature bears responsibility for orderings of the mind. Leontes' union of love, dream, and imagination reflects one ordering of the mind—one ruled by jealousy. Other orderings are reflected in Hermione's classification of statements and the values assigned to each, as well as in Leontes' warped sense of decorum by which he hits upon "just" punishments for his wife and infant daughter. Time, the Chorus, has depicted Perdita as "a shepherd's daughter, / And what to her adheres" (4.1.27–28). By "adheres," Time implies that Perdita has certain notions typical of a young woman nurtured by a shepherd in the country. Thus, her anxiety about the difference between her rank and Florizel's should not be surprising. Her strong sense of decorum makes the idea of marriage between a prince and a low-born girl intellectually disagreeable to her; her love must struggle to overcome this aversion. Perdita's idea of decorum, revealed in her debate with Polixenes and in her flower-welcome, indicates her special ordering of the mind. Like the Princes in *Cymbeline*, she has daily communed with nature, and its cycles and orders have impressed themselves directly upon her mind. A rigid—on occasion limiting—notion of what is fit has resulted from this impression. In this respect, Perdita resembles Guiderius, whose idea of decorum restrained Arviragus's synthetic and imaginative art. Florizel remarks that Perdita's costuming herself as the goddess of flowers gives her added life; she is "no shepherdess, but Flora," a queen, "peering in April's front" (4.4.1–5). But because of her fixed idea of decorum, she cannot wax enthusiastic about her artificial disguise. In her eyes, Florizel's shepherd's mask never obliterates his royalty. She politely addresses him as a subject might rather than as a lover would:

> Sir: my gracious lord,
> To chide at your extremes, it not becomes me—

O pardon, that I name them! Your high self,
The gracious mark o' th' land, you have obscur'd
With a swain's wearing, and me, poor lowly maid,
Most goddess-like prank'd up. . . .

(4.4.5–10)

Perdita dismisses any innocent grace potentially resulting from their festive roles. Florizel in her opinion appears "vilely bound up" (4.4.22) while she wears "borrowed flaunts" (l. 23). The decorum and temperance that are often Shakespeare's standards for success, especially in his dark comedies and later tragedies, become at times retarding traits in the world of his late romances. Nonetheless, Florizel attempts to instruct Perdita about the positive benefits of their masking. While she believes that false appearances often obscure true realities, he, on the contrary, knows that new identities can emerge from empathetic role-playing. For him, appearance and reality represent misleading categories; both merge into a third term, a refined state of being wholly new and unexpected. His listing of the shapes—a bull, a ram, a humble swain—that the gods assumed to satisfy their lusts makes two important points. The gods' disguisings reflected basic transformations of being, like those which the lovers might experience as Flora and Doricles. The transformations of the lovers, however, are chaste, unlike those of the gods. These points are lost upon Perdita. Because she does not vividly imagine Florizel as Doricles, she never *fully* experiences the innocent love associated with the pastoral realm. The perception of transcendental virtues, made possible by art, constitutes the noblest working of the erected wit, according to Sir Philip Sidney.[43] Perdita's natural sense of decorum denies her a vision of the unfallen nature that Sidney described in *An Apology for Poetry*. The imaginative artistry of the lovers' costumes and roles gives her no intuition of the innocent virtues associated with the pastoral mode. Primarily, the Art versus Nature conflict in *The Winter's Tale* becomes an epistemological issue rather than a genetic or philosophical problem. Can art overcome natural ways of thinking and speaking so that an ideal truth is known? Florizel's central love lyric, one of the most beautiful in Shakespearean drama, contains the answer.

During Perdita's distribution of her flowers and herbs, Florizel remains fascinated by her loveliness and her gracious movements. The artistic context created by Perdita's costume and play-acting transforms his mistress so that he knows her in a new way:

> What you do,
> Still betters what is done. When you speak, sweet,
> I'd have you do it ever: when you sing,
> I'd have you buy and sell so, so give alms,
> Pray so, and, for the ord'ring your affairs,
> To sing them too: when you do dance, I wish you
> A wave o'th' sea, that you might ever do
> Nothing but that, move still, still so,
> And own no other function. Each your doing,
> So singular in each particular,
> Crowns what you are doing, in the present deeds,
> That all your acts are queens.

(4.4.135–46)

S. L. Bethell's paraphrase of the rather obscure final sentence of the passage clarifies its significance: "'Your performance of it ('each your doing'), uniquely good in each detail, makes superior ('crowns') whatever you may be doing *at present* ('in the present deeds'), so that all your acts are (successively) preeminent.' In this interpretation the lover sees his mistress's deeds as a scale of rising perfections."[44] The deeds to which Florizel refers are mainly acts of expression. More precisely, he describes his beloved ascending from less to more nearly perfect kinds of self-expression. Florizel first would have Perdita speak forever because she speaks so exquisitely. But when he hears her sing, he would have song excellently translate her affairs, whether they involve buying, selling, giving charitably, or praying. And when she dances he would have her maintain such a ravishing image eternally, if that were possible. Then her movements would always be cast in an unchanging form, like a wave that does not appear to move because it keeps the same unbroken shape until reaching shore. Then Perdita would "move still, still so." The arresting phrase imitates the movement of the sea wave (motion crests with the first "still," suspends itself at the caesural pause, and sweeps downward again with the second "still" and ensuing "so"—an adverb suggesting the repetition of the process indefinitely). The wave provides Shakespeare's context for the dance in which motion and stillness mystically merge into something more than Nature and Art or their union.[45] Individual waves and dancers may grow, crest (approximate perfection), and die, but in their momentary attainment of beautiful forms they become suggestive of a permanence beyond flux. Such forms organize bewildering change and confer value upon it, becoming the tangible evidence of shadowy realities like Apollo's providence. Thus dance becomes a kind of communication more expressive than either song or ordinary speech. "'Tullie saith well' concludes Thomas Wilson in *The Arte of Rhetorique;* 'the gesture of man, is the speache of his bodie.'"[46] As a consummate metaphysical form of expression, dance amounts to a literal kind of speech act. Paradoxically, Perdita's deeds become physical words unintentionally excelling not only her restrictive ways of thinking and speaking but her special "flower speech" as well.

In summary, Shakespeare sets Perdita within four different but complementary contexts. As the goddess Flora, Perdita exists within the context of classical myth and art, which invests her with a mysterious fertility.[47] It is Flora who becomes Florizel's dancer, wedding mutability and eternity through hypnotic movement. The magnificent metaphor of the sea wave, in turn, provides a context for understanding this mystical wedding. Flora, the dancer, the sea wave—each provides a wider, a more valuable context for viewing Perdita and knowing Grace. Finally, Florizel's entire eleven-line lyric composes the largest enveloping context, which acquires its value from its contained images and their contexts. As an absolutely beautiful love poem, the ultimate romantic word, the lyric invests the enclosed images and contexts with added worth. As a construct of words, Florizel's speech testifies to the expressive potentiality of human utterance, infolding previous kinds of communication within itself before aesthetically transcending them. Perceived in an instant through all four contexts, Perdita stands like a jewel in the rarest place described thus far in *The Winter's Tale.* Art and Nature merge in Florizel's contemplative vision, making any debate about one or the other's superiority irrelevant. Florizel's rapture confirms the mutual working of Art and Nature in a way that the prudish Perdita and pedantic Polixenes cannot grasp.

Nevertheless, Perdita sharply recalls Florizel from his ecstasy of mind by telling him that his praise is "too large" for her. Like decorous Guiderius, she limits the effect of ravishing verbal art. The viewer may question the truth of Florizel's speech of praise, however, only as a pronouncement upon different kinds of expression. By implying that dancing best expresses virtue, Florizel qualifies not only his own poetry but also the traditional eloquence of all speech and song. Thus Shakespeare focuses upon the extraverbal dance that soon occurs onstage. Florizel's panegyric prepares the viewer for valuing the ensuing dance of shepherds and shepherdesses, a group that includes Doricles and Flora. The special dance constitutes the crescendo toward which the opening part of the pastoral scene builds and then falls away, like the swell of a sea wave.

Still, even though Shakespeare apparently has circumscribed the expressibility of speech by means of a nonverbal art, words obviously possess transformational power. They on occasion change our perspectives for viewing and valuing dramatic events. With Florizel's words of admiration ringing in his ears, the beholder of the pastoral dance agrees with the Prince's judgment that dance can be a kind of unparalleled report. Seen through the idealizing contexts created by Florizel's poetry, ravishing Perdita appears even lovelier in graceful movement. Paradoxically, words create a perspective within which the superior virtues of extraverbal communication can be appreciated. Upon hearing in the last act how the Old Shepherd found Perdita, Leontes and Polixenes become so transfixed that, in a courtier's words, "there was speech in their dumbness, language in their very gesture" (5.2.13–14). The belief that gesture can be a kind of language pervades *The Winter's Tale*.[48] The repeated "so's" in Florizel's speech of praise stand for dramatic gestures representing the inexpressible. Pervasive also is the opinion that silence—"dumbness"—can be a mode of expression. During the dance, the viewer may remember Paulina's idea of the benign effect that the infant Perdita might have upon Leontes: "The silence often of pure innocence / Persuades, when speaking fails." Perdita fulfills Paulina's prediction that she will be an "unspeakable comfort" when her dancing image silently conveys innocence better than any spoken words could.[49]

The marvellous image amounts to an unorthodox, literal example of a "speaking picture," that sixteenth-century aesthetic idea popularized by Sidney in his critical masterpiece. "Let but Sophocles bring you Ajax on a stage," Sidney writes, "killing and whipping sheep and oxen, thinking them the army of Greeks, with their chieftains Agamemnon and Menelaus, and tell me if you have not a more familiar insight into anger than finding in the schoolmen his genus and difference."[50] Sidney implies that imaginatively written, dramatic episodes (specifically those infused with *enargeia*) "picture" ideas and so "speak" to a viewer better than abstractly written, philosophical treatises can. Thus they are "speaking pictures." For Shakespeare in *The Winter's Tale*, however, visual images of virtues sometimes offer a preferred way of communicating ideals beyond the reach of words. As he does so often, Shakespeare originally interprets a celebrated idea of his age, in the process recharging it. For Florizel, the picture of Perdita truly is "speaking"; it takes the place of the word, assuming a special expressive role.

But the moment passes, the swell rolls onward, and the vision of love and innocence dissolves. Autolycus enters, directing attention to himself and destroying the highly wrought mood. A disruption occurs similar to Prospero's memory of Caliban's plot, which ruins the Masque of Ceres. Agents of disorder in their respective plays prevent an exceptional vision from being sustained. But before it dissolves, the dance in *The Winter's Tale* fulfills the extraordinary claims made for it. Both Florizel's and the viewer's affectionate imagining of dancing Perdita reflects a redemptive ordering of the mind—one that displaces Leontes' vile ordering as well as the image of his evilly dancing heart. During the dance, Shakespeare provides a base for measuring the degree of our appreciation of the artistic event. Polixenes unenthusiastically admits that Perdita "dances featly" (4.4.178). To Polixenes and to Camillo, and to others unaware of enriching dramatic contexts, the dance is mere "country footing." And so, considered flatly out of context, it is.

Stubborn in his plan for a secret marriage, Florizel tells the disguised Polixenes that he will neither notify his father of the wedding nor include him in it. The King in fury then reveals himself, forbids any meeting between the Prince and Perdita, and orders his son to return to court. Instead of returning, however, Florizel, upon Camillo's advice, flees with Perdita to Leontes' kingdom—an act that draws all characters together for their unexpected reunions. Occurring in the last two scenes of *The Winter's Tale*, the joyous reunions of the members of Leontes' separated family are brought about by acts of speech and vision given the highest dramatic priority. In fact, the penultimate scene of the play (5.2) focuses not upon the reunion itself but upon alternating words and visions mutually charging one another with a developing providential meaning. Such a dramatic focus is important, for Hermione's resurrection occurs only after Paulina's artfully calculated words alter and enlarge Leontes' idea of his wife until it fits the living woman.

Shakespeare begins by presenting the reunion of Leontes and Perdita through a series of staggered reports in which a later speaker supplements the partial knowledge of an earlier narrator. The emphasis thus falls upon the change in understanding that additional speech prompts. Answering Autolycus's desire for news about the Old Shepherd's discoveries, First Gentleman knows "no more but seeing" (5.2.17). Ordered from the royal chamber just as the Old Shepherd began speaking about his stumbling upon the infant princess, he had time to see only Leontes' and Camillo's stunned faces:

> a notable passion of wonder appeared in them; but the wisest be-holder, that knew no more but seeing, could not say if th' importance were joy or sorrow; but in the extremity of the one it must needs be.
>
> (5.2.15-19)

Further knowledge must clarify that given only by the eye. That clarification proceeds from the interpretation of the word in one of its most primitive forms—a riddle. Rogero, Second Gentle-man, enters and exclaims that the oracle is fulfilled—the King's daughter has been found, a fact that reveals that the ambiguous wonder observed in Leontes and Camillo was joyful. Paulina's steward, Third Gentleman, then satisfies all listeners by giving a detailed account of what followed the main discoveries: tokens confirmed Perdita's identity; Polixenes and Leontes embraced so wildly that only their clothing distinguished them; the Shepherd and his son described Antigonus's death and the shipwreck; and Leontes confessed his former tyranny.

While their chief value lies in adding to previous knowledge, Third Gentleman's speeches also have another function; they suggest that what is heard can radically transform what is seen. He insists that the proofs of Perdita's identity are so unified that "that which you hear you'll swear you see" (5.2.32–33). His next words testify to the truth of such alteration. Perdita, whom Leontes and everyone onstage have regarded as a lovely but low-class country girl, suddenly radiates nobility once the courtiers hear that she is royally born. Third Gentleman marvels that

> the majesty of the creature in resemblance of the mother, the affec-tion of nobleness which nature shows above her breeding, and many other evidences proclaim her, with all certainty, to be the king's daughter.
>
> (5.2.36–40)

These qualities of course have been visible in Perdita from the moment that she entered Leontes' court, but no one credits them until the courtiers acquire an idea of nobility that can detect and highlight the traits. Only when the courtiers hear that Perdita is a noblewoman do they swear that they see one. Through its epistemologically creative power, the word forges a redemptive context. By being explicit in the penultimate scene about how words can translate a visual image, Shakespeare prepares his viewer for Paulina's manner of creating Leontes' idea of Hermione in the final episode of the play. When Paulina tells him that Hermione is a statue, what the King hears becomes what he sees— a stunning work of art established mainly by Paulina's carefully chosen words.

Still, one must avoid making too large a claim for words in this respect. Words in *The Winter's Tale* create the possibility of visions; as in *Cymbeline*, they cannot as a medium for knowing reproduce the ideational message of vision. Obviously some extraordinary events can be understood only by being seen.[51] Shakespeare takes dramatic pains to remind his audience of this fact. Upon Second Gentleman's denial that he saw the meeting of Leontes and Polixenes, Third Gentleman exclaims, "Then have you lost a sight which was to be seen, cannot be spoken of" (5.2.43-44). And he goes on to say,

> I never heard of such another encounter, which lames report to follow it, and undoes description to do it.
>
> (5.2.57–59)

Words are often incapable of expressing outlandish truths; to dramatize this inadequacy, Shakespeare has a courtier narrate the reunions in unsatisfactory verbal images. These are worse when the act of seeing itself becomes his subject, as though Shakespeare wished to stress the idea that report at times remains inferior to vision for reliable knowledge.[52] For example, Paulina, transfixed between joy and sorrow, in Third Gentleman's words almost comically "had one eye declined for the loss of her husband, [and] another elevated that the Oracle was fulfilled" (5.2.74–76); moreover, the same courtier finds that "one of the prettiest touches of all, and that which angled for mine eyes (caught the water though not the fish) was, when at the relation of the queen's death . . . how attentiveness wounded his daughter" (5.2.81–86). It is through such grotesque and artificial verbal images as these, which explicitly focus upon acts of seeing, that report "lames" what should be seen.[53] From Archidamus's difficulty in stating his thanks to this latter scene, spoken report has on occasion inadequately conveyed rare truths in *The*

Winter's Tale. An unrivalled truth, such as Hermione's gracious-
ness, can only be fully understood in its own terms—when seen,
not known through the obscuring medium of words. And yet, as
previously mentioned, the insufficient word becomes crucially
efficacious when, in the last scene of the play, Leontes sees
Hermione's beauty only when special language creates the context for apprehending it.

By declaring that an Italian master carved Hermione's effigy
and by revealing her motionless upon a pedestal, Paulina forces
Leontes to regard his Queen within an artistic context. Considered as a rare *objet d'art*, Hermione literally stands in a rich
place. Paulina, in essence, first says to Leontes, "Know Hermione
as a priceless statue." The unveiled "statue" immediately strikes
Leontes dumb. "I like your silence," Paulina at length says; "it
the more shows off / Your wonder" (5.3.21–22). In Leonard
Barkin's opinion, "the silence of the statue reflects on the whole
action. Hermione's speech in the first act is, after all, the occasion for her downfall. . . . Thus the silence at the end of the play
in which the couple meet as statue and speechless viewer puri-
fies the disasters of speech."[54] Finally breaking this ethereal silence, Leontes responds to the imposed context with an artistic
cliché heard often during the Renaissance:

> Her natural posture!
> Chide me, dear stone, that I may say indeed
> Thou art Hermione.
>
> (5.3.23–25)

Art qualifies as outstanding, according to Renaissance theorists,
when its lifelikeness chides life for failing to be as vital.[55] Paulina
has provoked Leontes' commonplace by speaking these words
prior to her discovery of Hermione:

> But here it is: prepare
> To see the life as lively mock'd as ever
> Still sleep mock'd death. . . .[56]
>
> (5.3.18–20)

Significantly, Leontes yearns in the hush of expectation to hear
the healing spoken word, which would ring memorably in the
silent context of wonder. Leontes' sudden recollection of the actual Hermione, however, causes him to revise a conventional
idea about art's mockery:

> or rather, thou art she
> In thy not chiding; for she was as tender
> As infancy and grace.
>
> (5.3.25–27)

It is in contrast to the statue that Leontes vividly recreates the true Hermione. Shakespeare implies that art helps its beholder to understand life but only through its radical difference, not through any compelling and enlightening identity. Art supplies an attractive context that engages the beholder, causing him or her to value certain dimensions of life and reflect upon them. But the context must be transcended if art is to exert its proper effect. Florizel and Perdita do step out of their bewitching dance and pastoral make-believe to walk the path that leads to practical fulfillment. Leontes at first "knows no more but seeing" (the idea "Hermione" is only an art work appealing to his eyes); memory, however, soon qualifies his vision. Leontes' recollection of a youthful Hermione challenges his vision of an artifact until he prefers an image beyond art's compass:

> O, thus she stood,
> Even with such life of majesty, warm life,
> As now it coldly stands, when first I woo'd her!
> I am asham'd: does not the stone rebuke me
> For being more stone than it?
>
> (5.3.34–38)

Paradoxically, art succeeds when it encourages Leontes to replace its contexts with one of his own based upon personal experience. The King's new context is based upon a remembered moment of intimacy that has nothing to do with art. This personal memory of Leontes' first wooing proves transitory, however; the aesthetic context reforms, and the conventional mockery of art becomes a chiding for old sins:

> does not the stone rebuke me
> For being more stone than it? O royal piece!
> There's magic in thy majesty, which has
> My evils conjur'd to remembrance, and
> From thy admiring daughter took the spirits,
> Standing like stone with thee.
>
> (5.3.37–42)

Surprisingly the longed-for word, if capable of being spoken by the imagined artifact, would amount to a destructive rather than reconstitutive act.

Paulina begins dissolving the initially enabling aesthetic context once the petrifying qualities of art stupefy Perdita and threaten to destroy Leontes' promising recollection. Again, like the sea wave, art builds to its proper affective working, realizes it brilliantly in an instant, and then buries it in undesirable effects. The dangerous paralytic effect of art, most notably caught in the freezing of Ferdinand's spirits and in his wish that time and history would stop in a marvelous moment, is also felt by Perdita, who exclaims: "So long could I / Stand by, a looker on" (5.3.84–85). Contrary to the opinion of the Romantics, Shakespeare did not generally find life's *sustained* imitation of art valuable. Paradoxically, the admirer of art may unknowingly emulate it, becoming "lifeless"—an ironic "monument" indicting art's true, self-sacrificial working.

When Paulina cleverly commands Leontes to avert his gaze from the "stone" lest he think it moves, her words reassert the context of life. Obedient to his cue, the King sees the movement obvious from the time of Hermione's unveiling—her breathing, the pulse beating in her throat, the involuntary motions of her eyes and their lids (slight actions that the actress playing the Queen should not attempt to suppress). In one sense, Paulina's word creates life; it causes its auditors to see what was dead as alive. Leontes has not observed Hermione's vital signs because he, like Perdita, has been viewing the Queen within a special context in which life is impossible. But when music strikes and Hermione stirs and descends from her pedestal, that artistic context vanishes. Hermione, however, remains silent as she embraces and kisses ecstatic Leontes; a Christian ceremony for bringing the divine Word to mankind provides the model for her rebirth of speech. "Please you to interpose, fair madam, kneel," Paulina commands, "and pray your mother's blessing" (5.3.119–20). By interposing ("placing oneself between"), Perdita, like the Intercessor Mary, becomes the salvatory means for her mother's repentance—her turning to life. "Turn good lady," Paulina urges, "Our Perdita is found" (5.3.120–21). Surprisingly, the kneeling maiden maintains silence; instead, the patient sufferer (rather than the intercessor) invokes the divine word. The first, crystalline words of Hermione, ringing in the clarified atmosphere, form a prayer: "You gods, look down, / And from your sacred vials pour your graces / Upon my daughter's head!" (5.3.121–23). When the spoken word finally does issue from

Hermione's lips, it possesses, after the long silence, the signature of peace.

Having wrought within us the refined emotion that we hear communicated among the participants in Hermione's resurrection, the charged, final words of the statue scene have done all that they can do for us. They have evoked the tender affection that we read into the play's ultimate, nonverbal image. As William Matchett has noted, a still moment—a long, silent embrace—communicates the King's and Queen's reborn love.[57] These characters create their own moving tableau, which appears in stark outline on the hushed and inactive stage. Hermione and Leontes are free from contexts (verbal or otherwise) that might supplement or detract from a simple truth about love. A self-interpreting tableau, almost as old as Time itself, older perhaps than Apollo, carries the final message of this dramatic romance. The Winter's Tale, like all great works of art, transcends conventional contexts, upon which it necessarily depends for its remarkable meanings, yielding at last a pure and powerful image for our understanding of it.

5

The Tempest

Throughout *The Tempest* Shakespeare implies that one cannot know what one cannot formulate in words. In Whorfian terms, characters depend for their knowledge on their linguistic capacities (see chapter 1). This fact becomes most apparent in the sad case of Caliban. Miranda bitterly reminds Caliban that, upon meeting him, she pitied him and took pains to make him speak when he did not know his own meaning but would "gabble like / A thing most brutish" (1.2.358–59). She tells Caliban, "I endow'd thy purposes / With words that made them known" (1.2.359–60). Shakespeare focuses the notion that speech confers self-knowledge; what cannot be articulated cannot be known. A corollary of this view is that the quality of one's speech determines the quality of self-knowledge. Caliban dramatizes this consequence in his reply to Miranda's accusations:

> You taught me language; and my profit on't
> Is, I know how to curse. The red-plague rid you
> For learning me your language!
>
> (1.2.365–67)

Caliban believes that language has only allowed him to verbalize curses that mire him in brutishness. In his opinion, he has only wet his lips at the Pierian spring. After their meeting, Stephano uses Caliban's half-formed ideas to make him his political slave:

> *Cal.* Hast thou not dropp'd from heaven?
> *Ste.* Out o' the moon, I do assure thee: I was the man i'th' moon when time was.
> *Cal.* I have seen thee in her, and I do adore thee: My mistress show'd me thee, and thy dog, and thy bush.
>
> (2.2.137–41)

Caliban comically believes that a metaphor has actual identity. Miranda pointed out the traditional iconic features of the moon,

109

but apparently she broke off her instruction before she could explain the nature of metaphor and its uses. Caliban remains a metaphoric idiot; half-taught, he does not understand how the symbol constitutes a different reality. Thus, like political masses everywhere, he undergoes manipulation through his literal understanding of symbols.

Accepting Prospero's judgment that he is an absolute devil, Caliban regards curses as his typical speech. The more he curses, the more he becomes an animal (since the quality of self-knowledge is prescribed by the quality of the speech that realizes it). The specific nature of Prospero's tortures betrays the magician's belief that speech not only makes possible education but also amounts to the surest evidence of its failure. Caliban states that "for every trifle" Prospero's spirits are

> set upon me;
> Sometime like apes, that mow and chatter at me,
> And after bite me . . . .
> . . . .
> . . . . sometime am I
> All wound with adders, who with cloven tongues
> Do hiss me into madness.
>
> (2.2.8–14)

Chattering apes and adders hissing with "cloven tongues" are designed to remind Caliban of his linguistic failure. The malevolent and nonrational "speech" of brutes provokes Caliban to cursing, and his cursing, in a vicious cycle, incites the creatures to renewed noise. Prospero keeps Caliban in a bestial state, but the failure of language is partly Prospero's unadmitted responsibility.

In the early acts of The Tempest, curses and jests limit the comprehension of hearer and speaker alike; considered together, these polar forms of discourse reveal mankind's vulnerability to corrupting words. Imaginatively using words to shape a logical argument, Prospero refines Miranda's perspective on romantic love, neutralizing the threat posed by the potentially destructive language of courtship. Later, the epiphanic word of the Harpy's Banquet powerfully affects Alonso, ultimately transforming his knowledge of himself and his personal happiness. The ideal words of the Masque of Ceres seem to promise a similar intellectual alteration for Ferdinand and Miranda. And yet when passion explodes this magical creation, the master of verbal "shapes" discovers a surprising, mind-expanding lesson in their use from his servant Ariel, a use that can make unmagical artistic language "magical" in its humane effect.

In *The Tempest*, Caliban remains the most graphic example of a widespread restriction of understanding brought about by un-ideal speech. Verbal curses, for example, not only disrupt the efforts to preserve the ship during the tempest of act 1, scene 1; they also prevent men in danger of dying from understanding that they must cooperate and assume new roles for the good of community.[1] In the opening lines of the play, the Ship-Master commands the Boatswain to "speak to th' mariners": "fall to't, yarely, or we run ourselves aground" (1.1.3–4). When Alonso, Ferdinand, and the other courtiers fearfully erupt from below, the distracted Boatswain orders them "to cabin: silence! trouble us not" (1.1.17–18). Once below deck, the aristocrats, however, raise "*a cry within.*" "A plague upon this howling," the Boatswain exclaims; "they are louder than the weather or our office" (1.1.35–37). Finally the King's party reemerges and, in the general atmosphere of unkindness, vents curses that make social unity and individual survival apparently impossible:

> *Seb.* A pox o' your throat, you bawling, blasphemous, incharitable dog!
> *Boats.* Work you, then.
> *Ant.* Hang, cur! hang, you whoreson, insolent noisemaker. We are less afraid to be drowned than thou art.
>
> (1.1.40–45)

The Boatswain's envisioning of their imagined drowning— "What, must our mouths be cold?"—connects their death with a contributing cause: degenerate (cold) speech. Gonzalo extends the metaphor to the raging sea, whose drops of water "swear" against the Boatswain "and gape at wid'st to glut him" (1.1.57–58). The image represents an unintended but fitting inversion of baptism; water damns mankind rather than blesses him. Gonzalo's negative image and his own ungracious speech remain dramatically apt because cursing exists not simply as a cause but also as a result of men's inability to comprehend their saving relationships with one another. The *"confused noise within"* (a Folio stage direction), which the ship makes as it breaks up, echoes later in the play when the spirits acting the Masque of Ceres heavily vanish *"to a strange, hollow, and confused noise."* In each case, representatives of "killing" speech—

cursing Caliban and the courtiers—prematurely ruin something marvelously organized: a ship symbolic of human government and a harmonious vision. The virtually identical stage directions simply condense that fact and remind the viewer of the destructive word.

Shakespeare's idea that the quality of speech determines the quality of understanding especially applies to Antonio and Sebastian. In their case, the words in question make up the punning jest.[2] Shakespeare primarily evokes the essence of punning in The Tempest so that he can portray its retarding effect upon good understanding and communication. Once certain evils inherent in punning are apparent, the viewer can better comprehend why Shakespeare performs a catharsis upon the jesting spirit in the play. Major characters in the other late romances rarely exchange the labored wit that marks act 2, scene 1 of The Tempest. When Alonso's courtiers begin joking among themselves after their shipwreck, we may have the impression that we are watching a redacted play in which one passage was never cast out of the dramatic idiom by which an "upstart crow" had dutifully caught the sharp sounds of fashionable Elizabethan wit flights. The tediousness of the courtiers' jests can be definitely felt in the following passages:

> Gon. When every grief is entertain'd that's offer'd,
>   Comes to th' entertainer—
> Seb. A dollar.
> Gon. Dolour comes to him, indeed: you have spoken truer than you
>   purpos'd.
> . . . .
> Ant. Which, of he or Adrian, for a good wager, first begins to crow?
> Seb. The old cock.
> Ant. The cockerel.
> Seb. Done. The wager?
> Ant. A laughter.
> Seb. A match!
> Adr. Though this island seem to be desert,—
> Ant. Ha, ha, ha!
> Seb. So: you're paid.
> Adr. Uninhabitable, and almost inaccessible,—
> Seb. Yet,—
> Adr. Yet,—
> Ant. He could not miss't.
> Adr. It must be of subtle, tender and delicate temperance.
> Ant. Temperance was a delicate wench.

Seb. Ay, and a subtle; as he most learnedly deliver'd.
Adr. The air breathes upon us here most sweetly.
Seb. As if it had lungs, and rotten ones.
Ant. Or as 'twere perfum'd by a fen.

. . . .

Gon. But the rarity of it is,—which is indeed almost beyond credit,—
Seb. As many vouch'd rarities are.
Gon. That our garments, being, as they were, drenched in the sea,
hold, notwithstanding, their freshness and glosses, being rather
new-dyed than stained with salt water.
Ant. If but one of his pockets could speak, would it not say he lies?
Seb. Ay, or very falsely pocket up his report.

                                            (2.1.16–20, 27–47, 56–65)

The puns in these speeches are classical in form. Sister Miriam
Joseph observes that "Antanaclasis is a figure which in repeat-
ing a word shifts from one of its meanings to another," while
"Asteismus is a figure of reply in which the answerer catches a
certain word and throws it back to the first speaker with an unexpected twist, an unlooked for meaning."[3] Shakespeare's puns
upon "temperance," "delicate," and "subtle" are excellent examples of the former rhetorical trope, while those on "dolour"
and "pocket" nicely illustrate the latter figure. Shakespeare often
employs puns regardless of dramatic period to signify a certain
coarseness or deficiency within a society or character. Sebastian's and Antonio's puns are verbal rapier-thrusts revealing
their belligerent Machiavellian culture and their opportunistic
and cynical selves. Foolishly indecorous, Antonio and Sebastian
prove insensitive to Alonso's grief for his lost son and the party's
predicament. Through punning, they violate the courtier's mod-
erate art; "pleasantries and witticisms are the gift and bounty of
nature rather than of art," Castiglione remarks in *The Book of the
Courtier:*

> Yet there are many among these and other peoples who, out of an
> excessive loquacity, go beyond bounds and become insipid and inept
> because they pay no attention whatever to the kind of person they
> are speaking with, or to the place where they are, or to the occasion
> or the soberness and modesty which they themselves ought to prac-
> tice.[4]

A pun normally succeeds by calling attention to the embar-
rassing bedfellows of meaning that usually accompany a word's

intended significance. For example, Gonzalo has no control over the fact that in his statement—

> When every grief is entertain'd that's offer'd,
> Comes to th' entertainer—

the word "entertainer," divorced from its syntax, can legitimately mean "performer" as well as "sufferer." This is a verbal possibility that Sebastian hears and crystallizes into a pun by finishing Gonzalo's sentence with the word "dolour"; the noble stoic of Gonzalo's sentence suddenly becomes a cheap actor pandering for a small fee in Sebastian's completion of the remark.[5] In order to identify the inappropriate connotations of words, the punster must as a rule be more concerned with how words are put together into phrases and clauses than with the ideational meanings created by syntax. When Gonzalo remarks after being soaked by the tempest—"Is not, sir, my doublet as fresh as the first day I wore it? I mean, in a sort,"—the value of his statement for Antonio resides in "sort's" possible sixteenth-century meaning of "lot" or "quantity."[6] "That sort was well fish'd for" (2.1.98–100), he degenerately quibbles. Antonio insipidly jests that Gonzalo should insert the word "sort" at precisely the point that he does in his speech even as Sebastian jokes only in terms of isolated meanings. The latter has cynically rejoiced that the word "yet" should predictably appear (to begin a new grammatical clause infused with hope) after Adrian's initial observation on the island's bleakness (2.1.35–43). Antonio sarcastically agrees ("He could not miss't") that Adrian compulsively chooses this conjunction.

As Antonio and Sebastian listen for words upon which they can pun, they overlook not only the need to find cheer in the midst of darkness but also the higher conceptual meanings created mainly by the order—the syntax—of Adrian's and Gonzalo's speech.[7] They offer a deaf ear to Adrian's optimism, which stems from his perception of the island's benign climate. Their spiritual loss is an apt punishment for their maiming of speech. By concerning themselves only with the word's significance as pun, cultured Antonio and Sebastian limit their knowledge to a single, trivial dimension of speech meaning, much as Caliban does when he believes that Stephano is the man-in-the-moon. Antonio and Sebastian have been taught speech, and their profit reveals itself as merely knowing how to pun.

Partly because of his superficial focus, the jesting duper of others sometimes becomes the dupe of a masterful rhetorician. Once Alonso's exhausted party is asleep, Antonio, in Sebastian's opinion, begins speaking a "sleepy language." To draw out Antonio's allusive meaning, Sebastian casually suggests that he is ready for a guiding current in an unknown direction; he pronounces that he is "standing water" (2.1.216). Replying in the spirit of Sebastian's metaphor, Antonio reassures him: "I'll teach you how to flow."[8] Wary Sebastian, however, will not commit himself in a direct statement to any course of action, although he feebly jests to keep the likelihood alive: "Do so: to ebb / Hereditary sloth instructs me" (2.1.218–19). Antonio then tells Sebastian that he does not fully comprehend how his jest has revealed a special purpose:

> O,
> If you but knew how you the purpose cherish
> Whiles thus you mock it! how, in stripping it,
> You more invest it! Ebbing men, indeed,
> Most often do so near the bottom run
> By their own fear or sloth.
>
> (2.1.218–23)

Gonzalo declared when Sebastian made his pun upon dolour, "You have spoken truer than you purpos'd" (2.1.19–20); that essentially is what Antonio tells Sebastian about jesting's impact upon purpose. Sebastian's royal ambition has been for the most part dimly known to himself. Antonio begins forcing it into Sebastian's consciousness by shrewdly interpreting his jest for him. He thus makes a casual joke the point of departure for his duping. Sebastian will "flow" to kingship by "courageously" murdering sleeping men; the moment can free him from his cowardly "ebbing." Antonio's fiendish reversal of the verbal meanings of courage and cowardice escapes Sebastian's notice. Sebastian's intention becomes treacherous when a slippery mode of discourse, jesting, makes it intelligible to him. His next step lies in acknowledging the smoldering discontent that Antonio will blow into raging treason.

Furthermore, the innocent hearer of a pun on occasion becomes vulnerable to ideas introduced into dialogue by a joke's multiple meanings—more so, in fact, because the auditor neither partly colludes with a manipulating jester nor generally imagines the strength of language's controlling power. This feature of jesting appears in the love affair between Ferdinand and Miranda. Ferdinand's intentions toward Miranda remain morally

ambiguous as long as he employs the flattering language of courtship. On one occasion Ferdinand reveals that he understands the
hazards of the courtly idiom:

> Full many a lady
> I have ey'd with best regard, and many a time
> Th' harmony of their tongues hath into bondage
> Brought my too diligent ear. . . .
>
> (3.1.39–42)

The "diligent" ear's bondage in this instance presumably involves flattering speech. Yet, despite his worldly knowledge, Ferdinand surprisingly recreates a beguiling harmony of the tongue
when he meets Miranda:

> Most sure the goddess
> On whom these airs attend! Vouchsafe my prayer
> May know if you remain upon this island;
> And that you will some good instruction give
> How I may bear me here: my prime request,
> Which I do last pronounce, is, O you wonder!
> If you be maid or no?
>
> (1.2.424–30)

"*O dea certe!*" Ferdinand in effect pronounces, gallantly and
perhaps self-consciously invoking the context of Aeneas's meeting with Venus, hardly a figure of chastity.[9] In the final line of
the above quotation, Ferdinand makes a slightly bawdy pun
upon two meanings of the spoken word "maid." On one level he
questions Miranda's possible divinity. Is she a goddess or a
woman of heavenly beauty who has been "made" (conceived)
in the normal mortal manner? On another level he asks her if
she is an available virgin (a "maid").[10] The sexual overtones of
this pun suggest that Ferdinand neither genteelly nor abstractly
considers Miranda's eligibility for marriage. He quibbles at Miranda's potential expense while he protects himself from im-
propriety with the compliment that he literally pays her as a
goddess. The subterranean meaning of Ferdinand's word graphi-
cally reveals the sexuality of any courtship, no matter how refined the partners might be. Although it is admittedly harmless,
Ferdinand's pun darkly reflects the Caliban within him—the passions that his noble nature forbids him from expressing out-
right.[11] Miranda, nonetheless, seems hazardously unaware of the
innuendoes in Ferdinand's greeting. She in her naïveté naturally
recognizes only its more chaste meaning; she informs him
charmingly that she surely is no divinity, but merely a mortal:

"No wonder, sir; / But certainly a maid" (1.2.430–31). Despite her answer's charm, Miranda remains susceptible to verbal manipulation. (That "sir" in her reply reveals that, at this instant, Ferdinand sways her.) Even though Ferdinand proves magnanimous, his speech is fraught with suggestion when regarded in the light of Shakespeare's special portrayal of jesting in the play.

Caliban's release from a jesting spirit is a major business of the comic subplot of *The Tempest*. Separated, he stands free from a corrupter of speech and knowledge. While Antonio and Sebastian most consistently voice the jesting spirit, Trinculo, listed as a "Jester" in the "Names of Actors" that follow the Folio's Epilogue, personifies it in *The Tempest*. Caliban's derogatory observation concerning Trinculo—"what a pied ninny's this!"(3.2.62)—indicates that the actor playing this part should wear the jester's traditional motley. The comic action pertinent to our topic begins when Caliban mistakes the jester Trinculo for one of Prospero's spirits about to play a cruel joke upon him for bringing in his burden of wood too slowly. Consequently, he falls flat upon the stage in abject fear. The threat of a renewed tempest then drives terrified Trinculo to seek the only refuge for miles about—shelter beneath Caliban's large, odorous cloak. Trinculo's disappearance beneath Caliban's gabardine has the stage effect of placing a jesting spirit within Caliban. Once the two characters form a grotesque creature with four legs (Trinculo's protrude near Caliban's ears), Stephano, the drunken butler, enters and hears Caliban's frightened cry that the strange spirit beneath his garment torments him. So that he might preserve the monster and show him for a price to the curious in Naples, Stephano gives the forward mouth of the bizarre beast—Caliban's—some wine to calm his fear.

Since he remains certain that his comrade must have drowned, Trinculo believes that he hears an island devil who has adopted Stephano's voice to address Caliban; consequently, the lower part of the fantastic animal starts pleading for a miraculous rescue. Truly shaken, Stephano then marvels at his beast's double nature:

Four legs and two voices,—a most delicate monster! His forward voice, now, is to speak well of his friend; his backward voice is to utter foul speeches and to detract. If all the wine in my bottle will recover him, I will help his ague. Come:—Amen! I will pour some in thy other mouth.

(2.2.91–96)

In this horseplay we see comically dramatized the jesting spirit's derogatory effect upon coherent speech. At destructive cross purposes with Caliban's "forward" voice, Trinculo's backward voice calls into question the authority of the former's statements. Shakespeare anatomizes in this farcical image the jesting spirit's previous inner confusion of purpose. As Stephano pours his wine over Caliban's bottom, drenched Trinculo beneath the cloak calls in earnest to his friend by name; as a result, Stephano becomes even more convinced that this mouth belongs to a demon. He then finds, however, that the backward voice issues from Trinculo; he roughly pulls the Jester by his legs from under Caliban's garment, asking him in the process how he came to be the excrement of such a creature. Stephano thus performs a comic purgation upon Caliban's foul voice, symbolically liberating him from a spirit that has threatened good understanding in the serious action of *The Tempest*.

Caliban's dissociation from the Jester is even stronger in the comic subplot of act 3. Trinculo states the scenario that the first half of the second scene will demonstrate when he tells Caliban and Stephano that they will "lie, like dogs, and yet say nothing neither" (3.2.18–19).[12] Upon Caliban's dogmatic refusal to serve cowardly Trinculo, the Jester says in drunken wrath that Caliban lies: "Wilt thou tell a monstrous lie, being but half a fish and half a monster?" (3.2.27–28). Sympathetic to Caliban's plea that he prevent Trinculo from mocking him, Stephano warns the Jester to keep a good tongue in his head (3.2.33). Again Caliban's immunity from foul speech becomes the dramatic issue of the comic scene. Appeased for the moment, Caliban then presents his barbaric plan for seizing rule from Prospero. That plan is broken up several times by ventriloquism, which the invisible Ariel, prepared always to protect his master, practices upon Trinculo. Thus, when Caliban complains that he remains at the mercy of a sorcerer who has cheated him of the island's ownership, Trinculo seems to say "Thou liest." Enraged, Caliban turns upon the unfortunate clown:

> Thou liest, thou jesting monkey, thou:
> I would my valiant master would destroy thee!
> I do not lie.
>
> (3.2.44–46)

Stephano's warning to Trinculo contains an unintentional pun upon "tale" / "tail": "Trinculo, if you trouble him any more in's tale, by this hand, I will supplant some of your teeth"

(3.2.47–48). Thus the recollection of the backward voice and the comic matter of the previous subplot scene is evoked.[13] Shakespeare carefully formulates Caliban's accusation so that jesting amounts to a kind of false statement—here specifically lying. Dumbfounded, Trinculo replies, "Why, I said nothing" (3.2.49). We have had the impression in *The Tempest* that puns reflect the most minimal of meanings. The Jester's "nonexistent" sayings underscore that impression in this episode. Twice more Ariel interrupts Caliban's tale with accusations of lying that seem to emanate from Trinculo. Finally driven beyond his patience, Stephano beats Trinculo into submission, much to the delight of Caliban and the theater audience. As he moves resentfully to the other side of the stage to escape more abuse, Trinculo physically reveals how far removed Caliban now is from the jesting spirit—from, that is, the potentially corrupting word.

That Caliban has the ability to seek the fresh grace that his master offers him in act 5 is partly due to the purgation discussed. During the catharsis of the jesting spirit, Trinculo clearly assumes the dramatic role of a Parolles or Malvolio—the absolute comic butt in contrast to whom other characters define their virtues. Excused from a sacrificial part, Caliban expresses the abiding ingredients of his humanity, which is ultimately realized both in his knowledge of the thrice-double ass he has been to worship Stephano and Trinculo and in his humble determination always to sue in the future for Prospero's grace.[14] While bloodthirsty desires for political power and revenge appear bestial in Caliban, they also surface just as savagely in those whose natures have been nurtured. Caliban's capacities for speech, dream, imaginative vision, and service all mark him a man. Whether Prospero will ever strengthen these capacities by resuming his education of Caliban when they both reach Italy is a Bradleyan question that Shakespeare does not answer. Nonetheless, the dramatist, by means of the sophisticated comic subplot of *The Tempest*, certainly does make his viewer feel that Caliban is free from one danger of cultivated speech.

Thus far in our analysis, the molding of characters' ideas and attitudes through speech has occurred either extemporaneously or casually. In Prospero's pedagogy, however, the shaping word becomes the agent for systematic lessons. Theurgist, or white magician; Medean enchanter; wizard; "jugler," or sixteenth-century street magician; experimenter, or New Scientist—several Prosperos inhabit the desert isle of *The Tempest*.[15] In his capacity as schoolmaster, Prospero employs the word as part of an educational program for Miranda. Just after he has stirred up the sea tempest, Prospero designs a narrative lesson so that Miranda might deduce an idea important for understanding the humanity she is about to meet. Empathizing with the suffering of the mariners and travelers aboard the "brave vessel," she believes that the ship seen laboring in the tempest was "dash'd all to pieces." Prospero, however, assures her that no harm was done:

> I have done nothing but in care of thee,
> Of thee, my dear one; thee, my daughter, who
> Art ignorant of what thou art; nought knowing
> Of whence I am, nor that I am more better
> Than Prospero, master of a full poor cell,
> And thy no greater father.
>
> (1.2.16–21)

"More to know," Miranda protests, "did never meddle with my thoughts." As the Eve-like inhabitant of a closed world, Miranda has rarely experienced the push of curiosity; she has rested content in her placid love for her miraculous father. "'Tis time / I should inform thee farther" (1.2.22–23), Prospero announces. The word "farther" suggests her schoolmaster's planned stretching of Miranda's cloistered undertanding.

Prospero regards the story of betrayal that he is about to tell as a verbal force that can expand her mind. "You have often / Begun to tell me what I am," Miranda exclaims,

> but stopp'd,
> And left me to a bootless inquisition,
> Concluding "Stay: not yet. . . ."
>
> (1.2.33–36)

Hearing that her father once was Duke of Milan and that she was an infant royally attended, Miranda eagerly desires to know both the blessed and damnable reasons for their being on the desert isle. In her repetition of Prospero's "farther," we sense the contrived expansion of her consciousness:

> O, my heart bleeds
> To think o'th' teen that I have turn'd you to,
> Which is from my remembrance! Please you, farther.
>
> (1.2.63–65)

Prospero's words will give his daughter the context for understanding the value of Antonio's and Alonso's moral renewal, which he intellectually desires to effect that day. Knowing her history, Miranda might grasp fully the wrongs that Prospero has patiently endured and admire her father for choosing to be virtuous rather than vengeful toward a false brother. Prospero's aim, however, can only be surmised in retrospect. At the moment he tells his tale, neither Miranda nor the viewer is aware of this long-range purpose. As Prospero's lengthy story unfolds, it resembles an *exemplum* designed to impart a moral truth. An *exemplum*, whether appearing in a sermon or a work of secular literature, typically was framed by a text—a statement of the virtue or vice illustrated by the intervening narrative.[16] Prospero's repeated text frames his narrative of Antonio's betrayal:

> I pray thee, mark me, that a brother should
> Be so perfidious!—he whom next thyself
> Of all the world I lov'd . . . .
> Mark his condition, and th' event; then tell me
> If this might be a brother.
>
>   (1.2.67–69, 117–18)

Prospero thus makes his personal history illustrate a sad truth about supposed brotherhood, his *exemplum* representing a variant of the Cain and Abel motif.[17]

Given his *exemplum*, Prospero is not wholly successful. Like his pastoral counterpart Belarius, Prospero is a tutor who would have his royal pupil, brought up in a wilderness, deduce an abstract moral that experience in a sophisticated court usually teaches.[18] In his insistence that his own experience underscores a lesson about the deceit of others, Prospero again resembles Belarius, who believes that the outlining of his past misfortunes and suffered ignomity will cause Arviragus and Guiderius to apprehend the workings of "uncertain favour." The Princes, however, generally grumble about Belarius's lessons, pointing out in their isolation that they have no perspectives from which they can value their tutor's lessons. And while Miranda does not complain about the relevance of Prospero's lesson for her life, she avoids making the deduction about brotherhood and evil that Prospero designs. For her, Prospero's words initially fail; she never exclaims "Treacherous brotherhood" or "Perfidious uncle."

Pressed by Prospero to deny Antonio's status as her father's brother, Miranda refuses to focus upon the crime obsessing Prospero:

> I should sin
> To think but nobly of my grandmother:
> Good wombs have borne bad sons.
>
> (1.2.118–20)

Miranda acknowledges Antonio's badness, but she blunts the force of her recognition by choosing to concentrate upon her grandmother's virtue. If a good man may have an evil brother, a good woman may have a bad son. In her innocence, Miranda voices a surprisingly complex idea that Prospero is not prepared to pursue at this point in the play. If good wombs have borne bad sons, bad wombs need not always produce equally depraved sons; the Caliban presented in the play, while corrupt, is clearly more redeemable than Sycorax, his mother. While Miranda's insight prepares the viewer for this realization, Prospero's opinion of his demi-devil blinds him to Caliban's capacity for reason and thus for learning. Thus Miranda's strong pity and her instinctive tendency to think well of everything, while admirable traits, divert the educational program of her schoolmaster.

Nevertheless, Prospero succeeds remarkably in his second lesson for Miranda. He intends to educate Miranda in a proper love for Alonso's son, but his method must accommodate her potentially dangerous habit of naïvely fixing upon virtue in a world of mixed qualities. That Prospero succeeds in his second lesson is attributable mainly to the verbal shapes created and manipulated by reason—both his own and Miranda's. For Aristotle, reasoning is basically a matter of right speaking.[19] According to classical theory, the ordering of spoken words determines the reasonable conclusion of instruction. Prospero's use of words to create verbal shapes directing Miranda's reason to his predetermined end of instruction merits analysis.

Unfamiliar with suitors and courtship customs, Miranda, to use phrasing from The Winter's Tale, initially knows no more about a wondrous sight than seeing makes possible. "The fringed curtains of thine eye advance," Prospero commands his daughter with regard to Ferdinand, "and say what thou seest yond" (1.2.411–12). Miranda at first mistakenly knows the handsome prince as one of her father's spirits, who are daily seen upon magical errands:

> What is't? a spirit?
> Lord, how it looks about! Believe me, sir,
> It carries a brave form. But 'tis a spirit.

> (1.2.412–14)

Miranda perceives Ferdinand as a spirit because she has known
only mysterious sprites, her father, and Caliban, whom (as the
following quotation makes clear) she does not regard as a man.
Consequently she has difficulty gauging Ferdinand's nature by
contrast with those of other men whom she would inevitably
meet in ordinary society. In a central speech, she tells Ferdinand,

> I do not know
> One of my sex; no woman's face remember,
> Save, from my glass, mine own; nor have I seen
> More that I may call men than you, good friend,
> And my dear father: how features are abroad,
> I am skilless of; but, by my modesty,
> The jewel in my dower, I would not wish
> Any companion in the world but you;
> Nor can imagination form a shape,
> Besides yourself, to like of.

> (3.1.48–57)

Were she living in society, Miranda would possess some knowledge of mankind and thus a partial context for judging Ferdinand's nature. Deprived of this context by her isolated life on
the island, however, she must blindly trust her instincts for her
love. Were Ferdinand not the noble young man that he providentially is, but perhaps a handsome opportunist like Antonio, Miranda could not deduce truth from beauty; here she might be
choosing and loving a vicious man. The last lines of the above
passage imply that an abundance of imagined shapes can, by the
contrasting examples that they provide, help one to define more
precisely the nature of an object. As Miranda testifies, a dearth
of them conversely leaves one dangerously gullible.

Prospero initially adopts the role of the irate father so that this
problem might be corrected and Ferdinand and Miranda know
a more nearly perfect love. The principle that he employs in aid-
ing the progress of the love affair is expressed in *The Tempest*
by Gonzalo when the old counselor portrays his Golden Age to
Alonso and the other lords of his party: "I'th' commonwealth I
would by contraries / Execute all things" (2.1.143–44).[20] Gonzalo

simply means that primitive life on his island paradise would be contrary to busy existence in civilized states:[21]

> for no kind of traffic
> Would I admit; no name of magistrate;
> Letters should not be known; riches, poverty,
> And use of service, none; contract, succession,
> Bourn, bound of land, tilth, vineyard, none;
> No use of metal, corn, or wine, or oil;
> No occupation; all men idle, all;
> And women too, but innocent and pure:
> No sovereignty;—
>
> (2.1.144–52)

Hearing Gonzalo, the viewer may recollect a phrase from *Timon of Athens*. When saturnine Timon, deserted by his false friends, leaves Athens in rage for the woods, he commands the rich city to "decline to your confounding contraries" (4.1.20), to the raw materials from which its grandeur arose. In a state of nature contrary to a corrupt urban world, Gonzalo, however, believes that mankind could lead a better life. Still, the presence of Caliban argues for a modicum of cultivation. By means of verbal shapes embedded in contrary comparisons, Prospero directs Miranda's and Ferdinand's love so that humility and gentleness, the fruits of culture, are not sacrificed to passion.

The magician tells his daughter,

> Thou think'st there is no more such shapes as he,
> Having seen but him and Caliban: foolish wench!
> To th' most of men this is a Caliban,
> And they to him are angels.
>
> (1.2.481–84)

The contrary terms "Caliban" and "angels" help Miranda to construct an elementary ratio; as angels are to most men, so most men are to Ferdinand. Prospero's unorthodox instruction relies upon classical reason; the comparison of terms in a ratio typified analogical reasoning as it derived from Aristotle.[22] It has been claimed that Prospero "embodies the very definition of *temparare* . . . described by Leo Spitzer: 'Any purposeful activity which proceeds with a view to correcting excesses.'"[23] Prospero, like Hamlet, may prize classical virtues; yet his management of Ferdinand and Miranda reveals that he paradoxically articulates excessive comparisons in order to achieve temperance.

Upon first consideration, Prospero seems to be trying to play down Ferdinand's noble nature, apparently meaning to counter Miranda's unrealistic vision of the Prince as a spirit. Toward such a supposed end, he has already asserted that "the spirit"

> eats and sleeps and hath such senses
> As we have, such. This gallant which thou seest
> Was in the wrack; and, but he's something stain'd
> With grief (that's beauty's canker) thou mightst call him
> A goodly person: he hath lost his fellows,
> And strays about to find 'em.
>
> (1.2.415–20)

By calling Ferdinand a "gallant" and "a goodly person"—excessively colorless terms in contrast with Miranda's—and by likening him to an animal in the last two lines of the passage (livestock "stray" about to rejoin a herd), Prospero appears to be giving his daughter additional verbal categories—"shapes," to use her word—by which she might more accurately imagine her lover's nature.

Prospero's experience has shown him that limitless feelings of virtue can be dangerous. Was it not his confidence "sans bound" in Antonio that awakened in the latter a falsity of equal dimensions (1.2.93–97)? One concludes that as a result of her father's worldly portrait of Ferdinand, a shrewd devaluation, Miranda might somewhat qualify her enthusiasm and more precisely know the Prince not as a strange spirit but as a courtier who eats and sleeps and pursues the delights of the senses. Such an aim, however, has no effect upon Miranda. After Prospero has called Ferdinand a gallant, Miranda again strongly affirms his spiritual status, this time calling him "a thing divine" (1.2.420–21). Instead of qualifying his daughter's hyperbolic image of her lover, Prospero's rather cold account of him causes her ideal conception to inflate proportionally.

Prospero's verbal shaping of his daughter's thoughts has a different instructive end. When Prospero tells his daughter that Ferdinand is a Caliban compared to most men and that they, juxtaposed to him, are angels, she replies,

> My affections
> Are then most humble; I have no ambition
> To see a goodlier man.
>
> (1.2.484–86)

When Miranda imagines Ferdinand in the shape of Caliban, a humble condition suggests to her a humble love, and she has no ambition to see a better man. Prospero's playing with verbal shapes, with Caliban and angels, thus gives Miranda a perspective by which she might understand her passion for the Prince. Even though her love is limitless, Miranda now knows her affection as a humble passion and so avoids the ambitious desires that drive characters like Antonio, Sebastian, Trinculo, and Stephano toward vice.

Nevertheless, contraries in *The Tempest* do not always interact to produce valuable ideas and moral states. Prospero testifies early in the action, in a passage already mentioned, to extreme contraries that perniciously impacted each other. He says that he awakened an evil nature within Antonio when

> my trust,
> Like a good parent, did beget of him
> A falsehood in its contrary, as great
> As my trust was; which had indeed no limit,
> A confidence sans bound.
>
> (1.2.93–97)

The greatness of virtue can be destructive; Antonio's falsity was proportional to the contrary immensity of Prospero's faith. The same principle—that the intensity of one quality is created in reaction to that of its contrary—appears in the rhetoric that seduces Sebastian to Antonio's murderous purpose:

> O, out of that "no hope"
> What great hope have you! no hope that way is
> Another way so high a hope, that even
> Ambition cannot pierce a wink beyond,
> But doubt discovery there.
>
> (2.1.234–38)

No hope, according to Antonio, can boomerang to a contrary great hope. Thus the devilish brother insidiously converts dull Sebastian's lack of hope that Ferdinand has survived the shipwreck into the dawning thought that he suddenly has the opportunity to seize the crown of Naples.

Contraries, reacting to one another in the fashion described above, are similarly perilous for Caliban. He comes to know Miranda's beauty, after which he subsequently lusts, only be-

cause he can articulate rudimentary comparisons. Caliban tells
Stephano during their plotting to take over the island that Prospero proudly calls Miranda a "nonpareil":

> I never saw a woman,
> But only Sycorax my dam and she;
> But she as far surpasseth Sycorax
> As great'st does least.
>
> (3.2.97–101)

Like Miranda, Caliban imagines another's nature mainly by contrast with that of a parent. It is in comparison with degenerate
Sycorax that the maiden's beauty becomes knowable; she is ravishing to the intense degree that Sycorax is ugly. Shakespeare
presents in Caliban the human habit of verbalizing comparisons
and knowing ideas whenever two terms are available that can be
made into upper and lower values. When he educates Miranda
in an unambitious love, Prospero trusts this instinct in his
daughter, who has seen no other men but remarkable Prospero
and beastly Caliban. An articulated ratio creates Caliban's ideas,
just as it does those of Miranda. As greatest is to least, so Miranda is to Sycorax.

Caliban's problem involves his inability morally to control his
verbalization of comparisons. Shakespeare indicated in *Pericles*
that ideas created by indiscriminate or chance comparisons
could be dangerous. When Marina and Philoten appear together,
Dionyza through their physical contrast incidentally becomes
aware of her daughter's plainness. Consequently, in her maternal
jealousy she plots Marina's death in order to erase the uncomplimentary comparison that constantly embarrasses her (Chorus
4.5–45). Caliban suggests that the use of reason in the form of
a simple ratio is a way of knowing neither good nor bad in itself.
He merely cannot give his articulated, reasonable thought the
ethical direction of the man whose nature has been nurtured.
Caliban's reasonable use of comparisons, however, is major evidence of a human element in his abhorrently mixed character.
Among all the capacities of a man that Caliban expresses—those
for music, rich vision, power and its accompanying cruelty—the
ability to reason verbally must be included.[24]

Arguing that Caliban would have been better off without the
gift of language because it allows him to realize vicious desires
amounts to claiming that gabbling like a brutish thing categorically takes precedence over natural man's learning to think rea-

sonably and acquiring the capacity for self-knowledge and the
need for grace. These, too, are the fruits of language. Even
Caliban's most attractive natural trait, his rich awareness of the
isle's qualities (2.2.167–72), would remain dark both to himself
and others were he unable to frame it in poetic speech. As
Caliban's periodic eloquence suggests, his speech is not always
a curse; when love or gratitude animates him, he can become me-
lodious. His memory of Prospero's original instruction reveals
this fact:

> When thou cam'st first,
> Thou strok'st me, and made much of me; wouldst give me
> Water with berries in't; and teach me how
> To name the bigger light, and how the less,
> That burn by day and night: and then I lov'd thee,
> And show'd thee all the qualities o' th' isle,
> The fresh springs, brine-pits, barren place and fertile:
> Curs'd be I that did so!
>
> (1.2.334–41)

Kindness begets gratitude—"and then I lov'd thee." Caliban indicates that kind instruction, especially as speech creates the
world around the ignorant savage or the innocent child, gene-
rates love and the desire to serve. The gentleness of Caliban's
speech, exemplified by the sensitive image of water with berries
in it, reflects the momentary gentility of his thought as he recalls
a brief, happy episode in his life. His rhapsodic words about the
qualities of the isle, which he in gratitude will show Stephano,
make up a second instance of Caliban's poetry mirroring an affectionate attitude. The relationship between kindness and instruction has wide-ranging implications in The Tempest. Even
though Prospero's educational programs, like those of ruling
deities in other late romances, require adversity, Shakespeare
suggests (especially in act 5) that an element of kindness
can facilitate a pupil's use of language and expand his understanding.

And what of Alonso? Do words enlarge his understanding?
Critics have not remarked that the Harpy's Banquet focuses
and emphasizes the epiphanic word. Considering his complex
magical design, Prospero's most magnanimous expression of his
power will be his forgiving Alonso and Antonio their crimes
against him and Miranda. He will offer such forgiveness, how-

ever, only if his enemies comprehend a spiritual lesson—only if they recollect repressed evil and genuinely experience remorse, heart's sorrow, and the desire to lead a "clear life." Alonso's education, like that of Miranda, begins when he knows no more than seeing makes possible. By fabricating the Harpy's Banquet so that its images resist verbal interpretation, Shakespeare (and Prospero) prepare Alonso and the theater audience to be duly impressed by the powerful epiphanic word when it is uttered. While searching the island for Ferdinand, the King and his party suddenly see *"several strange Shapes, bringing in a banquet,"* about which they dance *"with gentle actions of salutations."* Inviting both Alonso and courtiers to eat, they depart. John Doebler has likened this feast to an abbreviated Banquet of Sense, or Medieval Banquet of Sins, and cited several iconographical analogues to it.[25] Such symbolic allusions, in Doebler's opinion, define Prospero's purposes in punishing Gluttony (Appetite), the sin that greedy Alonso, Antonio, and Sebastian have committed in a general sense and the fault most associated with the Banquet of Sense. Thus Doebler believes that producers of *The Tempest* can communicate Shakespeare's dramatic purpose by making the procession of the Shapes "like that of the Seven Deadly Sins in *Dr. Faustus*" . . . or that of "the Five Senses."[26] If Prospero's feast were a Banquet of Sense, Alonso and Antonio, being sinful men, should be attracted to it; they, however, show no signs of being drawn to it. Moreover, were the shapes traditional personifications, they presumably would be recognizable to Alonso and the courtiers and thus capable of relatively uniform explanation. Their appearance, however, must be extremely ambiguous, for they encourage diverse interpretations. In Sebastian's eyes they are "a living drollery," a puppet show with live actors. For Antonio and Gonzalo, they are islanders of "monstrous shape" whose manners are most gentle, that is, civilized. Critics have often judged that the Shapes and the banquet, like *The Tempest* as a whole, amount to ambiguous mirrors whose meanings depend upon the values of a perceiver's mind.[27] Thus humane Gonzalo sees kind gestures in the Shapes' behavior, while cynical and unimaginative Sebastian only sees controlled puppets like himself. If the Shapes had a familiar emblematic appearance, Shakespeare would be working against himself in establishing the epistemology of his play; the audience would think that his characters were blind rather than subject to different degrees of spiritual vision.

Unlike his courtiers, Alonso does not indicate how he sees the Shapes. Instead, he reacts to the strange music accompanying their delivery of the banquet:

> I cannot too much muse
> Such shapes, such gesture, and such sound, expressing—
> Although they want the use of tongue—a kind
> Of excellent dumb discourse.

(3.3.36–39)

The Shapes "speak" to Alonso, but they do not communicate an intelligible discourse. Prospero during his education of Miranda provided "shapes" (Caliban, angels) by which she might imagine her humble love for Ferdinand. Prospero's "Shapes," however, do not immediately stimulate Alonso's imagination into an act of interpretation. Gonzalo, in fact, dilutes the supernatural wonder surrounding their appearance by reminding Alonso of the Renaissance voyager's discoveries in the new world—of "mountaineers / Dew-lapp'd like bulls" and "men / Whose heads stood in their breasts." At this point Ariel appears "like a Harpy; claps his wings upon the table; and, with a quaint device, the banquet vanishes." The harpy was an emblem of greed for Shakespeare's age, one in which an erring mortal might see his sin's grotesqueness.[28] But while it may carry this meaning in the humanist's Aeneid, Dürer's woodcuts, and fifteenth-century emblem books, the harpy has an immediate locus for interpretation—Pericles. "Thou art like the harpy," Cleon tells Dionyza, "which, to betray, dost with thine angel's face / Seize with thine eagle's talons" (4.3.46–48). In this context the harpy becomes an archetype of duplicity and betrayal. As harpy, Ariel projects a grotesque amalgam of pity and wrath, angel and eagle—symbols for the respective spirits of the New Law and the Old. Such an unresolved image fits the dramaturgy of The Tempest; Prospero's state of mind at this moment reflects a mixture of intellectual compassion and emotional hatred. Ariel as harpy thus mirrors Prospero's wish (and plan) to forgive Alonso and Antonio as well as his savage desire to avenge his twelve-year-old pain. Not surprisingly, Alonso remains unable to translate the deepest meaning of the harpy into words. As a type of the Last Supper, the banquet represents the spiritual communion that Prospero's pardon would make possible.[29] "Bravely the figure of this Harpy hast thou / Perform'd, my Ariel," Prospero states; "a grace it had devouring" (3.3.83–84). The last words form at once an artistic compliment and a description of the blessedness gained by eating the feast. Mockingly snatched away before Alonso can taste it, the banquet, however, gives way to Ariel's terrific speech of destiny.

Like Posthumus's comprehension of Jupiter's dream-vision, Alonso's knowledge of the Harpy's Banquet appears to be less than that of the audience. In the King's ears, Ariel's ominous poetic words become the threatening sounds of the sea, wind, and thunder:

> O, it is monstrous, monstrous!
> Methought the billows spoke, and told me of it;
> The winds did sing it to me; and the thunder,
> That deep and dreadful organ-pipe, pronounc'd
> The name of Prosper: it did bass my trespass.
> Therefor my son i' th' ooze is bedded; and
> I'll seek him deeper than e'er plummet sounded,
> And with him there lie mudded.
>
> (3.3.95–102)

The single word "Prosper" represents the culmination of the elaborate Harpy's Banquet. Within that single epiphanic name lies stored the knowledge of guilt and retribution that now floods Alonso's consciousness. Ironically, the truncated form of the word conveys prosperity seemingly denied the shaken Alonso, and yet, within the scope of the play's action, it betokens truly the prosperity that will finally befall the guilty King. Like Gloucester in *Lear*, Alonso deduces that present suffering is just punishment for a crime committed long ago.[30] Like Gloucester again, he ambiguously responds to the spiritual program devised by his tutor—Edgar and Prospero, respectively. Connecting their losses with past crimes, both Gloucester and Alonso sink into a dangerous despair. Edgar attempts to cure his suicidal father through the trick of his fall from Dover Cliff—a "miracle" arranged to force Gloucester to believe that the "clearest gods" have preserved him for a natural death. The cure momentarily holds as Gloucester promises to bear "Affliction till it do cry out itself / 'Enough, enough,' and die" (4.6.76–77). But the remedy lapses when Gloucester, told by Edgar that Lear and Cordelia have lost the battle, resolves to "rot" where he sits. Edgar's stoic philosophy of ripeness draws a weak "and that's true too" from

the old man, an answer, in other words, at odds with the strength
of the religious conviction that Edgar intended.[31]

Similarly, Alonso's immediate reaction to Ariel's pronouncement is clearly different from the constructive sorrow attending
contrition and repentance. Alonso suffers life-threatening despair until the final act of the play.[32] Commentators on act 3,
scene 3 never observe that, when Alonso exits determined to lie
"mudded" with his son's body, it is Gonzalo rather than Ariel
who incites the younger members of the party to

> follow them swiftly,
> And hinder them from what this ecstasy
> May now provoke them to. . . .
>
> (3.3.107–9)

Significantly, Prospero and Ariel have exited *before* Alonso expresses his understanding of Ariel's grim speech. Consequently
Gonzalo's direction for preserving Alonso's life does not appear
to be inspired (or foreseen) by Prospero. We can only conclude
that Alonso would have drowned himself while Prospero was
visiting "young Ferdinand . . . And his and mine lov'd darling"
if Gonzalo had not intervened. This staging stresses Prospero's
conflicted allegiances and the less-than-perfect design of his program for Alonso's recovery. The magician has ominously stated,

> My high charms work,
> And these mine enemies are all knit up
> In their distractions: they now are in my power;
> And in these fits I leave them. . . .
>
> (3.3.89–91)

Such vagueness of purpose accords well with the surprising indifference to Alonso's fate that Prospero exhibits. Nevertheless,
the epiphanic word "Prosper" eventually alters Alonso's mind;
rather than immediately, the utterance works silently within him
over a course of time. Alonso's refined awareness reveals itself
in his later contrite words to Prospero, "Thy dukedom I resign,
and do entreat / Thou pardon me my wrongs—" (5.1.118–19). His
profound wish to lie "mudded in that oozy bed" so that Miranda
and Ferdinand might reign in Naples (5.1.149–52) reflects at
play's end not despair but an expanded awareness of the selfless
concern for others required for personal happiness. From the
seed-word "Prosper" grows and blooms this saving knowledge.

By promoting irrationality, the Harpy's Banquet qualifies as the grotesque antimasque to the Masque of Ceres, which, conforming to the Jonsonian aesthetic developed in 1609 in *The Masque of Queens*, celebrates reason and a rational ordering of experience.[33] The Jonsonian masque set the precedent for the entry of the presenter of the antimasque into the masque itself, in which he played an important role.[34] Iris, the character played by Ariel in the Masque of Ceres, was the sister of the harpies, according to Hesiod.[35] Visionary moments in other late romances occur when the novel use of expressive symbols such as flowers supersede fallen, courtly speech as a medium of communication. In keeping with this emphasis, Prospero commands, "No tongue! All eyes! be silent" (4.1.59), as Iris enters to soft music. The magician will not allow the disruptive human speech heard at various moments throughout *The Tempest* to ruin his visual lesson for the lovers. Despite Prospero's stress on vision as a way of knowing in this episode, the word translates and then interprets what is seen. Spoken by spirits assuming divine shapes, the words of the masque possess a rarefied tone, appropriate to the occasion; they transcend the corruption of mortal speech to convey authoritatively a message about fruitful marriage.

Consistent with the Johannine doctrine of creation through the Word, the gradual birth of life in the masque occurs primarily through words rather than symbolic action. Iris's description of Ceres' realm is at first surprisingly cold and barren. "*Turfy mountains*," "*flat meads thatch'd with stover*," "*banks with pioned and twilled brims*," a "*pole-clipt vineyard*," a "*seamarge, sterile and rocky-hard*"—such words and phrases describe remarkably colorless attributes of "*bounteous*" Ceres.[36] Taken as a whole, they portray a fit setting for "*cold nymphs*" with "*chaste crowns*" and "*the dismissed bachelor*." But this black-and-white world of potentiality—the world of late March or early April—suddenly breaks into vivid color when Ceres addresses Iris, the deity of the rainbow:

> *Hail, many colour'd messenger, that ne'er*
> *Dost disobey the wife of Jupiter;*
> *Who, with thy saffron wings, upon my flowers*
> *Diffusest honey-drops, refreshing showers;*
> *And with each end of thy blue bow dost crown*
> *My bosky acres and my unshrubb'd down,*
> *Rich scarf to my proud earth. . . .*
>
> (4.1.76–82)

Ceres speaks of the familiar myth of growth, of the miraculous springing of abundant life from the fallow ground. Shakespeare's intent and artistic procedure early in the masque loosely resemble those of Botticelli in the *Primavera*. Edgar Wind has described the Italian painter's dependence upon a Neo-Platonic idea of creation in which the divine spirit, depicted in the painting as the *inflatus* Zephyrus, inspires Flora, a figure of spring, so that flowers emerge.[37] In the painting, Zephyrus literally colors the barren Flora with new life, while in *The Tempest*, lifegiving Iris paints the plain earth—"*rich scarf to my proud earth.*" Ceres' words in Shakespeare's play essentially function as the vital spirit depicted by the painter's pigments. For Shakespeare, the divine word breathes a life of its own.

Shakespeare's poetic version of Neo-Platonic rebirth is appropriate because children will be the fruit of Miranda's and Ferdinand's betrothal, which the masque celebrates. "*Go with me / To bless this twain,*" Juno tells Ceres, "*that they may prosperous be, / And honour'd in their issue*" (4.1.103–5). Reference is twice made in the masque to Ceres' bounty (4.1.60, 103); her part in Juno's song for the betrothed couple extends the absolute marriage blessing:

> *Earth's increase, foison plenty,*
> *Barns and garners never empty;*
> *Vines with clust'ring bunches growing;*
> *Plants with goodly burthen bowing. . . .*
>
> (4.1.110–13)

Spoken by a goddess, these words attain the status of a mystical declaration rather than a hypothetical wish (a subjunctive statement).

Rapt by his vision of the goddesses, Ferdinand simply wonders at its beauty and wishes to live forever with Miranda and Prospero on the enchanted island. Paradoxically, the preferred medium of vision in the masque threatens to eclipse the crucial message conveyed by its ideal words. As Miranda prepares to echo Ferdinand's sentiments, Prospero again warns against disruptive speech:

> Sweet, now, silence!
> Juno and Ceres whisper seriously;
> There's something else to do: hush, and be mute,
> Or else our spell is marr'd.
>
> (4.1.124–27)

Iris then calls forth sunburned sicklemen of August, weary from harvesting, to dance with chaste and temperate Naiads. Figures symbolic of work and fertility join gracefully with nymphs poetically associated with dormant, relatively colorless early spring (4.1.64–70). By harmoniously joining the reapers and the nymphs, Ceres (and Prospero) physically enact the verbal benediction extended before Ferdinand's interruption:

> Spring come to you at the farthest
> In the very end of harvest!
>
> (4.1.114–15)

From this symbolic dance (which transforms the above words into deeds), Miranda and Ferdinand could see and know the idea that unaided nature cannot depict—that perpetual fertility should be the reward of married chastity. Spring and autumn dovetail in the dance; both barren winter and Venus Cupiditas have been banished. The vision thus depends upon erected wit, or nurtured reason, for not only its conception but also for the viewer's understanding of its hidden meaning. Its reasonable idea complements (and rectifies) the central point of the anti-masque—that the irrational breaking of a hallowed bond between brothers leads to the loss of an only son and so to the death of the father's name.[38] Perpetual fertility does not appear in the brazen world in which mankind lives. By rearranging the order of the seasons, Prospero artistically realizes an endless reaping; he apparently achieves the art above nature that makes nature, the art that Perdita rejected. Here Prospero projects the rich vision that Perdita lacked when she could find no spring flowers in late summer by which she might chastely and aptly express her love for Florizel.

Early seventeenth-century betrothal masques usually ended in a dance in which the masquers broke the fictional plane of the playing area and drew the aristocratic couple in whose honor the entertainment was staged into a stately dance, one often filled with mythological personages. Shakespeare indicated in The Winter's Tale that dance can be a means for participating in and communicating otherworldly ideas.[39] Mingled with the reapers and the nymphs, Miranda and Ferdinand could participate in the Idea of Chaste Fertility, which they might know by "doing."[40] The conventions of the kind of entertainment that Prospero has selected at least suggest this reconstruction. Prospero's recollection of Caliban's threat upon his life, however, precludes Miranda's and Ferdinand's performance of the artist's grand idea. The masque dissolves just as the symbolic dancers prepare to invite the lovers into its refined circle. Regarded from a linguistic viewpoint, the aborting of the masque implies that mankind cannot live indefinitely in a magical world of ideal words but must learn to cope with the reality of fallen speech (typified by Caliban's language).

The sequence of events in *The Tempest* most closely resembles that in the scene of Arviragus's elegy in *Cymbeline*. Guiderius breaks off the beautiful elegy, comparable to the Masque of Ceres in its place in its play, because its words are "wench-like"— without passion. The elegy's sweetness in Guiderius's view disqualifies it for commemorating bitter death. Passion, symbolized by Cupid and Venus, is also absent from Prospero's artifact. Caliban exemplifies passion (both in his speech and deeds), and Prospero's memory of him provokes the very passion associated with the slave. Prospero *"starts suddenly,"* electrified by his painful thought, and Ferdinand remarks that the magician is "in some passion / That works him strongly" (4.1.143–44). The abrupt infusion of energy portrayed early in the masque recurs unexpectedly with negative overtones. Miranda then identifies the kind of passion that her father feels: "Never till this day / Saw I him touch'd with anger, so distemper'd" (4.1.144–45). During Prospero's narration of Antonio's betrayal, Miranda witnessed her father's righteous wrath, the classical *virtu* that testifies to the magnanimous man's self-esteem. But as the character of King Lear reveals, the point at which righteous wrath becomes the distemper against which Seneca warns in *De Ira* is often difficult to define. Miranda's "distemper'd" thus signals a change in the nature of Prospero's anger. To be effective, ideal artistry must somehow integrate passion into its fabric. Since *The Tempest* is idealistic art of the highest order, Shakespeare must eventually incorporate passion—the Caliban within—into the total dramatic design.

That incorporation occurs during the opening dialogue of act 5, where a final verbal use of contrary comparison effects the integration within Prospero, resolving his conflicted thought and feeling in favor of forgiveness. There, Ariel shows Prospero a further refinement in his own educational methodology. As part of a dialogic ratio, the word accomplishes Prospero's change of attitude and thus his latent redemptive design. Ariel begins the conversion of Prospero's vengeful feelings into merciful desires when he paints a word picture of suffering Gonzalo, bruised and led astray by bewitching visions and voices:

> His tears run down his beard, like winter's drops
> From eaves of reeds. Your charm so strongly works 'em,
> That if you now beheld them, your affections
> Would become tender.
>
> (5.1.16–19)

Ariel's pathetic portrayal of Gonzalo moves Prospero chiefly because a simile, a verbal comparison, makes Gonzalo's distress more vivid. His tears run down his beard like winter's drops from eaves of reeds. Winter was unnaturally left out of Prospero's masque.[41] Admitted in the form of Ariel's simile, winter plays a role in harmonizing the self. Actually, Ariel does not give Prospero a direct vision of Gonzalo by which the magician might be led to new ideas. He requires that his master respond to the creative word by imagining how Gonzalo in his misery appears; the simile helps Prospero to perform that intellectual feat. Ariel's poetic image possesses *enargeia,* or what Henry Peacham termed Efficacy: "a power of speech which representeth a thing after an excellent manner, neither by bare words only, but by presenting to our minds the lively *ideas* or forms of things so truly as if we saw them with our own eyes. . . ."[42] Ariel performs for Prospero a service like that which the magician enacted for the lovers during their courtship. He gives his master another "shape"— the image of weeping Gonzalo—by which he might imagine new ideas and more refined affections. Unlike Ferdinand during his sojourn on the island, Prospero has not clearly served an ideal cause; consequently, ambiguity riddles the quality and goal of his magic. Prospero suddenly finds himself in the service of Ariel and his empathy when the spirit vividly describes old Gonzalo's tearful face.[43] Even as he released Miranda—only knowing a woman by gazing, Narcissus-like, upon herself in a mirror—from a constrictive emotion, a wiser teacher kindly educates Prospero out of his self-centered desire for revenge.

When Ariel says that Prospero's affections would become tender if the latter saw Gonzalo, the magician asks, "Dost thou think so, spirit?" And Ariel answers, "Mine would, sir, were I human" (5.1.19–20). The mortal then concludes:

And mine shall.
Hast thou, which art but air, a touch, a feeling
Of their afflictions, and shall not myself,
One of their kind, that relish all as sharply
Passion as they, be kindlier mov'd than thou art?
Though with their high wrongs I am struck to th' quick,
Yet with my nobler reason 'gainst my fury
Do I take part: the rarer action is
In virtue than in vengeance. . . .

(5.1.20–28)

Prospero's marvel that the spirit Ariel has a touch of human feeling for Gonzalo's pain nicely illustrates a contemporary criterion for fine art. Fine art for the Renaissance viewer was so lifelike that it approached the condition of real life and was even mistaken for it, as, in a famous example, the painted grapes in Zeuxis's tapestry so deceived birds that they assaulted it. For a moment, Ariel, who embodies Art throughout the play,[44] seems to Prospero to feel human passion. But his impression lasts only for a moment. Art that seems alive with passion only serves to remind Prospero that passion is exclusively the property of living men and women.[45]

Prospero's thinking transparently reflects Aristotle's assumption about the verbal basis of reasoning; using the topic of comparison (actually a ratio), the magician essentially "talks through" his apotheosis of character in a dialectical conversation ostensibly with Ariel but actually with himself. When he finds by comparison that something contrary to himself, the non-human Ariel, can experience a touch of human pity over a human plight, Prospero discovers that he, a man, should all the more intensely feel the same redemptive compassion. He should be "kindlier" moved than Ariel in both Renaissance senses of that word—more pitifully and more humanly. An understanding of brotherhood constituted the lesson that Prospero set Miranda while he recounted his past injuries. Ironically, that is what he himself must learn before he can forgive his enemies. As a result of Ariel's tutelage, the image of his "brother" Gonzalo displaces the picture of untrustworthy Antonio haunting his mind.

One last time in The Tempest an elementary ratio gives a character's thinking and the dramatic action a major turn. Just as a person is more than a nonhuman creature, so a person's affections should be more human than any felt by the creature. The limitations of language in *The Tempest* are memorably over-come; for it is through speech, both the lively simile of Ariel and the rational discourse of Prospero, that virtue prevails.[46] Un-equivocally the word has enlarged the magician's understand-ing. By his verbal reasoning, Prospero creates his knowledge in the play's last act, demonstrating that he is not the passive slave, depicted as mankind in the revels speech, who depends upon mysterious dreams for his deeper understanding. Because he has discovered a way of coordinating art, imagination, and reason through speech to arrive at one of mankind's most liberating ideas, Prospero can afford to break his sorcerer's staff and drown his book of spells. He can orchestrate the three qualities named above in the ordinary worlds of Naples and Milan.

Still, Shakespeare does not make the ending of *The Tempest* quite as sanguine as the previous statement suggests. While forgiving Antonio's "rankest fault," Prospero snarls, "whom to call brother / Would even infect my mouth" (5.1.130–31). The playgoer senses that extraordinary verbal orchestrations such as Prospero's occur infrequently, if only because cata-lytic Ariels are rare. For the most part, mankind communicates through curses, deceitful equivocations, corrupting (and cor-ruptible) words. Thus Prospero's idealistic desire to control fallen speech, one of his magic's last acts, appears slightly ri-diculous when considered in light of the unmagical world he will soon inhabit. Prospero's forgiveness of Sebastian and Stephano carries a penalty. "Most cruelly / Didst thou, Alonso, use me and my daughter," Prospero concludes:

> Thy brother was a furtherer in the act.
> Thou art pinch'd for't now, Sebastian. Flesh and blood,
> You, brother mine, that entertain'd ambition,
> Expell'd remorse and nature; whom, with Sebastian,—
> Whose inward pinches therefor are most strong,—
> Would here have kill'd your King, I do forgive thee. . . .
>
> (5.1.71–78)

"O, touch me not," Stephano later exclaims; "I am not Stephano, but a cramp" (5.1.286). While strange pinching and cramping signal Prospero's insistence that these characters possess a con-science, *ayenbite of inwit*, they also represent his efforts to restrict their capacity for foul talk. Prospero simply treats aristo-crats as he did Caliban.

When Caliban enters the play cursing, Prospero replies,

> For this, be sure, to-night thou shalt have cramps,
> Side-stitches that shall pen thy breath up; urchins
> Shall forth at vast of night, that they may work
> All exercise on thee; thou shalt be pinch'd
> As thick as honeycomb, each pinch more stinging
> Than bees that made 'em.
>
> (1.2.327–32)

Cramps pen up the breath, making scurrilous speech difficult if not impossible; under Prospero's regimen, blasphemy and false utterances cannot infect the ear. Yet once Prospero abandons his magic, supernatural methods for controlling language will have been forfeited. Corrupt speech will echo through the streets of Milan and Naples, assaulting Miranda's and Prospero's ears. By these final, skeptical suggestions, Shakespeare magnifies the importance of those special moments of rich verbal orchestration. Along with prayer, they constitute a person's means for transforming his or her attitudes and world (if not those of others). By forming a prayer, Prospero's epilogue fittingly concludes Shakespeare's romance of the word. The charity for which Prospero prays includes much more than the audience's good will, the plaudite. The prayer invokes the kind of grace that mysterious Ariel freely offered his master at the beginning of act 5, the grace that initiated Prospero's redemptive verbal reasoning. Salvatory art and grace both shape themselves in words, those of the artist and the suppliant. Together, they inspire those noteworthy spiritual revolutions won through speech.

6
Conclusion

In Sir Philip Sidney's *New Arcadia* (1593, 1621), when Pyrocles, determined to elope with Philoclea, hears her ravishing song, he pauses at her bedchamber's door. His pausing becomes the occasion for the author's reflections on the lover's timeless fascination with his beloved. "Whatsoever she doth is ever in his eyes best," the narrator begins,

> And that best, being by the continual motion of our changing life turned by her to any other thing, that thing again becometh best; so that nature in each kind suffering but one superlative, the lover only admits no positive. If she sit still, that is best, for so is the conspiracy of her several graces held best together to make one perfect figure of beauty. If she walk, no doubt that is best, for, besides the making happy the more places by her steps, the very stirring adds a pleasing life to her native perfections. If she be silent, that without comparison is best, since by that means the untroubled eye most freely may devour the sweetness of his object. But if she speak, he will take it upon his death that is best, the quintessence of each word being distilled down into his affected soul.[1]

Representing the ornate Arcadian style at its best, the passage builds gracefully through several superlative acts of the beloved—her sitting, walking, remaining silent, and her speaking. Significantly, the beloved's speech accounts for the greatest admiration, "the quintessence of each word being distilled down into his affected soul." For Sidney's Pyrocles, it is Philoclea's heavenly word that most enchants his soul.

In 1893 C. B. Mount noted a resemblance between Sidney's passage and Florizel's love lyric in act 4 of *The Winter's Tale:*[2]

> What you do
> Still betters what is done. When you speak, sweet,
> I'd have you do it ever: when you sing,

141

> I'd have you buy and sell so, so give alms,
> Pray so, and, for the ord'ring your affairs,
> To sing them too: when you do dance, I wish you
> A wave o' th' sea, that you might ever do
> Nothing but that, move still, still so,
> And own no other function. Each your doing,
> So singular in each particular,
> Crowns what you are doing, in the present deeds,
> That all your acts are queens.
>
> (4.4.135–46)

Both Sidney and Shakespeare imply that "the continual motion of our changing life" increases the beloved's beauty and grace by entailing ever-changing deeds that variously express his or her perfection. Because each passage's rhythm builds to a climax, the auditor concludes that speaking and dancing ideally convey the beloved's charms. Interestingly, Shakespeare starts where Sidney ends. For the playwright, the beloved's speech begins rather than concludes the list of his or her perfections. Basically, Shakespeare reverses the sequence of the prose writer's points. The general principle (amounting to a thesis) with which Sidney begins (that "the continual motion of our changing life" requires the manifold expression of a single grace) becomes in Shakespeare's poetry the culminating paradox of static motion, the dance of the sea wave moving "still, still so."

My motive for comparing two passages from the *Arcadia* and *The Winter's Tale* does not involve proving that the Sidney passage constitutes a source for Shakespeare's play. While Hallett Smith and R. S. White (among others) have shown that the *Arcadia* exerted a greater influence upon Shakespeare's romances than was previously supposed, the differences between the two passages suggest analogue rather than direct borrowing.[3] Instead, I wish to underscore the fit between romance and the portrayal of ideal speech. It was Northrop Frye who classified romance as the perennial genre of summer, of joy, and ideality.[4] Following the rationale of genre, Sidney and Shakespeare often focus upon the word's power and beauty during their romantic experimentations. The silver speech acts of the *Arcadia* help us to account for Shakespeare's emphasis upon characters' exceptional ways of speaking and expressing themselves in his last romances. Quite simply, they conform to the aesthetics of an idealizing kind of literature. Obviously revolutionary acts of speech occur in Shakespearean tragedy and comedy; one need only remember the liberating words on Portia's golden casket and Bassanio's verbal reasoning based upon them, a discourse that leads him to choose her and his own eventual fulfillment. But these acts neither consistently appear within the comedies, histories, and tragedies, nor do they proportionately weigh with the redemptive words and new, remarkable ways of communicating found in the last romances. Clearly, Shakespeare discovered in the genre of dramatic romance a form already defined as suited for the presentation of extraordinary speech acts.

Certainly my conclusions thus far do not suggest the artistic complexity of either the *Arcadia* or any one of Shakespeare's last romances (including the much maligned *Pericles*). While Sidney positively represents the force of eloquence, he just as often (perhaps more so) portrays the enticing flowers of rhetoric obscuring not only evil arguments but the self-centered, irrelevant pleas of basically good characters. While the atheism of Cecropia lurks beneath her powerful *carpe diem* speech to imprisoned Pamela, Euarchus in Book V rightfully disregards the eloquent rhetoric of Musidorus's and Pyrocles' pleas for their lives.[5] And we have seen the degree to which malicious speech and inherently inadequate words inform Shakespeare's last romances. Shakespeare's long-time interest in staging fallen speech and insufficient words, an interest defined by Sigurd Burckhardt, James Calderwood, and Lawrence Danson, resurfaces when the thrust of romance suggests dramatizing ideal or remarkable expressive alternatives to disastrous utterances and slippery words. The playwright's ingrained linguistic skepticism, a preoccupation as old at least as *Love's Labour's Lost*, reappears but within a new formal context.

One could argue that the atmosphere of pastoral rather than that of romance rarefies Philoclea's words; Sidney's *Arcadia* is, after all, a pastoral romance. Nevertheless, Shakespeare's focusing of the salvatory word in the nonpastoral play *Pericles* and his staging of language's reformative power in scenes such as Posthumus's dream-vision and Hermione's "resurrection" suggest that the idealizing ethos of romance, rather than that of pastoral, initially (or chiefly) sparked his imagination as regards a linguistic design. Certain events basic to romance presented Shakespeare with linguistic opportunities once he turned to a consideration of the literary form. For example, the ruinous consequence of the uttered magical spell, an original trapping of the genre,[6] takes the form of Antiochus's riddle's wasteland-like effect upon Pericles and the city of Tyre. By the early seventeenth-century, however, providence had generally displaced white magic as the supernatural agent responsible for the relatively harmonious conclusion of romance (although *The Tempest* may pose an exception to this judgment).[7] More often than not, Renaissance authors condensed the ideal (and idealizing) language of romance in the epiphanic properties of the providential word, whether uttered by a deity, read as an oracle, or inscribed on a tablet. The main complication of the *Arcadia* follows from Basilius's faithless misreading of a divine oracle, a pronouncement that, when at last known to be fulfilled, tells characters and readers alike that the foolish deeds prompted by a multitude of blind statements cannot cancel the prosperity projected by the heavenly word. In Shakespeare's case, the formal predictability of this romance motif perhaps incited (at least partly) the less predictable nature of his imaginative staging of deficient or destructive utterances in early parts of the last plays. It is as though Shakespeare's experimentations with empirical language in *Cymbeline* were forward-looking to the degree that the certainty of the providential word's ultimate revelation grounded them in an article of traditional faith.

Recently, literary theorists have argued that romance depends for fulfillment upon additional kinds of epiphanic speech acts. Frederic Jameson and Patricia Parker have claimed that "romance, from the twelfth century, necessitates the projection of an Other, a *projet* which comes to an end when that Other reveals his identity or 'name.'"[8] In *The Tempest*, Alonso's Other is Prospero, his political as well as familial alter ego, the comparatively un-Machiavellian, promising part of his character buried by his crime against Prospero. Hearing the revelation of the repressed Other in the epiphanic name "Prosper" (nominally a curse and etymologically a blessing), Alonso depends for his salvation upon a single uttered name. Parker remarks that "this connection between naming, identity, and closure or ending remains a persistent romance phenomenon, from the delaying of names in the narrative of Chrétien de Troyes to Keats's preference for the noumenal over the nominal, for 'half-knowledge' over 'certainty' or 'fact.'"[9] The delaying of identity-giving names intrinsic to romance provides Imogen and Posthumus with the space to earn the names Fidele and Leonatus. Finally, Parker notes that "the association between deviations of language and the 'errors' of romance is a very old one indeed. In Rabelais' *Tiers Livre*—itself a 'late' romance—the shape-shifting Panurge uses the multivalence of language for the same purpose he uses continual digression, to evade the damning certainty of a one-to-one correspondence between sign and meaning, and the whole of his quest becomes paradoxically a form of evasion."[10] Pericles' "errors," his wanderings from city to city, derive from his failure to fool Antiochus; the multivalence of language, its potential for deviations, is not sufficiently ambiguous to allow him (equivocate though he does) to give a safe answer to the King's riddle—itself deviant language in both form and matter. And we saw that the moral and physical wanderings of Posthumus partly proceeded from language's inability to weld "a one-to-one correspondence between sign and meaning."[11] Thus, certain essential features of romance facilitated Shakespeare's staging of a linguistic design in four of his last plays.

Still, I do not wish to deemphasize the importance of pastoral to Shakespeare's expressive conception. Critics such as Walter R. Davis, Richard Cody, and Humphrey Tonkin have described both the evolution and practice among Renaissance writers of depicting scenes of visionary, especially Neo-Platonic contemplation within the context of literary pastoral.[12] Undoubtedly, in scenes such as Prospero's Masque of Ceres, ideal language complements the mage's superlative vision. Moreover, the eclogues heard during Sidneyan shepherds' singing matches reinforce the notion that pastoral is a place of silver utterances, simply because it is less spoiled than the unnatural court. Along with "books in the running brooks" and "sermons in stones," Duke Senior finds "tongues in trees" in the pastoral forest of Arden (AYLI, 2.1.15–17). By this suggestive phrase, Rosalind's father adapts a pastoral motif as old as Virgil's first eclogue; the echoing song of a green-world singer appears to come from the forest itself.[13] Giving this convention a postmodernist twist, Jonathan Goldberg has argued that, in The Two Gentlemen of Verona, Silvia must end up silently after a series of troping metamorphoses in the silva that utters her name.[14] While many years separate this early romantic comedy from Cymbeline, the step is relatively short from this use of pastoral to Shakespeare's portrayal of Wales as a place where words like "faithfulness" and "brother" specially name characters.[15] Yet these aspects of Elizabethan pastoral account for neither the expressive dynamics nor the implications of events such as Arviragus's elegy, Perdita's flower-welcome, and Prospero's instruction through verbal shapes. In the cases of the elegy and flower-welcome, one could trace Shakespeare's preference of eloquent res over verba to Book IV of Augustine's De Doctrina Christiana.[16] As the realm of Nature, postclassical pastoral reflects divine creation through the Word more immediately (or with less distortion) than does the city or court. Thus, situating speaking things within the context of pastoral could be justified by the Elizabethan pastoralist. Nevertheless, a reading of English Renaissance pastorals such as *The Shepheardes Calender* fails to show either shepherds or courtiers using *res* in the complex symbolic manner of Arviragus and Perdita. In this respect, Shakespeare's achievement in *Cymbeline* and *The Winter's Tale* appears unprecedented.

In conclusion, it should be stressed that noteworthy acts of expression in the last romances neither eradicate the causes of fallen speech nor insure the future purity and efficacy of words. Stress falls upon the notion that remarkable speech can only be an alternative to flawed language, an alternative nonetheless that in special circumstances can renew characters' exhausted lives. In cases like Pericles' declaration of a monarch's fault, Paulina's verbal recreation of Hermione, and Prospero's saving discourse of reason, the gift of speech transforms a life. Such expressive moments print themselves in our memories, lingering long after their theatrical performance. Even when silently heard, revolutionary language warrants our calling four plays traditionally classified together romances of the word.

Notes

Chapter 1. Introduction

1. In general, see James Sutherland, "The Language of the Last Plays," *More Talking of Shakespeare*, ed. John Garrett (New York: Theatre Arts Books, 1959), 144–51. For *Pericles*, see Inga-Stina Ewbank, "'My Name is Marina': The Language of Recognition," *Shakespeare's Styles: Essays in Honour of Kenneth Muir*, ed. Philip Edwards, Inga-Stina Ewbank, and G. K. Hunter (Cambridge: Cambridge University Press, 1980), 111–30; and Stephen Dickey, "Language and Role in *Pericles*," *English Literary Renaissance* 16 (1986): 550–66. For *The Winter's Tale*, see M. M. Mahood, *Shakespeare's Wordplay* (1957; reprint, London: Methuen, 1968), 146–63; Michael Taylor, "Shakespeare's *The Winter's Tale*: Speaking in the Freedom of Knowledge," *Critical Quarterly* 14 (1972): 49–56; Carol Thomas Neely, "*The Winter's Tale*: The Triumph of Speech," *Studies in English Literature* 15 (1975): 321–28; Ann Barton, "Leontes and the Spider: Language and Speaker in Shakespeare's Last Plays," *Shakespeare's Styles: Essays in Honour of Kenneth Muir*, 131–50; and Russ McDonald, "Poetry and Plot in *The Winter's Tale*," *Shakespeare Quarterly* 36 (1985): 315–29. For *The Tempest*, see W. T. Jewkes, "'Excellent Dumb Discourse': The Limits of Language in *The Tempest*," *Essays on Shakespeare*, ed. Gordon Ross Smith (University Park: Pennsylvania State University Press, 1965), 196–210; Gayle Greene, "'Excellent Dumb Discourse': Silence and Grace in Shakespeare's *Tempest*," *Studia Neophilologica* 59 (1978): 193–205; and Stanton B. Garner, Jr., "*The Tempest*: Language and Society," *Shakespeare Survey* 32 (1979): 177–87.

2. Lawrence Danson, *Tragic Alphabet: Shakespeare's Drama of Language* (New Haven: Yale University Press, 1974).

3. Cited in Keir Elam, *Shakespeare's Universe of Discourse: Language-Games in the Comedies* (Cambridge: Cambridge University Press, 1984), 213.

4. Quoted by Terence Hawkes, *Shakespeare's Talking Animals: Language and Drama in Society* (1973; reprint, Totowa, NJ: Rowman and Littlefield, 1974), 43.

5. All quotations from the last romances are taken from the New Arden editions: *Pericles*, ed. F. D. Hoeniger (London: Methuen, 1963); *Cymbeline*, ed. J. M. Nosworthy (London: Methuen, 1955); *The Winter's Tale*, ed. J. H. P. Pafford (London: Methuen, 1965); *The Tempest*, ed. Frank Kermode (London: Methuen, 1954). Quotations from other Shakespearean plays refer to *The Riverside Shakespeare*, ed. G. Blakemore Evans (Boston: Houghton Mifflin, 1974).

6. William C. Carroll, *The Great Feast of Language in "Love's Labour's Lost"* (Princeton: Princeton University Press, 1976), 12–13.

7. *Language, Thought, and Reality: Selected Writings of Benjamin Lee Whorf*, ed. John B. Carroll (Cambridge: The Technology Press of Massachusetts Institute of Technology, 1956), 252. The following opinions also represent

Whorf's view: "Thinking . . . follows a network of tracks laid down in the given language, an organization which may concentrate systematically upon certain phases of reality, certain aspects of intelligence, and may systematically discard others featured by other languages" (p. 256). . . . "Because of the systematic, configurative nature of higher mind, the 'patternment' aspect of language always overrides and controls the 'lexation' . . . or name-giving aspect. Hence the meanings of specific words are less important than we fondly fancy" (p. 258). . . . "In more subtle matters we all, unknowingly, project the linguistic relationships of a particular language upon the universe, and see them there" (p. 262).

8. It was Edward Sapir who pioneered Whorf's view. Sapir, for example, claimed that "language is heuristic" in the "sense that its forms predetermine for us certain modes of observation and interpretation" (*Selected Writings of Edward Sapir in Language, Culture, and Personality*, ed. David G. Mandelbaum [Berkeley: University of California Press, 1949], 10). Taken as a whole, Sapir's and Whorf's uncollaborated writings form the Sapir-Whorf hypothesis.

9. For a survey of the principal objections to the Sapir-Whorf hypothesis, see D. Steinberg, *Psycholinguistics: Language, Mind, and World* (London: Longman, 1982), 106–10. Still, Steinberg, like other critics of the hypothesis, must admit that the jury is still out on several Sapir-Whorf claims. In fact, Steinberg concedes, after his survey of objections, that "(1) language may be used to provide new ideas; (2) language may be used to bring about a change in beliefs and values" (p. 116).

10. Marion Trousdale, *Shakespeare and the Rhetoricians* (Chapel Hill: University of North Carolina Press, 1982), esp. 3–38.

11. Ibid., 25–26.

12. Ibid., 33.

13. James L. Calderwood, *Metadrama in Shakespeare's Henriad: "Richard II" to "Henry V"* (Berkeley: University of California Press, 1979), 205.

14. Accounts of Elizabethan and Jacobean theories of speech and the relative truthfulness of the word are provided by Mahood, *Shakespeare's Wordplay*, 169–75; Danson, *Tragic Alphabet*, 1–21 passim; Hawkes, *Shakespeare's Talking Animals*, 37–52; Carroll, *Great Feast of Language*, 12–25; Calderwood, *Metadrama in Shakespeare's Henriad*, 183–220; Margreta De Grazia, "Shakespeare's View of Language: An Historical Perspective," *Shakespeare Quarterly* 29 (1978): 374–88; Jane Donawerth, *Shakespeare and the Sixteenth-Century Study of Language* (Urbana: University of Illinois Press, 1984), 1–140; Trousdale, *Shakespeare and the Rhetoricians*, 24–38; and by Elam, *Universe of Discourse*, 114–36, 166–76, 199–229. A more theoretical survey is made by Richard Waswo, *Language and Meaning in the Renaissance* (Princeton: Princeton University Press, 1987).

15. In the optimistic band of the spectrum are found pronouncements by Wilson (1560), Ficino (1561), Huarte (1594); among the skeptical demystifiers of the word as sign are counted Scot (1584), Perkins (1600), Bacon (1605, 1620), and Montaigne (1603). See, respectively, Calderwood, *Metadrama in Shakespeare's Henriad*, 196–97; Donawerth, *Sixteenth-Century Study of Language* 13–55; Elam, *Universe of Discourse*, 123–24, 168–71.

Chapter 2. Pericles, Prince of Tyre

1. Philip Edwards, *Shakespeare and the Confines of Art* (London: Methuen, 1968), 140.

2. The comic subplot's functions of foil and parody are exhaustively treated by Richard Levin, *The Multiple Plot in English Renaissance Drama* (Chicago: University of Chicago Press, 1971), 109–47. Also see Dean Frye, "The Question of Shakespearean 'Parody,'" *Essays in Criticism* 15 (1965): 22–26.

3. James O. Wood, in "Shakespeare and the Belching Whale," *English Language Notes* 11 (1973): 40–44, argues that a "pattern of imaginal and verbal associations" identifies 2.1 with Shakespeare rather than John Day, to whom F. D. Hoeniger in the New Arden edition of *Pericles* tentatively attributes the scene. The corrupt text and possible joint authorship of *Pericles* will always, for some critics, negatively affect any analysis of the play that implies artistic integrity. For a review of the play's textual problems, consult the New Arden edition, pp. xxiii–liv. The editorial problem, according to Hoeniger, "is incapable of being finally decided for the simple reason that external evidence is wholly wanting" (p. liii). Joan Hartwig, in "The Authorship of *Pericles*," cites Hoeniger's judgment with approval during her argument that a reading of *Pericles* can be meaningful without continual references to the textual difficulties (*Shakespeare's Tragicomic Vision* [Baton Rouge: Louisiana State University Press, 1972], 181–83). Quoting Northrop Frye, Hartwig notes that even "collaborated works may create 'a distinct and unified personality' as the artistic control" (p. 182). In this vein, also see G. Wilson Knight, *The Crown of Life* (1947; reprint, New York: Barnes and Noble, 1966), 32–34; and David Bergeron, *Shakespeare's Romances and the Royal Family* (Lawrence: University Press of Kansas, 1985), 117.

4. As a recurrent thematic element, the verbal motif presented in this chapter suggests a secondary design in *Pericles* that complements the primary romance pattern of loss-suffering-recovery-reconciliation. Derek Traversi, in *Shakespeare: The Last Phase* (1954; reprint, Stanford, CA: Stanford University Press, 1965), 19–42, traces the romance pattern in the play; and Douglas L. Peterson, in *Time, Tide and Tempest: A Study of Shakespeare's Romances* (San Marino, CA: Huntington Library Press, 1973), 71–107, bases his interpretation of the drama upon it. We shall see that Pericles' enacting of the focal idea helps make possible his recovery and his reunion with Thaisa. In this respect, the play's secondary design at points creates the major experience of romance.

5. F. David Hoeniger, "Gower and Shakespeare in *Pericles*," *Shakespeare Quarterly* 33 (1982): 471.

6. Norman Nathan, "'Pericles' and 'Jonah,'" *Notes and Queries* 201 (1956): 10–11. In addition to noting that Shakespeare's fishermen essentially retell the Jonah story, Nathan observes that "Pericles flees from the wrath of Antiochus to Tharsus, the same city to which Jonah fled, as Barker's 1583 printing of the Bible indicates." In Shakespeare's primary sources—*Confessio Amantis* and *The Patterne of Painefull Adventures*—neither Gower nor Twine allude to the Jonah story. Also see Wood, "The Belching Whale," 41–42.

7. Similarly, in *Pericles* sailors superstitiously consign Thaisa to the deep in order to calm a sea storm (Nathan, "'Pericles' and 'Jonah,'" 10).

8. For leviathan's maw as hellmouth, see James Hall, *Dictionary of Subjects and Symbols in Art* (New York: Harper and Row, 1974), 147.

9. Thomas Lodge and Robert Greene had dramatized Jonah's experience, including his onstage casting from the whale's belly, in *A Looking Glass for London and England* (1590?). Between 1598 and 1617, four reprints of the 1594 quarto appeared. *A Looking Glass* and *Pericles* are linked by Thomas B. Stroup, "The Testing Pattern in Elizabethan Tragedy," *Studies in English Literature* 3 (1963): 180, 186. Stroup also finds Jonah's experience in *Hamlet*, remarking

that in all three plays the main characters must withstand the "testing force of Providence." While *A Looking Glass* has traditionally been classified as an Elizabethan Morality play, miracle/morality features of *Pericles* have only recently been identified by Hoeniger, New Arden edition, lxxxviii–xci; by Knight, *Crown of Life*, 36–38, 52, 73–74; and by Howard Felperin, "Shakespeare's Miracle Play," *Shakespeare Quarterly* 18 (1967): 363–74. For a study of the parallels between the two plays (with special attention to the Jonah motif), see Maurice Hunt, "A Looking Glass for *Pericles*," *Essays in Literature* 13 (1986): 3–11.

10. By regarding Ophelia's corpse as a "whoreson dead body" (*Ham.* 5.1.172) rather than as "Ophelia," the Gravedigger makes a healthy distinction; he never equates base matter with the spirit once animating it. Hamlet, however, ignores this distinction and, in his imagination, disturbingly confuses remembered Ophelia and Yorick with skulls and dirt. In both cases, his compelling but dangerous juxtaposition of a beloved image with putrid matter blasts the memory of a loved one. Preserving the integrity of his affectionate memory of Yorick and his youthful lover, the Gravedigger, however, never makes this mistake.

11. For Pericles' passivity, see, for example, John Arthos, "*Pericles, Prince of Tyre*: A Study in the Dramatic Use of Romantic Narrative," *Shakespeare Quarterly* 4 (1953): 269; Knight, *Crown of Life*, 73–74; Norman Rabkin, *Shakespeare and the Common Understanding* (New York: Macmillan, 1967), 194; Thelma N. Greenfield, "A Re-Examination of the 'Patient' Pericles," *Shakespeare Studies* 3 (1967): 55; and Michael Taylor, "'Here is a thing too young for such a place': Innocence in *Pericles*," *Ariel* 13 (1982): 12–13.

12. See Maurice Hunt, "'Stir' and Work in Shakespeare's Last Plays," *Studies in English Literature* 22 (1982): 385–88.

13. See Stephen Dickey, "Language and Role in *Pericles*," *English Literary Renaissance* 16 (1986): 558.

14. Ernst Robert Curtius, *European Literature and the Latin Middle Ages*, trans. Willard R. Trask (1948; reprint, New York: Harper and Row, 1953), 332–40.

15. Northrop Frye, *A Natural Perspective: The Development of Shakespearean Comedy and Romance* (New York: Harcourt, Brace and World, 1965), 32.

16. For a different reading of visual deception in the riddle-solving scene, see Howard B. White, "*Copp'd Hills Towards Heaven*": *Shakespeare and the Classical Polity* (The Hague: Martinus Nijhoff, 1970), 99.

17. For a representative description of this impairment, see Robert Burton, *The Anatomy of Melancholy*, ed. Floyd Dell and Paul Jordan-Smith (New York: Tudor Publishing Co., 1927), 144–48.

18. Augustine's idea of the ideal relationship between mortal words and the Word is neatly represented by Donawerth with reference to *De Trinitate* and *De Doctrina Christiana*. See *Sixteenth-Century Study of Language*, 10.

19. Speech act theory was formulated by J. L. Austin in *How To Do Things With Words* (Cambridge: Harvard University Press, 1962) and refined by John R. Searle, principally in *Speech Acts: An Essay in the Philosophy of Language* (Cambridge: Cambridge University Press, 1969). For the relevance of speech acts for literature, see Mary Louise Pratt, *Toward a Speech Act Theory of Literary Discourse* (Bloomington: Indiana University Press, 1977). Besides Elam, critics who have applied speech act theory to Shakespeare's plays include Stanley E. Fish, "How To Do Things With Austin and Searle: Speech Act The-

ory and Literary Criticism," *Modern Language Notes* 91 (1976): 983–1025; and Joseph Porter, *The Drama of Speech Acts: Shakespeare's Lancastrian Tetralogy* (Berkeley: University of California Press, 1979).

20. Austin, *How To Do Things With Words*, 99.

21. Elam, *Universe of Discourse*, 6.

22. Ibid., 109.

23. Pericles embodies a viewpoint (expressed in 1.1.92–109) that Shakespeare undercuts and finally supersedes. Shakespeare exposes Pericles to the benefits of redemptive speech in four relatively early scenes (1.2, 1.4, 2.1, 2.5). However, the Prince is offstage at other times that a declaration proves reparative (1.3, 4.6). When Pericles religiously follows Diana's command in 5.1 to narrate a tale involving evil, he gives no sign of understanding that an act which he has denied plays a part in his restoration. The audience, rather than the hero, primarily appreciates the virtue of the idea repeatedly staged.

24. In the Taliart episode in Gower's *Confessio Amantis* as well as in the Taliarchus scene in Twine's *The Patterne of Painefull Adventures*, the deliberate speaking and hearing of a monarch's faults do not play a narrative role. See Geoffrey Bullough, ed., *Narrative and Dramatic Sources of Shakespeare*, (London: Routledge and Kegan Paul, 1966), vol. 6: 382, 429–30.

25. Theodore Spencer, in *Shakespeare and the Nature of Man* (1942; reprint, New York: Collier Books, 1966), 186–202, argues that the phenomenon of evil appearance/good reality distinguishes the last romances from Shakespeare's previous work.

26. John F. Danby, *Poets on Fortune's Hill* (1952; reprint, Port Washington, NY: Kennikat Press, 1966), 92.

27. Ibid., 81–97. Danby quotes *Paradise Lost* 2.28–33, for his definition of "Apathie" as a kind of mistaken Stoicism which Milton also terms "stubborn patience" (p. 82).

28. Ibid., 96.

29. See, for example, *Cymb.* 5.4.30–113. When the ghosts of the Leonati complain to the "Thunder-master" that the god has unjustly caused Posthumus to suffer, he simply says, "No more, you petty spirits of region low, / Offend our hearing; hush!" (5.4.93–94). Jupiter proceeds to explain that "Whom best I love, I cross; to make my gift, / The more delay'd, delighted" (101–2). Significantly, the god calls the ghosts' complaints "din" expressing "impatience" (111–12). Shakespeare most memorably links patience and silence in *Lear*. After indicting "rain, wind, thunder, [and] fire" for joining with his daughters to wage "battles 'gainst a head / So old and white as this" (3.2.14–24), Lear suddenly corrects himself: "No, I will be the pattern of all patience, / I will say nothing" (37–38). The mad king's resolution, however, soon breaks under the weight of his rage.

30. The gentlemen fleeing the brothel illustrate the wondrous effect of Marina's words upon immoral men:

1. Gent. But to have divinity preach'd there! did you ever dream of such a thing?
2. Gent. No, no. Come, I am for no more bawdy-houses.
   Shall's go hear the vestals sing?
1. Gent. I'll do anything now that is virtuous; but I am out of the road of rutting for ever.

(4.5.4–9)

31. In "'My name is Marina,'" Inga-Stina Ewbank explains how Marina's

eloquence has a therapeutic value for Lysimachus (pp. 116–17). Dickey's interpretation of the efficacy of Marina's language in the brothel resembles mine ("Language and Role in *Pericles*," 562–63).

32. For other kinds of understanding given by picture and word in Shakespearean drama, see Inga-Stina Ewbank, "'More Pregnantly than Words': Some Uses and Limitations of Visual Symbolism," *Shakespeare Survey* 24 (1971): 13–18.

33. For Ewbank ("'My name is Marina,'" 116, 118–21, 124–29), Marina's language in the first scene of act 5 is restorative. It "opens up Pericles' mind" but in a manner and for reasons different from those which I describe. Also see Robert W. Uphaus, *Beyond Tragedy: Structure and Experience in Shakespeare's Romances* (Lexington: University Press of Kentucky, 1981), 43–48.

34. The society is both that of Tyre, which will flourish under the restored Pericles, and that of the theater audience. In "Heritage in *Pericles*," *Shakespeare's Last Plays: Essays in Honor of Charles Crow*, ed. Richard C. Tobias and Paul G. Zolbrod (Athens: Ohio University Press, 1974), 93–95, Andrew Welsh offers another explanation of how the telling of a story in *Pericles* can be "a recognition device that brings about restoration."

35. Francis Berry discusses the relationship between word and vision in Gower's choruses in *The Shakespeare Inset: Word and Picture* (London: Routledge and Kegan Paul, 1965), 153–54. For this critic, the opposition and eventual coordination of seeing and hearing in *Pericles* are theatrical techniques rather than dramatic subjects in their own right. The words of a "downstage" presenter, such as those of Gower, provide a perspective upon a "backstage" spectacle, set by physical implication in a more remote time.

36. For an alternative view of the efficacy of Gower's choral words, see Donawerth, *Sixteenth-Century Study of Language*, 23–24.

37. See E. H. Gombrich, "*Icones Symbolicae*: The Visual Image in Neo-Platonic Thought," *Journal of the Warburg and Courtauld Institutes* 11 (1948): 163–92. For an example of the identification of the classical deities with Neo-Platonic Ideas, see Marsilio Ficino, *Commentary on Plato's Symposium*, ed. and trans. Sears Reynolds Jayne, The University of Missouri Studies in English, vol. 19 (Columbia: University of Missouri Press, 1944), 127–28. The classical deity as Idea has been discussed by D. J. Gordon, "The Imagery of Ben Jonson's *The Masque of Blacknesse* and *The Masque of Beautie*," *Journal of the Warburg and Courtauld Institutes* 6 (1943): 122–41.

38. Sir Thomas Elyot explains how classical ideas can be learned from dancing in *The Boke Named the Governour*, Everyman Edition (1937; reprint, London: Dent, 1962), 76–88. Ben Jonson gave the kind of value that I am ascribing to the dance in *The Tempest* to the revels of *Pleasure Reconciled to Virtue* (1618). Consult Stephen Orgel, *The Jonsonian Masque* (Cambridge: Harvard University Press, 1965), 176–80.

39. Diana teaches Chastity to the masquers of Ben Jonson's *Time Vindicated to Himself and to His Honours* (1623), ll. 373–432. *Ben Jonson: The Complete Masques*, ed. Stephen Orgel (New Haven: Yale University Press, 1969), 406–8.

40. Obviously, I do not agree with Mark Rose's judgment, expressed in *Shakespearean Design* (Cambridge: Harvard University Press, 1972), that in *Pericles* "the absence of overall design . . . is intentional and can be seen as symptomatic of a quest for technical liberty" (p. 169). This chapter describes a stricter plan for *Pericles* than that which usually emerges when the other late romances provide the terms for evaluation. The unified composition of the play

has been inferred from primary metaphors by James O. Wood, "The Running Image in *Pericles*," *Shakespeare Studies* 5 (1969), 240–52. The present essay suggests a dramatic strategy of thesis and sustained counterargument in *Pericles*. Madeleine Doran, in *Endeavors of Art: A Study of Form in Elizabethan Drama* (Madison: University of Wisconsin Press, 1964), 310–22, has defined statement and counterstatement as a major Renaissance dramatic form.

Chapter 3. *Cymbeline*

1. De Grazia, "Shakespeare's View of Language," 374–88. In his "Elizabethan Naming" appendix to *Metadrama in Shakespeare's Henriad*, Calderwood essentially subscribes to De Grazia's thesis concerning a marked revolution in attitude toward the speaker/speech relationship. Though not neatly corresponding to the Elizabethan/Jacobean historical division, Calderwood's idea of a shifting of responsibility from speaker to word occurs in the context of his analysis of the Henry IV and V plays; in this view, Shakespeare's late sixteenth-century nominalism is predictive (not reflexive) of Baconian skepticism about words' ability to record truth.

2. De Grazia, "Shakespeare's View of Language," 378.

3. Ibid., 381.

4. For example, Elam (*Universe of Discourse*, 166–76), identifies four forces at work during the sixteenth century (Aristotelian scholasticism, Protestant iconoclasm, philosophical skepticism, the Catholic campaign against the occult arts) promoting a nominalist view of language. In this respect, he analyzes well Shakespeare's sixteenth-century satirizing in *Love's Labour's Lost* of the sixteenth-century (optimistic) Neo-Platonic view of language (pp. 116–29). Ben Jonson's pronouncements on language, recorded in his Jacobean commonplace book and published in *Discoveries* (1640–41), represent sanguine views of language persisting well into James' reign. See Elam, p. 213. Explicitly critical of De Grazia's position is Jane Donawerth in *Shakespeare and the Sixteenth-Century Study of Language*, pp. 110–11. Donawerth judges that "the current critical debate on Shakespeare's view of language does not help much in elucidating these various attitudes in his characters. One group of critics . . . argues that Shakespeare anticipates a modern distrust of language, and that his plays bear the mark of his recognizing 'the limits of language.' Another group, approaching the issue through a study of Shakespeare's historical context, almost universally holds that Shakespeare, like most educated Elizabethans, trusted that words amply express thoughts and feelings, and so fully achieve the end of communication between human beings. . . . If there is a characteristic Elizabethan attitude toward language, it is not one or the other, but an amalgamation of doubt and trust" (pp. 108–9). Regarded from one perspective, Donawerth's judgment is valid; nonetheless, one can grant its truth and yet agree that De Grazia's historical distinction reflects a general revolution within which there are many exceptions to its explanatory key. Despite her syncretic approach, Donawerth in fact essentially adopts De Grazia's position when she writes, "Language reflects man's history, and his rational and irrational powers; one studies language to know oneself. Man is the measure in the sixteenth century, and judged by this subjective standard, language is not found wanting" (p. 6).

5. Cited by Elam, *Universe of Discourse*, 212–13.

6. *The Sermons of John Donne*, ed. George R. Potter and Evelyn M. Simpson (Berkeley: University of California Press, 1953–62), vol. 4, 102.

7. Diana T. Childress, in "Are Shakespeare's Late Plays Really Romances?" *Shakespeare's Late Plays: Essays in Honor of Charles Crow,* ed. Richard C. Tobias and Paul G. Zolbrod (Athens: Ohio University Press, 1974), 44–47, notes that the term "romance" in the sixteenth century apparently referred almost exclusively to "a tale in verse, embodying the adventures of some hero of chivalry, esp. of those of the great cycles of mediaeval legend, and belonging both in matter and form to the ages of knighthood (OED II. 2)." This definition could be stretched to fit *Pericles* perhaps, but the other three late plays resist it. Childress argues that the critical term "romance" did not acquire a meaning that could apply to Shakespeare's last plays until *circa* 1638 (see OED II. 3). Still, Sidney clearly knew what kind of play he was alluding to when in *An Apology,* he blasted the marvelous but tawdry fictions of the 1570s, replete with shipwrecks and hideous monsters belching fire and smoke. Shakespeare's last plays have traditionally been referred to as romances, even though Heminge and Condell did not group plays under this category in the First Folio.

8. *Johnson on Shakespeare,* vol. 7 of the *Yale Edition of the Works of Samuel Johnson,* ed. Arthur Sherbo (New Haven: Yale University Press, 1968), 73–74.

9. Ibid., 73.

10. For the critical investigations, consult Richard Fly, *Shakespeare's Mediated World* (Amherst: University of Massachusetts Press, 1976), esp. pp. ix–xv, 27–52; and T. McAlindon, "Language, Style, and Meaning in *Troilus and Cressida,*" *PMLA* 84 (1969): 29–43. Both Fly and McAlindon draw upon Una Ellis-Fermor, *The Frontiers of Drama* (London: Methuen, 1945). Ellis-Fermor was perhaps the first Shakespearean scholar to assume a purposefully discordant dramaturgy.

11. I have substituted "king" for Nosworthy's "king's" in the above passage because this widely accepted emendation makes better sense in the context of 1.1.1–15. This change constitutes my only departure from the New Arden text.

12. Frank Kermode, *Shakespeare, Spenser, Donne* (New York: Viking, 1971), 232.

13. "This passage is so difficult," Johnson in fact wrote about the gentleman's opening lines, "that commentators may differ concerning it without animosity or shame." In Johnson's opinion, the lines are a "licentious and abrupt expression" (*Johnson on Shakespeare,* vol. 8, 874). For an alternative account of the "semantic complexity" of First Gentleman's opening speech, see Michael Taylor, "The Pastoral Reckoning of *Cymbeline,*" *Shakespeare Survey* 36 (1983): 100.

14. Until the later decades of the seventeenth century and the earlier ones of the eighteenth, when empiricism denoted a philosophy linked to Locke, Berkeley, and Hume, the word usually carried pejorative meanings. For example, Northrop Frye points out that in *The Return from Parnassus,* "it is said of Jonson, that he is 'a mere empiric, one that gets what he hath by observation, and makes only nature privy to what he indites'" (*A Natural Perspective,* p. 6). Bacon, in his writings, does not think of himself as an empiricist. Still, events in *Cymbeline* are often intellectually acted upon in ways clarified by the writings of the New Scientist. Some of these ways can be listed: trusting the eyes and ears initially for knowledge; learning by trial and error, especially through experiments; crediting experience rather than reported knowledge as a reliable teacher; and avoiding prefabricated sayings and reductive words during intellectual inquiry and the creation of knowledge. These commonplaces,

recommended throughout Bacon's writings, make up an empirical method, a method with broad ramifications for understanding *Cymbeline*.

15. Posthumus's and Imogen's marriage may be a "handfast," an informal union that has not been consummated. At one point, Posthumus complains that Imogen has denied him his married rights by insisting upon her chastity (2.4.161–62). For the "handfast" in *Cymbeline*, see Carol Gesner, *Shakespeare and the Greek Romance: A Study of Origins* (Lexington: University Press of Kentucky, 1970), 102; for the unconsummated marriage, David M. Bergeron, "Sexuality in *Cymbeline*," *Essays in Literature* 10 (1983): 160.

16. Derek Traversi, in *Shakespeare: The Last Phase*, 44–46, notices a "complexity of expression" in the gentlemen's dialogue which he believes points to a "deep-seated dislocation of natural feeling." More precisely, problematic speech and feeling play back and forth in their dialogue, dislocating each other. James Sutherland, in "The Language of the Last Plays," believes that Shakespeare's parenthetical and difficult style in *Cymbeline* is basically uncalculated, resulting from intense mechanical efforts to compensate for flagging inspiration (pp. 144–51). However, Coburn Freer, in *The Poetics of Jacobean Drama* (Baltimore: Johns Hopkins University Press, 1981), explains how Shakespeare in *Cymbeline* employs an obscure style as a subtle means of characterization (pp. 103–35).

17. The psychological flaws in the character of Posthumus that make such doubts inevitable are identified and discussed by Freer, *Jacobean Drama*, 110–13.

18. Terence Hawkes makes the contrary claim concerning the spoken overtones of words in *Shakespeare's Talking Animals*, 17–18.

19. *The Works of Francis Bacon*, ed. James Spedding, Robert Ellis, and Douglas Denon Heath (London: Longman, 1875), vol. 4, 54–55, 61. See Karl Wallace, *Francis Bacon on the Nature of Man* (Urbana: University of Illinois Press, 1967), 161.

20. Shakespeare's Baconian point of view and his emphasis upon experiential knowledge in *Cymbeline* have been discussed by Geoffrey Hill, "'The True Conduct of Human Judgment': Some Observations on *Cymbeline*," *The Morality of Art*, ed. D. W. Jefferson (London: Routledge and Kegan Paul, 1969), 24, 27–30.

21. Shakespeare's preoccupation with this subject—the manner by which society's verbal currency (public words) debases unique private values expressed therein—has been treated by Sigurd Burckhardt, *Shakespearean Meanings* (Princeton: Princeton University Press, 1968), esp. 22–46, 260–84.

22. For an alternative account of how each allusion to the art objects "contributes to the establishment of Iachimo's character and ironically signals the futility of his schemes," see R. J. Schork, "Allusion, Theme, and Characterization in *Cymbeline*," *Studies in Philology* 69 (1972): 212–13.

23. See Erwin Panofsky, *Studies in Iconology: Humanistic Themes in the Art of the Renaissance* (1939; reprint, New York: Harper and Row, 1962), 95–169 and passim.

24. Shakespeare thus denies the popular humanist aesthetic *ut pictura poesis*. The significant meanings of painting and poetry cannot be recreated by the sister art. In *Cymbeline*, a painting is not a picture of poetry; nor does poetry comprise a painting. "Such, and such" are the bedchamber's paintings; "there the window, such / Th' adornment of her bed; the arras, figures, / Why,

such, and such; and the contents o' th' story" (2.2.25–27). The word "such" denotes that Iachimo's notation could not be more mundane. For the ut pictura poesis tradition, consult Rennselaer W. Lee, "Ut Pictura Poesis": The Humanist Theory of Painting (New York: Norton, 1967).

25. See, for example, Sir Gawain and the Green Knight, ll. 619–63. The pentangle's divinity has been explained by J. A. Burrow, A Reading of Sir Gawain and the Green Knight (London: Routledge and Kegan Paul, 1965), 187–89. Both Iachimo and Posthumus, in their spiritual ignorance, regard Imogen's mole as a "stain" (2.4.138–41).

26. Achilles Tatius, The Loves of Clitophon and Leucippe, trans. William Burton (Oxford: B. Blackwell, 1923), 19.

27. Trousdale, Shakespeare and the Rhetoricians, 24.

28. Ibid., 31.

29. In Shakespeare's Wordplay, 181, M. M. Mahood asserts that Shakespeare in the course of his career moved from a skeptical belief that words have no inherent magic to a conviction of their "immense connotative powers," best heard in Prospero's evocative speeches. I would argue that Shakespeare in his final period depicts extraordinary speech once the multiple nuances of words in a late play fail to convey special meanings.

30. For another discussion of perspective in this scene, see Hartwig, Shakespeare's Tragicomic Vision, 88–89.

31. Cymbeline confirms Imogen's melodic speech; when he realizes that Fidele is his daughter, he exclaims, "The tune of Imogen!" (5.5.238). Conversely, the pathologically impulsive Cloten is recognized by "the snatches in his voice, / And burst of speaking" (4.2.105–6). See Freer, Jacobean Drama, 116–17.

32. Robert G. Hunter, Shakespeare and the Comedy of Forgiveness (New York: Columbia University Press, 1965), 151.

33. The critical view of Imogen as the incarnation of feminine virtue is so widespread that only a few references are necessary: Algernon Charles Swinburne, A Study of Shakespeare (1879; reprint, New York: AMS Press, 1965), 226–27; Arthur Quiller-Couch, Shakespeare's Workmanship (1919; reprint, Cambridge: Cambridge University Press, 1931), 217–19; and Knight, The Crown of Life, 152–57.

34. Walter R. Davis, Idea and Act in Elizabethan Fiction (Princeton: Princeton University Press, 1969), 45–54, 60–62. Davis notes that "the pastoral disguise expresses the values of the pastoral place, and that place is itself symbolic of a possible state of mind. The action of the hero in dressing himself as a shepherd and going to live in this place therefore constitutes an extensive exploration of his mind, especially touching the relation between what his mind is and the state it might achieve" (p. 61). Dressed as the page Fidele, Imogen in Wales has the opportunity to know faithfulness by experiencing it.

35. Imogen does not feel Cymbeline's anger concerning her forbidden meeting with her husband because Posthumus's banishment pains her. In her words, "a touch more rare / Subdues all pangs, all fears" (1.2.66–67). That misery becomes nothing when she learns that Posthumus believes that she is a strumpet and has ordered her execution; and that grief, which appeared definitive, in turn becomes trivial when she thinks that Posthumus is dead. This process of emotional displacement gives force to Jupiter's precept: "Whom best I love I cross; to make my gift, / The more delay'd, delighted" (5.4.101–2). The ethical rationale for painful deception given earlier by Cornelius in this instance can

stand for that of the divine physician, Jupiter. Cornelius justified his substitution of a harmless drug for the Queen's poison with these words:

> there is
> No danger in what show of death it makes,
> More than the locking up the spirits a time,
> To be more fresh, reviving. She is fool'd
> With a most false effect: and I the truer,
> So to be false with her.
>
> (1.6.39–44)

By protracting his crossing of elected mortals, Jupiter accommodates his ethos to mankind. Abrupt grief was the cause of Posthumus's father's death. Sicilius, according to First Gentleman, "took such sorrow" upon learning of his sons' deaths in battle "that he quit being" (1.1.37–38). Gradual and thus more bearable grieving is one dramatic reason for the length and digressive nature of Iachimo's final story of the wager and his deceits. After the guilty Italian has verbally treaded water for sixteen lines, speaking of a clock, Rome, Philario's feast—anything but his role in the wager—Cymbeline quite naturally protests, "I stand on fire. / Come to the matter" (5.5.168–69). Iachimo's reponse—"All too soon I shall, / Unless thou wouldst grieve quickly" (ll. 169–70)—ironically relates his long speech to the Jovian ethic. Cymbeline can bear his grief because it, provoked by Iachimo's tale, does not come swiftly; the King delights more in Belarius's gifts—his children—because of the relatively great delay endured before receiving them.

36. For a divergent reading of Imogen as Fidele, see Nancy K. Hayles, "Sexual Disguise in *Cymbeline,*" *Modern Language Quarterly* 41 (1980): 231–47. Hayles relates "Imogen's disguise to the play's central problems of misleading experience and the disrupted family" (p. 231). I disagree with Hayles's assumption that "the more closely linked the disguise is with the character's identity, the more the heroine will tend to take a passive role" (p. 236).

37. The unusually conceited style of *Cymbeline* has been a special critical problem for some time. See Mark Van Doren, *Shakespeare* (New York: Henry Holt, 1939), 305–9; Harley Granville-Barker, *Prefaces to Shakespeare* (1946; reprint, Princeton: Princeton University Press, 1965), vol. 2, 114–18; Wolfgang Clemen, *The Development of Shakespeare's Imagery* (Cambridge: Harvard University Press, 1951), 207–8; and Traversi, *The Last Phase,* 66–70. I am interested in discrediting the critical assumption that the late Shakespeare reverted to conceits because he had not yet forged a dramatic style to express his new romance vision. The quality of the verse in *Cymbeline* is deliberately meant to express the quality of the characters' ideas. They speak conceitedly because they think conceitedly, until corrected by experience.

38. *The Novum Organum,* in *The Works of Francis Bacon,* 48.

39. Peggy Muñoz Simonds, in "'No more . . . Offend Our Hearing': Aural Imagery in *Cymbeline,*" *Texas Studies in Literature and Language* 24 (1982): 137–54, argues that Posthumus's penitent speech "reaches the divine ears and evokes the appearance of Jupiter on his eagle" (p. 148).

40. Shakespeare's tongue-in-cheek dramatization of Iachimo's confession may anticipate his humorous method in *The Tempest* where, perhaps provoked by a Jonsonian claim that he regularly violated the Unities, he has Prospero in such detail narrate crucial events prior to the circumscribed action of the play that Miranda almost dozes off.

41. See Giovanni Boccaccio, *The Decameron*, ed. W. E. Henley, The Tudor Translations (London: David Nutt, 1909), vol. 41, 209–10; and *Cymbeline*, New Arden edition, 201–2.

42. Cymbeline's and Imogen's trust is thoroughly discussed by Robert Y. Turner, "Slander in *Cymbeline* and Other Jacobean Tragicomedies," *English Literary Renaissance* 13 (1983): 192–202.

43. Prior to the last plays, Shakespeare negatively portrays knowledge given retrospectively by action. Hardened by crime, Macbeth states, "Strange things I have in head, that will to hand, / Which must be acted ere they may be scann'd" (*Macb.* 3.4.138–39). Macbeth's earlier, cowardly desire that his eye wink at the hand's bloody deeds is justly fulfilled. Fragmented by sin, he now must await the deed that plunges him further into guilt in order to know himself. And when Volumnia requests Coriolanus to beg votes in the marketplace, he refuses: "Lest I surcease to honor mine own truth, / And by my body's action teach my mind / A most inherent baseness" (*Cor.* 3.2.121–23). The continuity between Coriolanus's thoughts and actions is usually ragged, so much so that his lack of self-control destroys him in Corioli. Unlike that of these tragic heroes, the knowledge given retrospectively by action is not harmful for characters in *Cymbeline*.

44. Wilbur Sanders, *The Dramatist and the Received Idea* (Cambridge: Cambridge University Press, 1968), 117.

45. Sir Walter Raleigh, *Ralighes' History of Y^E World* (London: W. Stansby, 1617), 18.

46. Samuel Taylor Coleridge, *Lectures on Shakespeare, Etc.*, ed. Ernest Rhys (1907; reprint, London: Dent, 1951), 87.

47. The etymology apparently was coined by Isidore of Seville. Consult J. A. K. Thomson, *Shakespeare and the Classics* (London: George Allen and Unwin, 1952), 135. T. W. Baldwin notes the seventeenth-century criticism of it in *William Shakspere's Small Latine and Lesse Greeke* (Urbana: University of Illinois Press, 1944), vol. 1, 719–20.

48. Quoted by Nosworthy in the New Arden edition of *Cymbeline*, p. 185.

49. This aspect of *Cymbeline* has been discussed by, among others, Emrys Jones, "Stuart Cymbeline," *Essays in Criticism* 11 (1961): 84–89; Robin Moffet, "*Cymbeline* and the Nativity," *Shakespeare Quarterly* 13 (1962): 207–18; and Bernard Harris, "'What's past is prologue': *Cymbeline* and *Henry VIII*," *Later Shakespeare*, ed. John Russell Brown and Bernard Harris, Stratford-Upon-Avon Studies 8 (London: Edward Arnold, 1966), 207–9.

50. This point is also made by Judiana Lawrence, "Natural Bonds and Artistic Coherence in the Ending of *Cymbeline*," *Shakespeare Quarterly* 35 (1984): 449.

Chapter 4. *The Winter's Tale*

1. Fernando Peñalosa, *Introduction to the Sociology of Language* (Rowley, MA: Newbury House, 1981), 23. Linguists distinguish a word's context of situation (or situational context) from its context—its phonetic and grammatical sentence environment. In the present chapter, the term context is used in the sense of situational context.

2. J. R. Firth, "The Technique of Semantics," *Papers in Linguistics: 1934–51* (London: Oxford University Press, 1957), 27. Also see M. A. K. Halliday, *Language as Social Semiotic: The Social Interpretation of Language and Meaning* (London: Edward Arnold, 1978), 27–35, passim.

3. In a 1950 paper entitled "Personality and Language in Society" (*Papers in Linguistics: 1934–51* [London: Oxford University Press, 1957], 182), Firth most fully defines the notion of a context of situation. "A context of situation for linguistic work brings into relation the following categories:

A. The relevant features of participants: persons, personalities.
  (i) The verbal action of the participants
  (ii) The nonverbal action of the participants.
B. The relevant objects.
C. The effect of the verbal action."

4. The role of language in *The Winter's Tale* has been investigated by Neely, "*The Winter's Tale*," 321–28; by Barton, "Leontes and the Spider," 131–50; and by McDonald, "Poetry and Plot," 315–29.

5. For an alternative discussion of how characters in *The Winter's Tale* cannot (or do not) speak in the freedom of their knowledge (one that also takes Archidamus's speech as its point of departure), see Taylor, "*The Winter's Tale*," 49–56. The problem of linguistic indeterminacy in characters' speeches in this play has been explored by Howard Felperin, "'Tongue-tied Our Queen?': The Deconstruction of Presence in *The Winter's Tale*," *Shakespeare and the Question of Theory*, ed. Patricia Parker and Geoffrey Hartman (New York: Methuen, 1985), 8–11.

6. J. Griffiths, ed., *The Two Books of Homilies* (Oxford: Oxford University Press, 1859), 74.

7. Charles Frey has remarked that "all knowledge of the play, of course, must be contextual. Locus follows focus, that is, what one makes of the play depends upon the purposive environment of one's study. There is no way to apprehend 'the play itself' freed from burdens of generic classification, historical origins, linguistic ambiguities, meanings as myth and ritual, psychoanalytic implications, vagaries of affective response, and the like. Strategies for attaining a single cohesive view [of *The Winter's Tale*] range from reductive concentration upon 'the text per se,' or upon 'what the author meant,' or upon themes or structures or spatial designs or archetypal meanings, to complete histories of staging and criticism, studies of sources, analogues, and influences, accounts of the drama's probable effect upon an Elizabethan or modern audience, and various combinations of 'approaches'" ("Interpreting *The Winter's Tale*," *Studies in English Literature* 18 [1978], 323). The manner in which situational context creates meaning in Shakespeare's poems and plays has recently become a critical subject. "In the Reynaldo scene (2.1) and Hamlet's first talk with Rosencrantz and Guildenstern," Stephen Booth notes that "the power of rhetoric and context to make a particular either good or bad at will is also a topic in the play" ("On the Value of *Hamlet*," *Reinterpretations of Elizabethan Drama*, ed. Norman Rabkin [New York: Columbia University Press, 1969], 172). Booth systematically applies this insight to *Hamlet*, revealing how the fluctuating values of the tragedy emerge from manipulated contexts.

8. Consult Paul A. Jorgensen, "*Much Ado About Nothing*," in *Redeeming Shakespeare's Words* (Berkeley: University of California Press, 1962), 22–42. Jorgensen cites several theological treatises, including De Mornay's *A Worke Concerning the Trewnesse of Christian Religion* (1592), which affirm "the essential nothingness of all temporal things" (pp. 24–26). According to the Protestant view of a Sidney or De Mornay, Adam's fallen heir is a cipher: "an O without a figure" (*Lear* 1.4.192–93), to use the words of Lear's Fool. For a dis-

cussion of mankind as "cipher," see Fly, *Shakespeare's Mediated World*, esp. 92, 112–13.

9. Refer to Burckhardt, *Shakespearean Meanings*, 260–84.

10. This possible interpretation is suggested by Nevill Coghill, "Six Points of Stage-Craft in *The Winter's Tale*," *Shakespeare Survey* 11 (1958): 32–33. For other readings of Polixenes' speech, see Mahood, *Shakespeare's Wordplay*, 146–47; William H. Matchett, "Some Dramatic Techniques in *The Winter's Tale*," *Shakespeare Survey* 22 (1969): 96; Mary L. Livingston, "The Natural Art of *The Winter's Tale*," *Modern Language Quarterly* 30 (1969): 342; and Louis L. Martz, "Shakespeare's Humanist Enterprise: *The Winter's Tale*," *English Renaissance Studies Presented to Dame Helen Gardner in Honour of Her Seventieth Birthday*, ed. John Carey (Oxford: Clarendon Press, 1980), 121.

11. Hilda Hulme, *Explorations in Shakespeare's Language* (London: Longman, 1962), 79.

12. Pastoral is an additional context undergirding Polixenes' speech (1.2.1–3). This context establishes the harmonious rhythms of natural time and life, which contrast with the frenzied mood of Leontes' court. Concerning these three lines, Mahood writes: "the whole image is the first of many taken from country things and the pastoral life, which persist throughout the Sicilian scenes of the play and so help to bridge the 'great gap' of time and place over which we pass later to the shepherd kingdom of Bohemia" (*Shakespeare's Wordplay*, 147).

13. As illocutionary (performative) speech acts, saying and swearing in Hermione's conception are (in John Searle's revision of Austin's typology) "representatives"—"acts which commit the speaker in varying degrees to something's being the case, to the truth of the expressed proposition" ("A Taxonomy of Illocutionary Acts," *Language, Mind, and Knowledge*, ed. Keith Gunderson, Minnesota Studies in the Philosophy of Science, vol. 7 [Minneapolis: University of Minnesota Press, 1975] 354). An oath possesses stronger perlocutionary force (its testimonial power) than a saying because it receives the additional linguistic charge of a nonlinguistic guarantor (God, saints, sometimes the self). Michel Foucault analyzes oaths as speech acts in *The Archaeology of Knowledge*, trans. A. M. Sheridan Smith (1969; reprint, New York: Harper and Row, 1976), 83.

14. When Leontes claims that Polixenes has made Hermione pregnant, the Queen defends herself by swearing and alluding to the supremacy of oaths: "But I'd say he had not; / And I'll be sworn you would believe my saying, / How e'er you lean to th' nay-ward" (2.1.62–64). Such an appeal is effective only when the listener (as Leontes does not) shares the speaker's assumption about the relative values of kinds of utterances (as will be discussed further).

15. See Norman Nathan, "Leontes' Provocation," *Shakespeare Quarterly* 19 (1968): 21.

16. The verbal fencing match begins when Hermione says: "Tell him, you are sure / All in Bohemia's well: this satisfaction / The by-gone day proclaim'd: say this to him, / He's beat from his best ward" (1.2.30–33). The fencing metaphor for speech is explicit here in the orthographic pun on "word"/"ward."

17. See A. F. Bellette, "Truth and Utterance in *The Winter's Tale*," *Shakespeare Survey* 31 (1978): 69–71.

18. David Patterson, *The Affirming Flame: Religion, Language, Literature* (Norman: University of Oklahoma Press, 1988), 8. Patterson quotes Susan Handelman (*The Slayers of Moses*, 1982), who concludes that, in the Hebraic

view, the word "'is not simply *thing* . . . but also *action, efficacious fact, event, matter, process*'" (*The Affirming Flame*, 8). For a description of the evolution and nature of the Johannine idea of the creative word (logos), consult Patterson's chapter "The Johannine Logos and Literary Criticism," 21–23.

19. Fish, "How To Do Things With Austin and Searle," 1002–3.

20. Pauline elements in Paulina's characterization are discussed by J. A. Bryant, Jr., *Hippolyta's View: Some Christian Aspects of Shakespeare's Plays* (Lexington: University Press of Kentucky, 1961), 216–17; and by Roy Battenhouse, "Theme and Structure in *The Winter's Tale*," *Shakespeare Survey* 33 (1980): 137.

21. 2 Corinthians 12:7.

22. The design of the hourglass has been noted in *The Winter's Tale* by David Young, *The Heart's Forest: A Study of Shakespeare's Pastoral Plays* (New Haven: Yale University Press, 1972), 119, 125, 133–45; and by Ernest Schanzer, "The Structural Pattern of *The Winter's Tale*," *Review of English Literature* 5 (1964): 79.

23. Thematic and stylistic repetitions in *The Winter's Tale* have been explored by Fitzroy Pyle, "*The Winter's Tale*": *A Commentary on the Structure* (London: Routledge and Kegan Paul, 1969); by James E. Siemon, "'But It Appears She Lives': Iteration in *The Winter's Tale*," *PMLA* 89 (1974): 10–16; by Richard Proudfoot, "Verbal Reminiscence and the Two-Part Structure of *The Winter's Tale*," *Shakespeare Survey* 29 (1976): 67–78; and by Schanzer, "Structural Pattern of *The Winter's Tale*," 72–82.

24. Charles Frey, *Shakespeare's Vast Romance: A Study of "The Winter's Tale"* (Columbia: University of Missouri Press, 1980), 77. Frey (p. 78) notes Shakespeare's repeated linking of "affection" with "infection" (*MV.* 2.2.115; *LLL.* 2.1.222–26; *Ado.* 2.3.118; *Tro.* 2.2.59).

25. Van Doren, in *Shakespeare*, judges, for example, that Leontes "is sometimes so difficult that we cannot follow the twists of his thinking" (p. 316). For Knight, in *The Crown of Life* (pp. 81–82), Leontes' speech is a "vitriolic spasm." Pafford, who paraphrases the speech in an appendix to his edition, nonetheless believes that "the speech is meant to be incoherent, as is shown by Polixenes' question" (p. 166). Polixenes' question—"What means Sicilia?"—appears, however, to refer only to Leontes' troubled face, for the King's appearance clearly becomes the subject of Polixenes' and Hermione's anxious questions (ll. 145–50), which follow Leontes' musing. Only the audience overhears Leontes' words.

26. Readings of the passage different from mine are given by Pafford, New Arden edition, 165–67; Harold C. Goddard, *The Meaning of Shakespeare* (Chicago: University of Chicago Press, 1951), 650–51; J. V. Cunningham, *Woe or Wonder* (Denver: University of Denver Press, 1951), 113–14; Jonathan Smith, "The Language of Leontes," *Shakespeare Quarterly* 19 (1968): 317–18; Neely, "*The Winter's Tale*," 324–27; Marjorie G. Garber, *Dream in Shakespeare: From Metaphor to Metamorphosis* (New Haven: Yale University Press, 1974), 165–66; and David Ward, "Affection, Intention, and Dreams in *The Winter's Tale*," *Modern Language Review* 82 (1987): 545–54. The speech receives extended commentary in *The New Variorum Edition of The Winter's Tale*, ed. Horace Howard Furness (Philadelphia: Lippincott, 1891), 27–31.

27. Smith, "Language of Leontes," 317–18. Smith points out that the affection speech makes up the second part of a larger passage (1.2.128–46), which breaks at line 137. In the first half of the greater passage, the language of

"blood" predominates. Key words in this half—"pash," "shoots," "full," "eggs," "o'er-dy'd blacks," "wind," "waters," "dice," "bourn," "welkin eye," "sweet villain," and "most dear'st, my collop"—are common or colloquial. They are mainly Anglo-Saxon in origin. In the Latinate half of the passage, however, Smith hears the language of "grace." Leontes struggles to impose reason upon his seething emotions, but the language of "blood"—"infection," "brain," "hard'ning," and "brows"—breaks through his defensive diction. "Leontes' psychological state is mirrored in this tension between the pseudo-rational and the 'hysterica passio'" (p. 318).

28. "We must . . . realize that 'affection' and 'intention' are technical terms in Elizabethan psychology: affection = natural tendency, instinct, (here) the sexual instinct . . . intention = the mental aim or purpose based upon the physical 'affection' . . ." (*The Winter's Tale*, ed. Sir Arthur Quiller-Couch and John Dover Wilson [1931; reprint, Cambridge: Cambridge University Press, 1968], 134–35).

29. Hallett Smith, "Leontes' *Affectio*," *Shakespeare Quarterly* 14 (1963): 163–66.

30. For the possible glosses, see OED, especially 3, 7, and 10. Pafford (New Arden edition, 166–67) and Hallett Smith (ibid., 163) review the many meanings proposed for the term "affection" in the passage under discussion. They cite no fewer than seven different interpretations ("emotion," "burning love," "lustful passions," "troubles," "mental seizure," "passion," and "natural propensity").

31. See Peter Lindenbaum, "Time, Sexual Love, and the Uses of Pastoral in *The Winter's Tale*," *Modern Language Quarterly* 33 (1972): 10–11. Actually, the first evidence of the jealous seizure may be Leontes' negative phrases "three crabbed months" and "sour'd themselves to death" in verse 102.

32. Mahood, *Shakespeare's Wordplay*, 153–54.

33. Ibid., 151.

34. Paul Oskar Kristeller, *The Philosophy of Marsilio Ficino*, trans. Virginia Conant (New York: Columbia University Press, 1943), 235.

35. Shakespeare's use of the vocabulary of Renaissance Platonism has been cogently discussed by A. P. Riemer, *Antic Fables: Patterns of Evasion in Shakespeare's Comedies* (New York: St. Martin's Press, 1980), 113, 116, 143–92 passim.

36. William O. Scott, in "Seasons and Flowers in *The Winter's Tale*," *Shakespeare Quarterly* 14 (1963): 411–17, discusses the symbolic values of Perdita's flowers and herbs. Also see Richard W. Hillman, "The 'Gillyvors' Exchange in *The Winter's Tale*," *English Studies in Canada* 5 (1979): 16–23.

37. See F. W. Bateson, "How Old Was Leontes?" *Essays and Studies* n.s., 31 (1978): 65–74; and Maurice Hunt, "The Three Seasons of Mankind: Age, Nature, and Art in *The Winter's Tale*," *Iowa State Journal of Research* 58 (1984): 300–2.

38. Concerning the symbolic value of the flowers, Scott remarks that "Polixenes would do well to repent in advance of his plans to sever the lovers (suggested, though not yet explicit, in 4.2), and remembrance of his former idyllic relations with Leontes . . . would prepare well for the marriage which will unite the two kingdoms and join country and court in full harmony. Or we could take the flower gifts another way: that Polixenes needs the grace to repent of what he is about to do and Camillo should remember his homeland where Perdita and Polixenes must return after sixteen years to heal all rifts. However

she distributes the flowers—some of each to both characters or rue to Polixenes and rosemary to Camillo—Perdita unknowingly offers wise admonitions" ("Seasons and Flowers," 412). Ironically, Perdita's flowers are metaphorically apt, even though she realizes that Polixenes and Camillo deserve hybrids of autumn (4.4.79–85).

39. Ibid.

40. For the argument that the events of the pastoral scene must occur in September, see Hunt, "The Three Seasons of Mankind," 303–4.

41. Mahood, Shakespeare's Wordplay, 159.

42. Knight, The Crown of Life, 90.

43. Sir Philip Sidney, An Apology for Poetry, ed. Geoffrey Shepherd (London: Thomas Nelson, 1965), 101, 104.

44. S. L. Bethell, "The Winter's Tale": A Study (London: The Staples Press, 1947), 25.

45. This merger is fully discussed by Murray Krieger, "The Ekphrastic Principle and the Still Movement of Poetry; or Laokoon Revisited," in The Play and Place of Criticism (Baltimore: Johns Hopkins University Press, 1967), 105–28.

46. Quoted by Donawerth, Sixteenth-Century Study of Language, 75.

47. For Flora's mysterious fertility, see Edgar Wind, Pagan Mysteries in the Renaissance (New Haven: Yale University Press, 1958), 101–2.

48. For more on this belief, see David Bevington, Action is Eloquence: Shakespeare's Language of Gesture (Cambridge: Harvard University Press, 1984); and Harold Fisch, "Shakespeare and the Language of Gesture," Shakespeare Studies 19 (1987): 239–51.

49. Sir Thomas Elyot, in The Boke Named the Governour, explains how dancing can teach Ideas (pp. 76–88).

50. Sidney, An Apology for Poetry, 108.

51. For example, after Hermione has enfolded Leontes in her arms, Paulina says, "That she is living, / Were it but told you, should be hooted at / Like an old tale" (5.3.115–17). That fact must be seen to be believed. In order to make this truth stronger, Shakespeare perhaps wanted his viewer to hoot (intellectually, of course) in the previous scene at the gentleman's lame telling of events so bizarre that they must be seen to be credited.

52. See Bellette, "Truth and Utterance in The Winter's Tale," 72–73; Bevington, Action is Eloquence, 19; and Uphaus, Beyond Tragedy, 86–88. Concerning 5.2, Uphaus observes: "this scene reports the silence of innocence through the failure of speech, perhaps because it was speech, after all, that set off the tragedy of Act I (e.g., 'Tongue-tied, our Queen? Speak you' . . .)."

53. That Shakespeare wrote "bad" poetry when dramatic meaning dictated it constitutes the thesis of Hardin Craig, "Shakespeare's Bad Poetry," Shakespeare Survey 1 (1948): 51–56. Bethell believes that the water-angle-fish conceit amounts to a burlesque of courtly speech (p. 42). For another verdict against the speech of 5.2, this time because it has a Euphuistic cast, see Charles Barber, "The Winter's Tale and Jacobean Society," in Shakespeare in a Changing World, ed. Arnold Kettle (London: Lawrence and Wishart, 1964), 241–42. The gentlemen's affected speech has traditionally posed a knotty critical problem of The Winter's Tale. (For a review of the problem, see Kenneth Muir, "The Conclusion of The Winter's Tale," in The Morality of Art, ed. D. W. Jefferson [London: Routledge and Kegan Paul, 1969] 88.)

54. Leonard Barkin, "'Living Sculptures': Ovid, Michelangelo, and The Winter's Tale," Journal of English Literary History 48 (1981): 658–59.

55. See W. Moelwyn Merchant, *Shakespeare and the Artist* (London: Oxford University Press, 1959), 171–76.

56. Peter Berek, in "'As We Are Mock'd with Art': From Scorn to Transfiguration," *Studies in English Literature* 18 (1978): 289–305, discusses the importance of "mocking" in Shakespeare's last plays.

57. Matchett, "Some Dramatic Techniques in *The Winter's Tale*," 104–5.

Chapter 5. *The Tempest*

1. The limitations of language in *The Tempest* have been described by Jewkes, "'Excellent Dumb Discourse,'" 196–210; by Hawkes, *Shakespeare's Talking Animals*, 194–212; by Greene, "'Excellent Dumb Discourse,'" 193–205; and by Garner, "*The Tempest*," 177–87.

2. A pun is of course only one kind of jest; it is a species of an inclusive genus. Because the word "pun" had not been coined (the OED gives an original date of c. 1660), Renaissance playwrights regularly refer to puns by their generic title. Trinculo's pun upon "line and level" and "lime-tree," for example, is called a "jest" by Stephano (4.1.235–45). Joseph Addison declared in *The Spectator* that a homonymic pun is "a Conceit arising from the use of two Words that agree in Sound, but differ in the Sense" (Ed. Donald F. Bond [Oxford: Clarendon Press, 1965], vol. 1, 262–63). While my focus is upon the double-entendres in *The Tempest*, I refer at times to puns and the punning habit as "jests" and "the jesting spirit."

3. Sister Miriam Joseph, *Shakespeare's Use of the Arts of Language* (New York: Columbia University Press, 1947), 165, 167.

4. Baldesar Castiglione, *The Book of the Courtier*, trans. Charles S. Singleton (Garden City, NY: Doubleday, 1959), 141.

5. "Dolour" and "dollar" were pronounced similarly in Renaissance London according to Fausto Cercignani, *Shakespeare's Works and Elizabethan Pronunciation* (Oxford: Clarendon Press, 1981), 189, 262.

6. See the OED definition 18A, in which it is noted that this special usage of "sort" was popular from c. 1530 to 1600.

7. Stanton Garner, Jr., in "*The Tempest*," observes that Antonio and Sebastian "play with non-referential language, severing words from a concern for truth" (p. 179), and that the flatness of the puns in 2.1 reveals that trivialized language used destructively isolates a speaker (pp. 179–80). For another account of linguistic dislocation in this scene, see A. Lynne Magnusson, "Interruption in *The Tempest*," *Shakespeare Quarterly* 37 (1986): 53–54.

8. "Jocose sayings are very useful as taunts, even as are grave sayings for the purpose of praise; and so are well-turned metaphors, and especially if used in repartee and if the one who replies keeps the same metaphor the other person used" (Castiglione, *The Book of the Courtier*, 163). Regarded from the courtier's perspective, Sebastian's continuation of Antonio's tide metaphor is a "jocose saying."

9. Virgil, *Aeneid*, I. 328ff.

10. A history of the commentary on this pun is given in *The New Variorum Edition of The Tempest*, ed. Horace Howard Furness (Philadelphia: Lippincott, 1892), 84–85.

11. See David Sundelson, "So Rare a Wonder'd Father: Prospero's *Tempest*," in *Representing Shakespeare: New Psychoanalytic Essays*, eds. Murray M.

Schwartz and Coppélia Kahn (Baltimore: Johns Hopkins University Press, 1980), 48; and Stephen Orgel, "Prospero's Wife," *Representations* 8 (1984): 5.

12. At the beginning of the scene, Trinculo makes several puns—upon "set," "standard," and "lie" itself (3.2.10–19)—thus identifying himself again as the jester. Consult the gloss on these puns in *The Riverside Shakespeare*, ed. G. Blakemore Evans, p. 1625.

13. The similar and dissimilar Renaissance meanings of "lying" and "excreting" suggested by Trinculo's pun, coalesce in the humorous idea of a backward voice.

14. In regard to the comic purgation of act 2, R. A. Foakes notes that "the re-appearance of Trinculo, pulled forth by Stephano, serves to emphasize how much less of a 'monster' Caliban himself is" (*Shakespeare: The Dark Comedies to the Last Plays* [Charlottesville: University Press of Virginia, 1971], 152).

15. For Prospero as theurgist, see Walter Clyde Curry, *Shakespeare's Philosophical Patterns* (Baton Rouge: Louisiana State University Press, 1937), 163–99; and D. G. James, *The Dream of Prospero* (Oxford: Clarendon Press, 1967), 45–71. For Prospero as Medean enchanter, wizard, and familiar Renaissance sleight-of-hand man—the trickster with his boy apprentice—see Barbara A. Mowat, "Prospero, Agrippa, and Hocus Pocus," *English Literary Renaissance* 11 (1981): 281–303. Frances A. Yates, in *Shakespeare's Last Plays: A New Approach* (London: Routledge and Kegan Paul, 1975), writes that "*The Tempest* would be one of the supreme expressions of that vitally important phase in the history of the European mind, the phase which borders on, and presages, the so-called scientific revolution of the seventeenth century. Prospero is clearly the magus as scientist, able to operate scientifically within his world view" (pp. 96–97). Gary Schmidgall asserts that *The Tempest* is Shakespeare's most Baconian play: "The play mounts in theatrical dress Bacon's arguments for the advancement of useful knowledge. The characterizations of the play are virtually all reflected in Bacon's theorem that true learning 'doth make the minds of men gentle, generous, maniable, and pliant to government; whereas ignorance makes them churlish, thwart, and mutinous'" (*Shakespeare and the Courtly Aesthetic* [Berkeley: University of California Press, 1981], 247–48).

16. For an explanation of how text and *exempla* interact to create a literary effect, see G. R. Owst, *Literature and Pulpit in Medieval England* (1933; reprint, New York: Barnes and Noble, 1961), esp. 149–209. The text-*exempla* structure of the medieval sermon survived in the Elizabethan homily, which exerted considerable influence upon Shakespeare's art. See Alfred Hart, *Shakespeare and the Homilies* (1934; reprint, New York: Octagon Books, 1977), 9–76. The type of Prospero's *exemplum* is "the moralized anecdote" (Owst, 149).

17. Robert Egan, in "This Rough Magic: Perspectives of Art and Morality in *The Tempest*," *Shakespeare Quarterly* 23 (1972): 176, notes that Prospero "was, and is still, unable to conceive of the contradiction between what a brother should be and what his brother was . . . primarily his amazement centers on the fact that his brother should have acted contrary to all logical and ideal norms of brotherhood—that his own kind could return hate where love was owed. The lapse of time has brought him no new understanding of this." The reader shall see that Prospero prefers virtue to vengeance once he experiences brotherly feelings for the weeping Gonzalo. This catalyst is both psychologically and poetically apt because it has been a brother's betrayal that has preoccupied Prospero and filled him with rage. The image of Gonzalo and Prospero's feelings toward it displace the idea of vicious Antonio.

18. Obviously, many more differences than similarities exist between these two characters. Belarius never attains Prospero's magisterial role as theurgist; the details of the schoolmaster's story never engross Arviragus and Guiderius as fully as they do Miranda. In fact, in her craving to know the next episode of Prospero's tale, she contrasts with the bored Princes. Both tutors, however, can appear rather pedantic, warning their pupils to pay close attention and to profit from the schoolmaster's painful experience in a distant court.

19. Walter J. Ong, Ramus, Method, and the Decay of Dialogue (1958: reprint, New York: Octagon Books, 1974), 107–8.

20. Contrariety has been defined and discussed in Shakespeare's plays by Robert Grudin, Mighty Opposites: Shakespeare and Renaissance Contrariety (Berkeley: University of California Press, 1979). Grudin applies the principle of contrariety to Prospero and The Tempest (pp. 185–211); yet his treatment of the subject and mine are substantially different. Also see Karen Flagstad, "'Making this Place Paradise': Prospero and the Problem of Caliban in The Tempest," Shakespeare Studies 18 (1986): 207–8 and passim.

21. Contraria was an Aristotelian category in Renaissance formal logic. Baldwin cites Gonzalo's speech as an example (Shakspere's Small Latine, vol. 2, 115–16).

22. Consult Aristotle, Topica 1. 17, trans. E. S. Forster (Cambridge: Harvard University Press, 1960), 323.

23. Schmidgall, Shakespeare and the Courtly Aesthetic, 90.

24. Knight observes in The Crown of Life that Sycorax is mentioned "to define, by contrast, the higher intuition" of Miranda (p. 238). Knight does not, however, explore the contrast or indicate that for Caliban it is a reasonable one. Knight discusses several of Caliban's human qualities and his gradual progression "from black magic, through nature and man, to grace" (pp. 235–40). Another positive view of Caliban is provided by Foakes, Shakespeare, 151–56. Also see Stephen J. Miko, "Tempest," English Literary History 49 (1982): 13–14.

25. John Doebler, Shakespeare's Speaking Pictures (Albuquerque: University of New Mexico Press, 1974), 148–57.

26. Ibid., 152.

27. Howard Felperin typically expresses this view in Shakespearean Romance (Princeton: Princeton University Press, 1972), 250, 257–59. Also see Greene, "'Excellent Dumb Discourse,'" 199–200.

28. Doebler, Shakespeare's Speaking Pictures, 153–55. A reading of Ariel as harpy personifying the courtiers' greed appears in John Gillies, "Shakespeare's Virginian Masque," English Literary History 53 (1986): 684, 701.

29. In Shakespeare and the Comedy of Forgiveness, Hunter suggests that "Prospero's banquet . . . is a type, not of Satan's temptations, but of the commonest of all symbolic banquets: the Communion table" (p. 234). For a divergent reading of the Harpy's Banquet, see Jacqueline Latham, "The Magic Banquet in The Tempest," Shakespeare Studies 12 (1979): 215–17.

30. Cf. Lear 4.1.66–69:

> Glou.   heavens, deal so still!
>   Let the superfluous and lust-dieted man,
>   That slaves your ordinance, that will not see
>   Because he does not feel, feel your pow'r quickly.

Also cf. Lear 5.3.170–74.

31. Cf. Gloucester's apathetic "and that's true too" (*Lear* 5.2.11) with Alonso's indifference: "I will stand to, and feed, / Although my last: no matter, since I feel / The best is past" (*Temp.* 3.3.49–51).

32. Cf. Harry Berger, Jr., "Miraculous Harp: A Reading of Shakespeare's *Tempest*," *Shakespeare Studies* 5 (1969): 265, 273–74.

33. See Glynne Wickham, "Masque and Anti-masque in *The Tempest*," *Essays and Studies* n.s., 28 (1975): 1–14. Wickham explains that "contrary to the conventions of Jonson's masques, some ninety lines of dialogue divorce anti-masque from masque in *The Tempest*" (p. 4). Ernest B. Gilman discusses the "rearrangement of the masquing structure" in *The Tempest*, in "'All eyes': Prospero's Inverted Masque," *Renaissance Quarterly* 33 (1980): 214–30.

34. Orgel, *Jonsonian Masque*, 84–87.

35. Karol Berger, "Prospero's Art," *Shakespeare Studies* 10 (1977): 239.

36. A similar point is made by Kevin McNamara, "Golden Worlds at Court: *The Tempest* and Its Masque," *Shakespeare Studies* 19 (1987): 193.

37. Wind, *Pagan Mysteries*, 101–3, 105.

38. Orgel, in *The Jonsonian Masque*, remarks that "the antimasque . . . becomes, both to its characters and to us, an education for the concluding revels" (p. 84). Orgel demonstrates that it does so mainly by dramatizing disorder so that the viewer can imagine a complementary idea of order required in the later masque. See his discussion of *The Masque of Queens*, pp. 133ff. In one sense, the maze that Alonso, Gonzalo, and the maddened courtiers tread (5.1.242) functions as the dance of the antimasque, a contrast to the nymphs' and reapers' gracious footing.

39. Beholders of the allegorical dances of the masque apprehended not only heavenly harmonies but also divine ideas in dancers' hieroglyphic movements and designs (John C. Meagher, *Method and Meaning in Jonson's Masques* [Notre Dame, IN: University of Notre Dame Press, 1966], 81–106). Orgel comments that "the masque dances [of *The Masque of Queens*] are a form of wisdom, as they are in *Pleasure Reconciled to Virtue* and in a more famous Renaissance poem about dancing, Davies' 'Orchestra'" (*The Jonsonian Masque*, 141).

40. Catherine M. Shaw, "*The Tempest* and *Hymenaei*," *Cahiers Élisabéthains* 26 (1984): 33–34.

41. The bearing of winter upon the Masque of Ceres has been discussed by Peterson, *Time, Tide and Tempest*, 240–42.

42. Henry Peacham, *The Complete Gentleman, The Truth of Our Times, and The Art of Living*, ed. Virgil B. Heltzel (Ithaca: Cornell University Press, 1962), 96.

43. A Shakespearean character often knows ideas by seeing them reflected in the face of another. Cassius, for example, states that he will be a mirror by which Brutus might know his inner worth (*Julius Caesar* 1.2.52–93). The notion that compassion can be learned from seeing pity mirrored in a face such as imagined Gonzalo's has a long history. Gordon Worth O'Brien, *Renaissance Poetics and the Problem of Power* (Chicago: University of Chicago Press, 1956) and Frederick Goldin, *The Mirror of Narcissus in the Courtly Love Lyric* (Ithaca: Cornell University Press, 1967) reveal that the reflection of ideas from the face of another is an important concept from Plotinus to Milton. Augustine is a major source for the idea that self-knowledge comes from the reflected sight of one's own visage, in which incarnate divinity is latent.

44. Shakespeare's sustained use of the endearative "are" works to identify Ariel with art ("which art but air" . . . "Kindlier moved than thou art").

45. David Horowitz, in *Shakespeare: An Existential View* (London: Tavistock, 1965), similarly believes that Prospero's new idea of humanity is made possible by passion: "Here Prosper names the well-spring of his pardon, which is to follow. It is his kind-ness, his nature which he shares with them. For he feels afflictions as they do, passions as they (where 'passions' has a verbal emphasis, suggesting 'to experience feelingly') and thus is moved to mercy by the image of himself, suffering in their agony" (p. 87). Also see D'Orsay W. Pearson, "'Unless I Be Reliev'd by Prayer': *The Tempest* in Perspective," *Shakespeare Studies* 7 (1974): 271–73; and Cosmo Corfield, "Why Does Prospero Abjure His 'Rough Magic'?" *Shakespeare Quarterly* 36 (1985): 40, 46–47.

46. In "*The Tempest*: Gratuitous Movement or Action Without Kibes and Pinches," *Shakespeare Studies* 14 (1981), Margreta De Grazia writes: "at the opening of Act Five, Prospero decides to take the action that will free him and his enemies to move and act again. He does so in response to sheer words, all the more insubstantial because spoken by 'spirit,' by 'air,' by Ariel. The play's pivotal action, then, is prompted by something of no more causal significance than breath. . . . What prompts the play's turning point and scene of discovery, then, is words not actions, as delivered by an onlooker (and an inhuman one at that) rather than a participant, describing external signs rather than the event itself and primarily as it affected bystanders" (pp. 249–50).

Chapter 6. Conclusion

1. Sir Philip Sidney, *The Countess of Pembroke's Arcadia*, ed. Maurice Evans (Harmondsworth: Penguin, 1977), 682.

2. C. B. Mount, "Sir Philip Sidney and Shakespeare," *Notes and Queries*, 8th series, vol. 3 (1893), 305.

3. Smith, *Shakespeare's Romances*, 63, 234; and R. S. White, "*Let Wonder Seem Familiar*": *Endings in Shakespeare's Romance Vision* (Atlantic Highlands, NJ: Humanities Press, 1985), 122, 139–41.

4. Northrop Frye, *Anatomy of Criticism: Four Essays* (Princeton, NJ: Princeton University Press, 1957), 186–206, esp. 187–88.

5. Sidney, *Arcadia*, 484–92, 834.

6. For the "baleful spell" as a romance motif subject to later cultural displacement, see Frederic Jameson, "Magical Narratives: Romance as Genre," *New Literary History* 7 (1975–76): 154.

7. For this historical displacement, consult Jameson, "Magical Narratives," 140–44.

8. Patricia Parker, *Inescapable Romance: Studies in the Poetics of a Mode* (Princeton: Princeton University Press, 1979), 4. Parker's sentences paraphrase an idea of Jameson's (ibid., 161).

9. Parker, *Inescapable Romance*, 5.

10. Ibid., 221–22.

11. This illustration confers a Baconian significance upon Parker's insight, extending the implications of her idea.

12. See, respectively, Davis, *Elizabethan Fiction*, 59; Richard Cody, *The Landscape of the Mind: Pastoralism and Platonic Theory in Tasso's "Aminta" and Shakespeare's Early Comedies* (Oxford: Clarendon Press, 1969), 3–11, 23–24, 51, 155–57; Humphrey Tonkin, *Spenser's Courteous Pastoral* (Oxford: Clarendon Press, 1972), 247–57.

13. Concerning the opening verses of Virgil's first eclogue, Paul Alpers, in

"What is Pastoral?" *Critical Inquiry* 8 (1982): 452, remarks that "here the responsiveness of man and landscape is unusually intense and intimate. The singer teaches the woods to sound his beloved's name, but on the other hand, the making of sound is attributed to the woods alone, so that the song is not what he utters but what he hears."

14. Jonathan Goldberg, *Voice Terminal Echo: Postmodernism and English Renaissance Texts* (New York: Methuen, 1986), 68–100, esp. 68–72, 81.

15. In this instance, the naming dimensions of romance cooperate with and reinforce Shakespeare's adaptation of a pastoral motif.

16. According to Joseph A. Mazzeo in "St. Augustine's Rhetoric of Silence: Truth vs. Eloquence and Things vs. Signs," *Journal of the History of Ideas* 23 (1962), "the theme that underlies the whole of Book IV [of *De Doctrina Christiana*] is that of the eloquence of words *(verba)* versus the immeasurably greater eloquence of realities *(res)* . . ." (p. 177). "Book IV, on the *modus proferendi*, has little to say of technique but stresses 'an eloquence in which words are supplied by things and by wisdom itself and the speaker is unlearnedly wise'" (p. 187).

Bibliography

Addison, Joseph. *The Spectator*. Vol 1. Edited by Donald F. Bond. Oxford: Clarendon Press, 1965.

Alpers, Paul. "What is Pastoral?" *Critical Inquiry* 8 (1982): 437–60.

Aristotle. *Topica*. Translated by E. S. Forster. Cambridge: Harvard University Press, 1960.

Arthos, John. "*Pericles, Prince of Tyre*: A Study in the Dramatic Use of Romantic Narrative." *Shakespeare Quarterly* 4 (1953): 257–70.

Austin, J. L. *How To Do Things With Words*. Cambridge: Harvard University Press, 1962.

Bacon, Francis. *The Works of Francis Bacon*. Vol. 4. Edited by James Spedding, Robert Ellis, and Douglas Denon Heath. London: Longman, 1875.

Baldwin, T. W. *William Shakspere's Small Latine and Lesse Greeke*. 2 vols. Urbana: University of Illinois Press, 1944.

Barber, Charles. "*The Winter's Tale* and Jacobean Society." In *Shakespeare in a Changing World*, edited by Arnold Kettle, 233–52. London: Lawrence and Wishart, 1964.

Barkin, Leonard. "'Living Sculptures': Ovid, Michelangelo, and *The Winter's Tale*." *Journal of English Literary History* 48 (1981): 639–67.

Barton, Ann. "Leontes and the Spider: Language and Speaker in Shakespeare's Last Plays." In *Shakespeare's Styles: Essays in Honour of Kenneth Muir*, edited by Philip Edwards, Inga-Stina Ewbank, and G. K. Hunter, 131–50. Cambridge: Cambridge University Press, 1980.

Bateson, F. W. "How Old Was Leontes?" *Essays and Studies*, n.s., 31 (1978): 65–75.

Battenhouse, Roy W. "Theme and Structure in *The Winter's Tale*." *Shakespeare Survey* 33 (1980): 123–38.

Bellette, A. F. "Truth and Utterance in *The Winter's Tale*." *Shakespeare Survey* 31 (1978): 65–75.

Berek, Peter. "'As We Are Mock'd with Art': From Scorn to Transfiguration." *Studies in English Literature* 18 (1978): 289–305.

Berger, Harry, Jr. "Miraculous Harp: A Reading of Shakespeare's *Tempest*." *Shakespeare Studies* 5 (1969): 253–83.

Berger, Karol. "Prospero's Art." *Shakespeare Studies* 10 (1977): 211–39.

Bergeron, David M. "Sexuality in *Cymbeline*." *Essays in Literature* 10 (1983): 159–68.

———. *Shakespeare's Romances and the Royal Family*. Lawrence: University Press of Kansas, 1985.

Berry, Francis. *The Shakespeare Inset: Word and Picture.* London: Routledge and Kegan Paul, 1965.

Bethell, S. L. *"The Winter's Tale": A Study.* London: The Staples Press, 1947.

Bevington, David. *Action is Eloquence: Shakespeare's Language of Gesture.* Cambridge: Harvard University Press, 1984.

Boccaccio, Giovanni. *The Decameron.* Edited by W. E. Henley. The Tudor Translations, no. 41. London: David Nutt, 1909.

Booth, Stephen. "On the Value of *Hamlet*." In *Reinterpretations of Elizabethan Drama*, edited by Norman Rabkin, 137–76. New York: Columbia University Press, 1969.

Bryant, J. A., Jr. *Hippolyta's View: Some Christian Aspects of Shakespeare's Plays.* Lexington: The University Press of Kentucky, 1961.

Bullough, Geoffrey, ed. *Narrative and Dramatic Sources of Shakespeare.* Vol. 6, *Other "Classical" Plays: "Titus Andronicus," "Troilus and Cressida," "Timon of Athens," "Pericles, Prince of Tyre."* London: Routledge and Kegan Paul, 1966.

Burckhardt, Sigurd. *Shakespearean Meanings.* Princeton: Princeton University Press, 1968.

Burton, Robert. *The Anatomy of Melancholy.* Edited by Floyd Dell and Paul Jordan-Smith. New York: Tudor Publishing Co., 1927.

Calderwood, James L. *Metadrama in Shakespeare's Henriad: "Richard II" to "Henry V."* Berkeley: University of California Press, 1979.

Carroll, William C. *The Great Feast of Language in "Love's Labour's Lost."* Princeton: Princeton University Press, 1976.

Castiglione, Baldesar. *The Book of the Courtier.* Translated by Charles S. Singleton. Garden City, NY: Doubleday, 1959.

Cercignani, Fausto. *Shakespeare's Works and Elizabethan Pronunciation.* Oxford: Clarendon Press, 1981.

Childress, Diana T. "Are Shakespeare's Late Plays Really Romances?" In *Shakespeare's Late Plays: Essays in Honor of Charles Crow*, edited by Richard C. Tobias and Paul G. Zolbrod, 44–55. Athens: Ohio University Press, 1974.

Clemen, Wolfgang. *The Development of Shakespeare's Imagery.* Cambridge: Harvard University Press, 1951.

Cody, Richard. *The Landscape of the Mind: Pastoralism and Platonic Theory in Tasso's "Aminta" and Shakespeare's Early Comedies.* Oxford: Clarendon Press, 1969.

Coghill, Nevill. "Six Points of Stage-Craft in The Winter's Tale." *Shakespeare Survey* 11 (1958): 31–41.

Coleridge, Samuel Taylor. *Lectures on Shakespeare, Etc.* Edited by Ernest Rhys. 1907. Reprint. London: Dent, 1951.

Corfield, Cosmo. "Why Does Prospero Abjure his 'Rough Magic'?" *Shakespeare Quarterly* 36 (1985): 31–48.

Craig, Hardin. "Shakespeare's Bad Poetry." *Shakespeare Survey* 1 (1948): 51–56.

Cunningham, James V. *Woe or Wonder: The Emotional Effect of Shakespearean Tragedy.* Denver: University of Denver Press, 1951.

Curry, Walter Clyde. *Shakespeare's Philosophical Patterns*. Baton Rouge: Louisiana State University Press, 1937.

Curtius, Ernst Robert. *European Literature and the Latin Middle Ages*. Translated by Willard R. Trask. 1948. Reprint. New York: Harper and Row, 1953.

Danby, John F. *Poets on Fortune's Hill: Studies in Sidney, Shakespeare, Beaumont and Fletcher*. 1952. Reprint. Port Washington, NY: Kennikat Press, 1966.

Danson, Lawrence. *Tragic Alphabet: Shakespeare's Drama of Language*. New Haven: Yale University Press, 1974.

Davis, Walter R. *Idea and Act in Elizabethan Fiction*. Princeton: Princeton University Press, 1969.

De Grazia, Margreta. "Shakespeare's View of Language: An Historical Perspective." *Shakespeare Quarterly* 29 (1978): 374–88.

———. "*The Tempest*: Gratuitous Movement or Action Without Kibes and Pinches." *Shakespeare Studies* 14 (1981): 249–65.

Dickey, Stephen. "Language and Role in *Pericles*." *English Literary Renaissance* 16 (1986): 550–66.

Doebler, John. *Shakespeare's Speaking Pictures*. Albuquerque: University of New Mexico Press, 1974.

Donawerth, Jane. *Shakespeare and the Sixteenth-Century Study of Language*. Urbana: University of Illinois Press, 1984.

Donne, John. *The Sermons of John Donne*. Vol 4. Edited by George R. Potter and Evelyn M. Simpson. Berkeley: University of California Press, 1959.

Doran, Madeleine. *Endeavors of Art: A Study of Form in Elizabethan Drama*. Madison: University of Wisconsin Press, 1964.

Edwards, Philip. *Shakespeare and the Confines of Art*. London: Methuen, 1968.

Egan, Robert. "This Rough Magic: Perspectives of Art and Morality in *The Tempest*." *Shakespeare Quarterly* 23 (1972): 171–82.

Elam, Keir. *Shakespeare's Universe of Discourse: Language-Games in the Comedies*. Cambridge: Cambridge University Press, 1984.

Ellis-Fermor, Una. *The Frontiers of Drama*. London: Methuen, 1945.

Elyot, Sir Thomas. *The Boke Named the Governour*. 1937. Reprint. London: Dent, 1962.

Ewbank, Inga-Stina. "'More Pregnantly than Words': Some Uses and Limitations of Visual Symbolism." *Shakespeare Survey* 24 (1971): 13–18.

———. "'My name is Marina': The Language of Recognition." In *Shakespeare's Styles: Essays in Honour of Kenneth Muir*, edited by Philip Edwards, Inga-Stina Ewbank, and G. K. Hunter, 111–30. Cambridge: Cambridge University Press, 1980.

Felperin, Howard. *Shakespearean Romance*. Princeton: Princeton University Press, 1972.

———. "Shakespeare's Miracle Play." *Shakespeare Quarterly* 18 (1967): 363–74.

———. "'Tongue-tied Our Queen?': The Deconstruction of Presence in *The Winter's Tale*." In *Shakespeare and the Question of Theory*, edited by Patricia Parker and Geoffrey Hartman, 3–18. New York: Methuen, 1985.

Ficino, Marsilio. *Commentary on Plato's Symposium*. Edited and Translated by Sears Reynolds Jayne. The University of Missouri Studies in English, no. 19. Columbia: University of Missouri Press, 1944.

Firth, J. R. "Personality and Language in Society." In *Papers in Linguistics: 1934–51*, 177–89. London: Oxford University Press, 1957.

———. "The Technique of Semantics." In *Papers in Linguistics: 1934–51*, 7–33. London: Oxford University Press, 1957.

Fisch, Harold. "Shakespeare and the Language of Gesture." *Shakespeare Studies* 19 (1987): 239–51.

Fish, Stanley E. "How To Do Things With Austin and Searle." *Modern Language Notes* 91 (1976): 983–1025.

Flagstad, Karen. "'Making this Place Paradise': Prospero and the Problem of Caliban in *The Tempest*." *Shakespeare Studies* 18 (1986): 205–33.

Fly, Richard. *Shakespeare's Mediated World*. Amherst: University of Massachusetts Press, 1976.

Foakes, R. A. *Shakespeare: The Dark Comedies to the Last Plays*. Charlottesville: The University Press of Virginia, 1971.

Foucault, Michel. *The Archaeology of Knowledge*. Translated by A. M. Sheridan Smith. 1969. Reprint. New York: Harper and Row, 1976.

Freer, Coburn. *The Poetics of Jacobean Drama*. The Johns Hopkins University Press, 1981.

Frey, Charles. "Interpreting *The Winter's Tale*." *Studies in English Literature* 18 (1978): 307–29.

———. *Shakespeare's Vast Romance: A Study of "The Winter's Tale"*. Columbia: University of Missouri Press, 1980.

Frye, Dean. "The Question of Shakespearean 'Parody.'" *Essays in Criticism* 15 (1965): 22–26.

Frye, Northrop. *Anatomy of Criticism: Four Essays*. Princeton: Princeton University Press, 1957.

———. *A Natural Perspective: The Development of Shakespearean Comedy and Romance*. New York: Harcourt, Brace and World, 1965.

Garber, Marjorie G. *Dream in Shakespeare: From Metaphor to Metamorphosis*. New Haven: Yale University Press, 1974.

Garner, Stanton B., Jr. "*The Tempest*: Language and Society." *Shakespeare Survey* 32 (1979): 177–87.

Gesner, Carol. *Shakespeare and the Greek Romance: A Study of Origins*. Lexington: The University Press of Kentucky, 1970.

Gillies, John. "Shakespeare's Virginian Masque." *Journal of English Literary History* 53 (1986): 673–707.

Gilman, Ernest B. "'All Eyes': Prospero's Inverted Masque." *Renaissance Quarterly* 33 (1980): 214–30.

Goddard, Harold C. *The Meaning of Shakespeare*. Chicago: University of Chicago Press, 1951.

Goldberg, Jonathan. *Voice Terminal Echo: Postmodernism and English Renaissance Texts*. New York: Methuen, 1986.

Goldin, Frederick. *The Mirror of Narcissus in the Courtly Love Lyric.* Ithaca: Cornell University Press, 1967.

Gombrich, E. H. "*Icones Symbolicae:* The Visual Image in Neo-Platonic Thought." *Journal of the Warburg and Courtauld Institutes* 11 (1948): 163–92.

Gordon, D. J. "The Imagery of Ben Jonson's *The Masque of Blacknesse* and *The Masque of Beautie.*" *Journal of the Warburg and Courtauld Institutes* 6 (1943): 122–41.

Granville-Barker, Harley. *Prefaces to Shakespeare.* Vol. 2, "*King Lear,*" "*Cymbeline,*" "*Julius Caesar.*" 1946. Reprint. Princeton: Princeton University Press, 1965.

Greene, Gayle. "'Excellent Dumb Discourse': Silence and Grace in Shakespeare's *Tempest.*" *Studia Neophilologica* 59 (1978): 193–205.

Greenfield, Thelma N. "A Re-Examination of the 'Patient' Pericles." *Shakespeare Studies* 3 (1967): 51–61.

Griffiths, J., ed. *The Two Books of Homilies.* Oxford: Oxford University Press, 1859.

Grudin, Robert. *Mighty Opposites: Shakespeare and Renaissance Contrariety.* Berkeley: University of California Press, 1979.

Hall, James. *Dictionary of Subjects and Symbols in Art.* New York: Harper and Row, 1974.

Halliday, M. A. K. *Language as Social Semiotic: The Social Interpretation of Language and Meaning.* London: Edward Arnold, 1978.

Harris, Bernard. "'What's past is prologue': *Cymbeline* and *Henry VIII.*" In *Later Shakespeare,* edited by John Russell Brown and Bernard Harris, 203–34. Stratford-Upon-Avon Studies, no. 8. London: Edward Arnold, 1966.

Hart, Alfred. *Shakespeare and the Homilies.* 1934. Reprint. New York: Octagon Books, 1977.

Hartwig, Joan. *Shakespeare's Tragicomic Vision.* Baton Rouge: Louisiana State University Press, 1972.

Hawkes, Terence. *Shakespeare's Talking Animals: Language and Drama in Society.* 1973. Reprint. Totowa, NJ: Rowman and Littlefield, 1974.

Hayles, Nancy K. "Sexual Disguise in *Cymbeline.*" *Modern Language Quarterly* 41 (1980): 231–47.

Hill, Geoffrey, "'The True Conduct of Human Judgment': Some Observations on *Cymbeline.*" In *The Morality of Art: Essays Presented to G. Wilson Knight by His Colleagues and Friends,* edited by D. W. Jefferson, 18-32. London: Routledge and Kegan Paul, 1969.

Hillman, Richard W. "The 'Gillyvors' Exchange in *The Winter's Tale.*" *English Studies in Canada* 5 (1979): 16–23.

Hoeniger, F. David. "Gower and Shakespeare in *Pericles.*" *Shakespeare Quarterly* 33 (1982): 461–79.

Horowitz, David. *Shakespeare: An Existential View.* London: Tavistock, 1965.

Hulme, Hilda. *Explorations in Shakespeare's Language.* London: Longman, 1962.

Hunt, Maurice. "A Looking Glass for *Pericles*." *Essays in Literature* 13 (1986): 3–11.

———. "'Stir' and Work in Shakespeare's Last Plays." *Studies in English Literature* 22 (1982): 285–304.

———. "The Three Seasons of Mankind: Age, Nature, and Art in *The Winter's Tale*." *Iowa State Journal of Research* 58 (1984): 299–309.

Hunter, Robert Grams. *Shakespeare and the Comedy of Forgiveness*. New York: Columbia University Press, 1965.

Jameson, Frederic. "Magical Narratives: Romance as Genre." *New Literary History* 7 (1975–76): 135–63.

Jewkes, W. T. "'Excellent Dumb Discourse': The Limits of Language in *The Tempest*." In *Essays on Shakespeare*, edited by Gordon Ross Smith, 196–210. University Park: Pennsylvania State University Press, 1965.

Johnson, Samuel. *Yale Edition of the Works of Samuel Johnson*. Edited by Arthur Sherbo. Vols. 7 and 8, *Johnson on Shakespeare*. New Haven: Yale University Press, 1968.

Jones, Emrys. "Stuart Cymbeline." *Essays in Criticism* 11 (1961): 84–89.

Jonson, Ben. *Ben Jonson: The Complete Masques*. Edited by Stephen Orgel. New Haven: Yale University Press, 1969.

Jorgensen, Paul A. "Much Ado About Nothing." In *Redeeming Shakespeare's Words*, 22–42. Berkeley: University of California Press, 1962.

Joseph, Sister Miriam. *Shakespeare's Use of the Arts of Language*. New York: Columbia University Press, 1947.

Kermode, Frank. *Shakespeare, Spenser, Donne*. New York: Viking, 1971.

Knight, G. Wilson. *The Crown of Life: Essays in Interpretation of Shakespeare's Final Plays*. 1947. Reprint. New York: Barnes and Noble, 1966.

Krieger, Murray. "The Ekphrastic Principle and the Still Movement of Poetry; or *Laokoon* Revisited." In *The Play and Place of Criticism*, 105–28. Baltimore: The Johns Hopkins University Press, 1967.

Kristeller, Paul Oskar. *The Philosophy of Marsilio Ficino*. Translated by Virginia Conant. New York: Columbia University Press, 1943.

Latham, Jacqueline E. M. "The Magic Banquet in *The Tempest*." *Shakespeare Studies* 12 (1979): 215–27.

Lawrence, Judiana. "Natural Bonds and Artistic Coherence in the Ending of *Cymbeline*." *Shakespeare Quarterly* 35 (1984): 440–60.

Lee, Rennselaer W. *"Ut Pictura Poesis": The Humanist Theory of Painting*. New York: Norton, 1967.

Levin, Richard. *The Multiple Plot in English Renaissance Drama*. Chicago: University of Chicago Press, 1971.

Lindenbaum, Peter. "Time, Sexual Love, and the Uses of Pastoral in *The Winter's Tale*." *Modern Language Quarterly* 33 (1972): 3–22.

Livingston, Mary L. "The Natural Art of *The Winter's Tale*." *Modern Language Quarterly* 20 (1969): 340–55.

Magnusson, A. Lynne. "Interruption in *The Tempest*." *Shakespeare Quarterly* 37 (1986): 52–65.

Mahood, M. M. *Shakespeare's Wordplay.* 1957. Reprint. London: Methuen, 1968.

Martz, Louis L. "Shakespeare's Humanist Enterprise: *The Winter's Tale.*" In *English Renaissance Studies Presented To Dame Helen Gardner in Honour of Her Seventieth Birthday,* edited by John Carey, 114–31. Oxford: Clarendon Press, 1980.

Matchett, William H.   "Some Dramatic Techniques in *The Winter's Tale.*" *Shakespeare Survey* 22 (1969): 93–107.

Mazzeo, Joseph A. "St. Augustine's Rhetoric of Silence: Truth vs. Eloquence and Things vs. Signs." *Journal of the History of Ideas* 23 (1962): 175–96.

McAlindon, T. "Language, Style, and Meaning in *Troilus and Cressida.*" *Publications of the Modern Language Association* 84 (1969): 29-43.

McDonald, Russ.   "Poetry and Plot in *The Winter's Tale.*" *Shakespeare Quarterly* 36 (1985): 315–29.

McNamara, Kevin R. "Golden Worlds at Court: *The Tempest* and Its Masque." *Shakespeare Studies* 19 (1987): 183–202.

Meagher, John C. *Method and Meaning in Jonson's Masques.* Notre Dame: University of Notre Dame Press, 1966.

Merchant, W. Moelwyn. *Shakespeare and the Artist.* London: Oxford University Press, 1959.

Miko, Stephen J. "Tempest." *Journal of English Literary History* 49 (1982): 1–17.

Moffet, Robin. "*Cymbeline* and the Nativity." *Shakespeare Quarterly* 13 (1962): 207–18.

Mount, C. B. "Sir Philip Sidney and Shakespeare." *Notes and Queries.* 8th series, vol. 3 (1893): 305.

Mowat, Barbara A. "Prospero, Agrippa, and Hocus Pocus." *English Literary Renaissance* 11 (1981): 281–303.

Muir, Kenneth. "The Conclusion of *The Winter's Tale.*" In *The Morality of Art: Essays Presented to G. Wilson Knight by His Colleagues and Friends,* edited by D. W. Jefferson, 87–101. London: Routledge and Kegan Paul, 1969.

Nathan, Norman. "Leontes' Provocation." *Shakespeare Quarterly* 19 (1968): 19-24.

———. "'Pericles' and 'Jonah.'" *Notes and Queries* 201 (1956): 10–11.

Neely, Carol Thomas. "*The Winter's Tale:* The Triumph of Speech." *Studies in English Literature* 15 (1975): 321–38.

O'Brien, Gordon Worth. *Renaissance Poetics and the Problem of Power.* Chicago: University of Chicago Press, 1956.

Ong, Walter J. *Ramus, Method, and the Decay of Dialogue.* 1958. Reprint. New York: Octagon Books, 1974.

Orgel, Stephen. *The Jonsonian Masque.* Cambridge: Harvard University Press, 1965.

———. "Prospero's Wife." *Representations* 8 (1984): 1–13.

Owst, G. R. *Literature and Pulpit in Medieval England.* 1933. Reprint. New York: Barnes and Noble, 1961.

Panofsky, Erwin. *Studies in Iconology: Humanistic Themes in the Art of the Renaissance.* 1939. Reprint. New York: Harper and Row, 1962.

Parker, Patricia. *Inescapable Romance: Studies in the Poetics of a Mode.* Princeton: Princeton University Press, 1979.

Patterson, David. *The Affirming Flame: Religion, Language, Literature.* Norman: University of Oklahoma Press, 1988.

Peacham, Henry. *The Complete Gentleman, The Truth of Our Times, and The Art of Living.* Edited by Virgil B. Heltzel. Ithaca: Cornell University Press, 1962.

Pearson, D'Orsay W. "'Unless I Be Reliev'd by Prayer': *The Tempest* in Perspective." *Shakespeare Studies* 7 (1974): 253–82.

Peñalosa, Fernando. *Introduction to the Sociology of Language.* Rowley, MA: Newbury House, 1981.

Peterson, Douglas L. *Time, Tide and Tempest: A Study of Shakespeare's Romances.* San Marino, CA: Huntington Library, 1973.

Porter, Joseph. *The Drama of Speech Acts: Shakespeare's Lancastrian Tetralogy.* Berkeley: University of California Press, 1979.

Pratt, Mary Louise. *Toward a Speech Act Theory of Literary Discourse.* Bloomington: Indiana University Press, 1977.

Proudfoot, Richard. "Verbal Reminiscence and the Two-Part Structure of *The Winter's Tale.*" *Shakespeare Survey* 29 (1976): 67–78.

Pyle, Fitzroy. *"The Winter's Tale": A Commentary on the Structure.* London: Routledge and Kegan Paul, 1969.

Quiller-Couch, Sir Arthur. *Shakespeare's Workmanship.* 1919. Reprint. Cambridge: Cambridge University Press, 1931.

Rabkin, Norman. *Shakespeare and the Common Understanding.* New York: Macmillan, 1967.

Raleigh, Sir Walter. *Ralighes' History of Y^E World.* London: W. Stansby, 1617.

Riemer, A. P. *Antic Fables: Patterns of Evasion in Shakespeare's Comedies.* New York: St. Martin's Press, 1980.

Rose, Mark. *Shakespearean Design.* Cambridge: Harvard University Press, 1972.

Sanders, Wilbur. *The Dramatist and the Received Idea: Studies in the Plays of Marlowe and Shakespeare.* Cambridge: Cambridge University Press, 1968.

Sapir, Edward. *Selected Writings of Edward Sapir in Language, Culture, and Personality.* Edited by David G. Mandelbaum. Berkeley: University of California Press, 1949.

Schanzer, Ernest. "The Structural Pattern of *The Winter's Tale.*" *Review of English Literature* 5 (1964): 72–82.

Schmidgall, Gary. *Shakespeare and the Courtly Aesthetic.* Berkeley: University of California Press, 1981.

Schork, R. J. "Allusion, Theme, and Characterization in *Cymbeline.*" *Studies in Philology* 69 (1972): 210–16.

Scott, William O. "Seasons and Flowers in *The Winter's Tale.*" *Shakespeare Quarterly* 14 (1963): 411–17.

Searle, John R. *Speech Acts: An Essay in the Philosophy of Language.* Cambridge: Cambridge University Press, 1969.

————. "A Taxonomy of Illocutionary Acts." In *Language, Mind, and Knowledge*, edited by Keith Gunderson, 344–69. Minnesota Studies in the Philosophy of Science, no. 7. Minneapolis: University of Minnesota Press, 1975.

Shakespeare, William. *Cymbeline*. Edited by J. M. Nosworthy. London: Methuen, 1955.

————. *The New Variorum Edition of "The Tempest."* Edited by Horace Howard Furness. Philadelphia: Lippincott, 1892.

————. *The New Variorum Edition of "The Winter's Tale."* Edited by Horace Howard Furness. Philadelphia: Lippincott, 1891.

————. *Pericles*. Edited by F. D. Hoeniger. London: Methuen, 1963.

————. *The Riverside Shakespeare*. Edited by G. Blakemore Evans. Boston: Houghton Mifflin, 1974.

————. *The Tempest*. Edited by Frank Kermode. London: Methuen, 1954.

————. *The Winter's Tale*. Edited by J. H. P. Pafford. London: Methuen, 1965.

————. *The Winter's Tale*. Edited by Sir Arthur Quiller-Couch and John Dover Wilson. 1931. Reprint. Cambridge: Cambridge University Press, 1968.

Shaw, Catherine M. "*The Tempest* and *Hymenaei*." *Cahiers Élisabéthains* 26 (1984): 29–39.

Sidney, Sir Philip. *An Apology for Poetry*. Edited by Geoffrey Shepherd. London: Thomas Nelson, 1965.

————. *The Countess of Pembroke's Arcadia*. Edited by Maurice Evans. Harmondsworth: Penguin, 1977.

Siemon, James E. "'But It Appears She Lives': Iteration in *The Winter's Tale*." *Publications of the Modern Language Association* 89 (1974): 10–16.

Simonds, Peggy Muñoz. "'No more . . . Offend Our Hearing': Aural Imagery in *Cymbeline*." *Texas Studies in Literature and Language* 24 (1982): 137–54.

Smith, Hallett. "Leontes' *Affectio*." *Shakespeare Quarterly* 14 (1963): 163–66.

————. *Shakespeare's Romances: A Study of Some Ways of the Imagination*. San Marino, CA: Huntington Library, 1972.

Smith, Jonathan. "The Language of Leontes." *Shakespeare Quarterly* 19 (1968): 317–27.

Spencer, Theodore. *Shakespeare and the Nature of Man*. 1942. Reprint. New York: Collier Books, 1966.

Steinberg, D. *Psycholinguistics: Language, Mind, and World*. London: Longman, 1982.

Stroup, Thomas B. "The Testing Pattern in Elizabethan Tragedy." *Studies in English Literature* 3 (1963): 175–90.

Sundelson, David. "So Rare a Wonder'd Father: Prospero's *Tempest*." In *Representing Shakespeare: New Psychoanalytic Essays*, edited by Murray M. Schwartz and Coppélia Kahn, 33–53. Baltimore: The Johns Hopkins University Press, 1980.

Sutherland, James. "The Language of the Last Plays." In *More Talking of Shakespeare*, edited by John Garrett, 144–51. New York: Theatre Arts Books, 1959.

Swinburne, Algernon Charles. *A Study of Shakespeare*. 1879. Reprint. New York: AMS Press, 1965.

Tatius, Achilles. *The Loves of Clitophon and Leucippe*. Translated by William Burton. Oxford: Basil Blackwell, 1923.

Taylor, Michael. "'Here is a thing too young for such a place': Innocence in *Pericles*." *Ariel* 13 (1982): 3–19.

———. "Shakespeare's *The Winter's Tale*: Speaking in the Freedom of Knowledge." *Critical Quarterly* 14 (1972): 49–56.

———. "The Pastoral Reckoning of *Cymbeline*." *Shakespeare Survey* 36 (1983): 97–106.

Thomson, J. A. K. *Shakespeare and the Classics*. London: George Allen and Unwin, 1952.

Tonkin, Humphrey. *Spenser's Courteous Pastoral*. Oxford: Clarendon Press, 1972.

Traversi, Derek. *Shakespeare: The Last Phase*. 1954. Reprint. Stanford, CA: Stanford University Press, 1965.

Trousdale, Marion. *Shakespeare and the Rhetoricians*. Chapel Hill: University of North Carolina Press, 1982.

Turner, Robert Y. "Slander in *Cymbeline* and Other Jacobean Tragicomedies." *English Literary Renaissance* 13 (1983): 194–202.

Uphaus, Robert W. *Beyond Tragedy: Structure and Experience in Shakespeare's Romances*. Lexington: The University Press of Kentucky, 1981.

Van Doren, Mark. *Shakespeare*. New York: Henry Holt, 1939.

Wallace, Karl. *Francis Bacon on the Nature of Man*. Urbana: University of Illinois Press, 1967.

Ward, David. "Affection, Intention, and Dreams in *The Winter's Tale*." *Modern Language Review* 82 (1987): 545–54.

Waswo, Richard. *Language and Meaning in the Renaissance*. Princeton: Princeton University Press, 1987.

Welsh, Andrew. "Heritage in *Pericles*." In *Shakespeare's Last Plays: Essays in Honor of Charles Crow*, edited by Richard C. Tobias and Paul G. Zolbrod, 89–113. Athens: Ohio University Press, 1974.

White, Howard B. *"Copp'd Hills Towards Heaven": Shakespeare and the Classical Polity*. The Hague: Martinus Nijhoff, 1970.

White, R. S. *"Let Wonder Seem Familiar": Endings in Shakespeare's Romance Vision*. Atlantic Highlands, NJ: Humanities Press, 1985.

Whorf, Benjamin Lee. *Language, Thought, and Reality: Selected Writings of Benjamin Lee Whorf*. Edited by John B. Carroll. Cambridge: The Technology Press of Massachusetts Institute of Technology, 1956.

Wickham, Glynne. "Masque and Anti-masque in *The Tempest*." *Essays and Studies*, n.s., 28 (1975): 1–14.

Wind, Edgar. *Pagan Mysteries in the Renaissance*. New Haven: Yale University Press, 1958.

Wood, James O. "The Running Image in *Pericles*." *Shakespeare Studies* 5 (1969): 240–52.

———. "Shakespeare and the Belching Whale." *English Language Notes* 11 (1973): 40–44.

Yates, Frances A. *Shakespeare's Last Plays: A New Approach.* London: Routledge and Kegan Paul, 1975.

Young, David P. *The Heart's Forest: A Study of Shakespeare's Pastoral Plays.* New Haven: Yale University Press, 1972.

Index